The Place Beyond the Winds

Cornstoc

THE PLACE BEYOND THE WINDS

"It was a beautiful thing, that dance, grotesque, pagan and yet divine"

THE PLACE BEYOND
THE WINDS

BY

HARRIET T. COMSTOCK

AUTHOR OF
JOYCE OF THE NORTH WOODS
A SON OF THE HILLS
JANET OF THE DUNES, ETC.

ILLUSTRATED BY
HARRY SPAFFORD POTTER

GROSSET & DUNLAP
PUBLISHERS : NEW YORK

Copyright, *1914*, by
DOUBLEDAY, PAGE & COMPANY

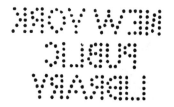

FOREWORD

The In-Place cannot be found; you must happen upon it! Hidden behind its rugged red rocks and hemlock-covered hills, it lies waiting for something to happen. It has its Trading Station, to and from which the Canadian Indians paddle their canoes — sometimes a dugout — bearing rare, luscious blue berries invitingly packed in small baskets with their own green leaves. And to the Station, also, go the hardy natives — good English, Scotch, or "Mixed" — with their splendid loads of fish.

"White fish go: pickerel come" — but always there is fish through summer days and winter's ice.

There is a lovely village Green, around which the modest homes cluster sociably. Poor, plain places they may be, but never dirty nor untidy. And the children and dogs! Such lovely babies; such human animals. They play and work together quite naturally and are the truest friends.

A little church, with a queer pointed spire and a beautiful altar, stands with open doors like a kindly welcome to all. Back of this, and apologetically placed behind its stockade fence, is the jail.

To have a jail and never need it! What more can be said of a community? But you are told — if you insist upon it — that the building is preserved as a warning, and if any one should by chance be forced to occupy it, "he will have the best the

v

place affords" — for justice is seasoned with mercy in the In-Place.

If you would know the aristocracy of the hamlet you must leave the friendly Green and the pleasant water of the Channel, climb the red rocks, tread the grassy road between the hemlocks and the pines, and find the farms. For, be it understood, by one's ability to wrench a living from the soil instead of the water is he known and estimated. To fish is to gamble; to plant and reap is conservative business.

Dreamer's Rock and One Tree Island, Far Hill Place and Lonely Farm, safely sheltered they lie, and from them, in obedience to the "Lure of the States," comes now and again an adventurous soul to make his way, if so he may; and never was there a braver, truer wanderer than Priscilla of Lonely Farm. Equipped with a great faith, a straight method of thinking, and an ideal that never faded from her sight, she, by the help of the Poor Property Man, found her place and her work awaiting her. Love, she found, too — love that had to be tested by a man's sense of honour and a woman's determination, but it survived and found its fulfilment before the Shrine in the woods beyond Lonely Farm, where, as a little child, Priscilla had set up her Strange God and given homage to it.

HARRIET T. COMSTOCK.

LIST OF ILLUSTRATIONS

The Place Beyond the Winds

CHAPTER I

PRISCILLA GLENN stood on the little slope leading down from the farmhouse to the spring at the bottom of the garden, and lifted her head as a young deer does when it senses something new or dangerous. Suddenly, and entirely subconsciously, she felt her kinship with life, her relation to the lovely May day which was more like June than May — and a rare thing for Kenmore — whose seasons lapsed into each other as calmly and sluggishly as did all the other happenings in that spot known to the Canadian Indians as The Place Beyond the Wind — the In-Place.

Across Priscilla's straight, young shoulders lay a yoke from both ends of which dangled empty tin pails, destined, sooner or later, to be filled with that peculiarly fine water of which Nathaniel Glenn was so proud. Nathaniel Glenn never loved things in a human, tender fashion, but he was proud of many things — proud that he, and his before him, had braved the hardships of farming among the red, rocky hills of Kenmore instead of wrenching a live-

3

lihood from the water. This capacity for tilling the soil instead of gambling in fish had made of Glenn, and a few other men, the real aristocracy of the place. Nathaniel's grandfather, with his wife and fifteen children, had been the first white settlers of Kenmore. So eager had the Indians been to have this first Glenn among them that it is said they offered him any amount of land he chose to select, and Glenn had taken only so much as would insure him a decent farm and prospects. This act of restraint had further endeared him to the natives, and no regret was ever known to follow the advent of the estimable gentleman.

The present Glenn never boasted; he had no need to; the plain statement of fact was enough to secure his elevated position from mean attack.

Nathaniel had taught himself to read and write — a most unusual thing — and naturally he was proud of that. He was proud of his stern, bleak religion that left no doubt in his own mind of his perfect interpretation of divine will. He was proud of his handsome wife — twenty years younger than himself. Inwardly he was proud of that, within himself, which had been capable of securing Theodora where other men had failed. Theodora had caused him great disappointment, but Nathaniel was a just man and he could not exactly see that his disappointment was due to any deliberate or malicious act of Theodora's; it was only when his wife showed weak tendencies toward making light of the matter that he hardened his heart.

In the face of his great desire and his modest aspirations — Theodora had borne for him (that was the only way he looked at it) five children — all girls, when she very well knew a son was the one thing, in the way of offspring, that he had expected or wanted.

The first child was as dark as a little Indian, "so dark," explained Nathaniel, "that she would have been welcome in any house on a New Year's Day." She lasted but a year, and, while she was a regret, she had been tolerated as an attempt, at least, in the right direction. Then came the second girl, a soft, pale creature with ways that endeared her to the mother-heart so tragically that when she died at the age of two Theodora rebelliously proclaimed that she wanted no other children! This blasphemy shocked Nathaniel beyond measure, and when, a year later, twin girls were born on Lonely Farm, he pointed out to his wife that no woman could fly in the face of the Almighty with impunity and she must now see, in this double disgrace of sex, her punishment.

Theodora was stricken; but the sad little sisters early escaped the bondage of life, and the Glenns once again, childless and alone, viewed the future superstitiously and with awe. Even Nathaniel, hope gone as to a son, resignedly accepted the fate that seemed to pursue him. Then, after five years, Priscilla was born, the lustiest and most demanding of all the children.

"She seems," said Long Jean, the midwife, "to be made of the odds and ends of all the others. She has the clear, dark skin of the first, the blue eyes of the second, and the rusty coloured hair and queer features of the twins."

Between Long Jean and Mary Terhune, midwives, a social rivalry existed. On account of her Indian taint Long Jean was less sought in aristocratic circles, but so great had been the need the night when Priscilla made her appearance, that both women had been summoned, and Long Jean, arriving first, and, her superior skill being well known, was accepted.

When she announced the birth and sex of the small stranger, Nathaniel, smoking before the fire in the big, clean, bare, living-room, permitted himself one reckless defiance:

"Not wanted!" Long Jean made the most of this.

"And his pretty wife at the point of death," she gossiped to Mrs. McAdam of the White Fish Lodge; "and there is this to say about the child being a girl: the lure of the States can't touch her, and Nathaniel may have some one to turn to for care and what not when infirmity overtakes him. Besides, the lass may be destined for the doing of big things; those witchy brats often are."

"The lure don't get all the boys," muttered Mary McAdam, cautiously thinking of her Sandy, aged five, and Tom, a bit older.

"All as amounts to much," Long Jean returned.

And in her heart of hearts Mary McAdam knew this to be true. The time would come to her, as it had to all Kenmore mothers, when she would have to acknowledge that by the power of the "lure" were her boys to be tested.

But Priscilla at Lonely Farm showed a hardened disregard of her state. She persisted and grew sturdy and lovely in defiance of tradition and conditions. She was as keen-witted and original as she was independent and charming. Still Theodora took long before she capitulated, and Nathaniel never succumbed. Indeed, as years passed he grew to fear and dislike his young daughter. The little creature, in some subtle way, seemed to have "found him out"; she became, though he would not admit it, a materialized conscience to him. She made him doubt himself; she laughed at him, elfishly and without excuse or explanation.

Once they two, sitting alone before the hearth — Nathaniel in his great chair, Priscilla in her small one — faced each other fearsomely for a time; then the child gave the gurgling laugh of inner understanding that maddened the father.

"What you laughing at?" he muttered, taking the pipe from his mouth.

"You!" Priscilla was only seven then, but large and strong.

"Me? How dare you!"

"You are so funny. If I screw my eyes tight I see two of you."

Then Nathaniel struck her. Not brutally, not maliciously; he wanted desperately to set himself right by — old-time and honoured methods — force of authority!

Priscilla sprang from her chair, all the laughter and joyousness gone from her face. She went close to her father, and leaning toward him as though to confide the warning to him more directly, said slowly:

"Don't you do that or Cilla will hate you!"

It was as if she meant to impress upon him that past a certain limit he could not go.

Nathaniel rose in mighty wrath at this, and, white-faced and outraged, darted toward the rebel, but she escaped him and put the width of the room and the square deal table between them. Then began the chase that suddenly sank into a degrading and un-dignified proceeding. Around and around the two went, and presently the child began to laugh again as the element of sport entered in

So Theodora came upon them, and her deeper understanding of her husband's face frightened and spurred her to action. In that moment, while she feared, she loved, as she had never loved before, her small daughter.   If the child was a conscience to her stern father, she was a materialization of all the suppressed defiance of the mother, and, ignoring consequences, she ran to Priscilla, gathered her in her arms, and over the little, hot, panting body, confronted the blazing eyes of her husband.

And Nathaniel had done — nothing; said nothing! In a moment the fury, outwardly, subsided, but deep in all three hearts new emotions were born never to die.

After that there was a triangle truce.   The years slipped by. Theodora taught her little daughter to read by a novel method which served the double purpose of quickening the keen intellect and arousing a housewifely skill.

The alphabet was learned from the labels on the cans of vegetables and fruits on Theodora's shelves. There was one line of goods made by a firm, according to its own telling, high in the favour of "their Majesties So and So," that was rich in vowels and consonants.   When Priscilla found that by taking innocent looking little letters and stringing them together like beads she could make words, she was wild with delight, and when she discovered that she could further take the magic words and by setting them forth in orderly fashion express her own thoughts or know another's thoughts, she was happy beyond description.

"Father," she panted at that point, her hands

clasped before her, her dark, blue-eyed face flushing and paling, "will you let me go to Master Farwell to study with the boys?"

Nathaniel eyed her from the top step of the porch; "with the boys" had been fatal to the child's request.

"No," he said firmly, the old light of antagonism glinting suddenly under his brow, "girls don't need learning past what their mothers can give them."

"I — do! I'm willing to suffer and *die*, but I do want to know things." She was an intense atom, and from the first thought true and straight.

A sharp memory was in her mind and it lent fervour to her words. It related to the episode of the small, fat mustard jar which always graced the middle of the dining table. They had once told her that the contents of the jar "were not for little girls."

They had been mistaken. She had investigated, suffered, and learned! Well, she was ready to suffer — but learn she must!

Nathaniel shook his head and set forth his scheme of life for her, briefly and clearly.

"You'll have nothing but woman ways — bad enough you need them — they will tame and keep you safe. You'll marry early and find your pleasure and duty in your home."

Priscilla turned without another word, but there was an ugly line between her eyes.

That night and the next she took the matter before a higher judge, and fervently, rigidly prayed. On the third night she pronounced her ultimatum. Kneeling by the tiny gable window of her grim little bedchamber, her face strained and intense, her big eyes fixed on a red, pulsing planet above the hemlocks outside, she said:

"Dear God, I'll give you three days to move his stony heart to let me go to school; if you don't do it by then, I'm going to worship graven images!"

Priscilla at that time was eight, and three days seemed to her a generous time limit. But Nathaniel's stony heart did not melt, and at the end of the three days Priscilla ceased to pray for many and many a year, and forthwith she proceeded to worship a graven image of her own creation.

A mile up the grassy road, beyond Lonely Farm and on the way toward the deep woods, was an open space of rich, red rock surrounded by a soft, feathery fringe of undergrowth and a few well-grown trees. From this spot one could see the Channel widened out into the Little Bay: the myriad islands, and, off to the west, the Secret and Fox Portages, beyond which lay the Great Bay, where the storms raged and the wind — such wind as Kenmore never knew — howled and tore like a raging fiend!

In this open stretch of trees and rock Priscilla set up her own god. She had found the bleached skull of a cow in one of her father's pastures; this gruesome thing mounted upon a forked stick, its empty eye-sockets and ears filled with twigs and dried grasses, was sufficiently pagan and horrible to demand an entirely unique form of worship, and this Priscilla proceeded to evolve. She invented weird words, meaningless but high-sounding; she propitiated her idol with wild dances and an abandon of restraint. Before it she had moments of strange silence when, with wonder-filled eyes, she waited for suggestion and impression by which to be guided. Very young was she when intuitively she sensed the inner call that was always so deeply to sway her. Through the years from eight to fourteen Priscilla worshipped more or less frequently before her secret shrine. The uncanny ceremony eased many an overstrained hour and did for the girl what should have been done in a more normal way. The place on the red rock became her sanctuary. To it she carried her daily task of sewing and dreamed her long dreams.

The Glenns rarely went to church — the distance was too great — but Nathaniel, looming high and stern across the table in the bare kitchen, morning and night, set forth the rigid, unlovely creed of his belief. This fell upon Priscilla's unheeding ears, but the hours before the shrine were deeply, tenderly religious, although they were bright and merry hours.

Of course, during the years, there were the regular Kenmore happenings that impressed the girl to a greater or lesser degree, but they were like pictures thrown upon a screen — they came, they went, while her inner growth was steady and sure.

Two families, one familiar and commonplace, the other more mystical than anything else, interested Priscilla mightily during her early youth.   Jerry and Michael McAlpin, with little Jerry-Jo, the son of old Jerry, were vital factors in Kenmore.   They occupied the exalted position of rural expressmen, and distributed, when various things did not interfere, the occasional freight and mail that survived the careless methods of the vicinity.

The McAlpin brothers were hard drinkers, but they were most considerate.   When Jerry indulged, Michael remained sober and steady; when Michael fell before temptation, Jerry pulled himself together in a marvellous way, and so, as a firm, they had surmounted every inquiry and suspicion of a relentless government and were welcomed far and wide, not only for their legitimate business, but for the amount of gossip and scandal they disbursed along with their load.   Jerry-Jo, the son of the older McAlpin, was four years older than Priscilla and was the only really young creature who had ever entered her life intimately.

The other family, of whom the girl thought vaguely, as she might have of a story, were the Travers of the Far Hill Place.

Now it might seem strange to more social minds

that people from a distant city could come summer after summer to the same spot and yet remain unknown to their nearest neighbours; but Kenmore was not a social community. It had all the reserve of its English heritage combined with the suspicion of its Indian taint, and it took strangers hard. Then, added to this, the Traverses aroused doubt, for no one, especially Nathaniel Glenn, could account for a certain big, heavy-browed man who shared the home life of the Hill Place without any apparent right or position. For Mrs. Travers, Glenn had managed to conjure up a very actual distrust. She was too good-looking and free-acting to be sound; and her misshapen and delicate son was, so the severe man concluded, a curse, in all probability, for past offences. The youth of Kenmore was straight and hearty, unless — and here Nathaniel recalled his superstitions — dire vengeance was wreaked on parents through their offspring.

With no better reason than this, and with the stubbornness he mistook for strength, Glenn would have nothing to do with his neighbours, four miles back in the woods, and had forbidden the sale of milk and garden stuff to them.

All this Priscilla had heard, as children do, but she had never seen any member of the family from the Far Hill Place, and mentally relegated them to the limbo of the damned under the classification of "them, from the States." Their name, even, was rarely mentioned, and, while curiosity often swayed her, temptation had never overruled obedience.

The McAlpins, with all their opportunity and qualifications, found little about the strangers from which to make talk. The family were reserved, and Tough Pine, the Indian guide they had impressed into summer service, was either bought or, from natural inclination, kept himself to himself.

So, until the summer when she was fourteen, Priscilla Glenn knew less about the Far Hill people than she did about the inhabitants of heaven and hell, with whom her father was upon such intimate and familiar terms.

Once, when Priscilla was ten, something had occurred which prepared her for following events. It was a bright morning and the McAlpin boat stopped at the wharf of Lonely Farm. While old Jerry went to the farmhouse with a package, Jerry-Jo remained on guard deeply engrossed in a book he had extracted from a box beneath the seat. He appeared not to notice Priscilla, who ran down the path to greet him in friendly fashion.

The boy was about fifteen then, and all the bloods of his various ancestors were warring in his veins. His mother had been a full-blooded Indian from Wyland Island, had drawn her four dollars every year from the English Government, and ruled her family with an iron hand; his father was Scotch-Irish, hot-blooded and jovial; Jerry-Jo was a composite result. Handsome, moody, with flashes of fun when not crossed, a good comrade at times, an unforgiving enemy.

He liked Priscilla, but she was his inferior, by sex, and she sorely needed discipline. He meant to keep her in her place, so he kept on reading. Priscilla at length, however, attracted his attention.

"Hey-ho, Jerry-Jo!"

"Hullo!"

"Where did you get the book?"

"It's for him up yonder."

And with this Jerry-Jo stood up, turned and twisted his lithe body into such a grotesque distortion that he was quite awful to look upon, and left no doubt in the girl's mind as to whom he referred. He brought the Far Hill people into focus, sharply and suddenly.

"He has miles of books," Jerry-Jo went on, "and a fiddle and pictures and gewgaws. He plays devil tunes, and he's bewitched!"

This description made the vague boy of the woods real and vital for the first time in Priscilla's life, and she shuddered. Then Jerry-Jo generously offered to lend her one of the books until his father came back, and Priscilla eagerly stepped from stone to stone until she could reach the volume. Once she had obtained the prize she went back to the garden and made herself comfortable, wholly forgetting Jerry-Jo and the world at large.

It was the oddest book she had ever seen. The words were arranged in charming little rows, and when you read them over and over they sang themselves into your very heart. They told you, lilting along, of a road that no one but you ever knew — a road that led in and out through wonders of beauty and faded at the day's end into your heart's desire. Your Heart's Desire!

And just then Jerry-Jo cried:

"Hey, there! you, Priscilla, come down with that book."

"Your Heart's Desire!" Priscilla's eyes were misty as she repeated the words. Indeed, one large, full tear escaped the blue eyes and lay like a pitiful kiss on the fair page, where there was a broad, generous space for tears on either side of the lines.

"Hist! Father's coming!"

Then Priscilla stood up and a demon seemed to possess her.

"I'm not going to give it back to you! It's mine!" she cried shrilly.

Jerry-Jo made as if he were about to dash up the path and annihilate her, but she stayed him by holding the book aloft and calling:

"If you do I'll throw it in the Channel!" She looked equal to it, too, and Jerry-Jo swore one angry word and stopped short. Then the girl's mood changed. Quite gently and noiselessly she ran to Jerry-Jo and held the opened book toward him.

His keen eye fell upon the tear-stain, but his coarser nature wrongly interpreted it.

"You imp!" he cried; "you spat upon it!"

But Priscilla shook her head.   "No — it's a tear," she explained; "and, oh! Jerry-Jo, it is mine — listen! — you cannot take it away from me."

And standing there upon the rock she repeated the words of the poem, her rich voice rising and falling musically, and poor Jerry-Jo, hypnotized by that which he could not comprehend, listened open-mouthed.

And now, again, it was spring and Priscilla was fourteen. Standing in the garden path, her yoke across her shoulders, her ears straining at the sound she heard, the old poem returned to her as it had not for years. She faltered over the words at the first attempt, but with the second they rushed vividly to her mind and seemed set to the music of that "pat-pat-pat" sound on the water. An un-accountable excitement seized her — that new but thrilling sense of nearness and kinship to life and the lovely meaning of spring. She was no longer a little girl looking *on* at life; she was part of it; and some-thing was going to happen after the long shut-in winter!

And presently the McAlpin boat came in sight around Lone Tree Island and in it stood Jerry-Jo quite alone, paddling straight for the landing-place!

For a moment Priscilla hardly knew him.   The winter had worked a wonder upon him.   He was almost a man!   He had the manners, too, of his kind — he ignored the girl on the rocks.

But he had seen her; seen her before she had seen him.   He had noted the wonderful change in her, for eighteen is keen about fourteen, particularly when fourteen is full of promise and belongs, in a sense, to one.

The short, ugly frock Priscilla wore could not hide the beauty and grace of her young body — the winter had wiped out forever her awkward length of limb.   Her reddish hair was twisted on the top of her head and made her look older and more mature.   Her uplifted face had the shining radiancy that was its chief charm, and as Jerry-Jo looked he was moved to admiration, and for that very reason he assumed indifference and gave undivided attention to his boat.

CHAPTER II

WITH skill and grace Jerry-Jo steered his boat to the landing-place at the foot of the garden. He leaped out and tied the rope to the ring in the rocks, then he waited for Priscilla to pay homage, but Priscilla was so absorbed with her own thoughts that she overlooked the expected tribute of sex to sex. At last Jerry-Jo stood upright, legs wide apart, hands in pockets, and, with bold, handsome face thrown back, cried:

"Well, there!"

At this Priscilla started, gave a light laugh, and readjusting her yoke, walked down to the young fellow below.

"It's Jerry-Jo," she said slowly, still held by the change in him; "and alone!"

"Yes." Jerry-Jo gave a gleaming smile that showed all his strong, white teeth — long, keen teeth they were, like the fangs of an animal.

"Where are the others?" asked Priscilla.

"Uncle's dead," the boy returned promptly and cheerfully; "dead, and a good thing. He was getting cranky."

Priscilla started back as if the mention of death on that glorious day cast a cloud and a shadow.

"And your father, Jerry-Jo, is he, too, dead?"

"No. Dad, he is in jail!"

"In — jail!" Never in her life before had Priscilla known of any one being in Kenmore jail. The red, wooden house behind its high, stockade fence was at once the pride and relic of the place. To have a jail and never use it! What more could be said for the peaceful virtues of a community?

"Yes. Dad's in jail and in jail he will stay, says he, till them as put him there begs his pardon humble and proper."

Priscilla now dropped the yoke upon the rocks and gave her entire thought to Jerry-Jo, who, she could see, was bursting with importance and a sense of the dramatic.

"What did your father do, Jerry-Jo?"

"It was like this: Uncle Michael died and the wake we had for him was the most splendid you ever saw. Bottles and kegs from the White Fish and money to pay for all, too! Every one welcome and free to say his say and drink his fill. I got drunk myself! Long about midnight Big Hornby he said as how he once licked Uncle Michael, and Dad he cried back that to blacken a man's name when he was too dead to stand up for it was a dirty trick, and so it was! Then it was forth and back for a time, with compliments and what not, and if you please just as Dad sent a bit of a stool at Big Hornby, who should come in at the door but Mr. Schoolmaster, him as had no invite and was not wanted! The stool took him full on the arm and broke it — the arm — and folks took sides, and some one, after a bit, got Dad from under the pile and tried to make him beg pardon! Beg pardon at his own wake in his own home, and Schoolmaster taking chances coming when he was not invited! Umph!"

Jerry-Jo's eyes flashed superbly.

"'I'll go to jail first and be damned,'" said Dad, and that put it in the mind of Big Hornby, and he up and says, 'To jail with him!' And so they takes Dad, thinking to scare him, and claps him into jail, not even mending the lock or nailing up the boards. That's three days since, and yesterday Hornby he comes to Dad and says as how a steamer was in with mail and freight and who was to carry it around? And Dad says as how I was a man now and could hold up the honour of the family, says he, and moreover, says Dad, 'I'll neither eat nor come out till you come to your senses and beg pardon for mistaking a joke for an insult!'"

Jerry-Jo paused to laugh. Then:

"So here am I with the boatload — there's a box of seeds for your father — and then I'm off to the Hill Place, for them as stays there has come, and there are boxes and packages for them as usual."

Jerry-Jo proceeded to extract Mr. Glenn's box

from the boat, and Priscilla, her clear skin flushed with excitement, drew near to examine the cargo.

"More books!" she gasped. "Oh, Jerry-Jo, do you remember the first book?"

"Do I?" Jerry-Jo had shouldered the box of seeds and now bent upon the girl a glad, softened look.

"Do I? You was a wild thing then, Priscilla. And I told him about the slob of a tear and he laughed in his big, queer way, and he said, I remember well, that by that token the book was more yours than his, and he wanted me to carry it back, but I knew what was good for you, and I would not! See here, Priscilla, would you like to have a peek at this?" And then Jerry-Jo put his burden down, and, returning to the boat, drew from under the seat a book in a clean separate wrapper and held it out toward her.

"Oh!" The hands were as eager as of old.

"What will you give for it?" A deep red mounted to the young fellow's cheeks.

"Anything, Jerry-Jo."

"A — kiss?"

"Yes" — doubtfully; "yes."

The book was in the outstretched hands, the hot kiss lay upon the smooth, girlish neck, and then they looked at each other.

"It — is *his* book?"

"No. Yours — I sent for it, myself."

"Oh! Jerry-Jo. And how did you know?"

"I copied it from that one of his."

Priscilla tore the wrappings asunder and saw that the book was a duplicate of the one over which, long ago, she had loved and wept.

"Thank you, Jerry-Jo," the voice faltered; "but I wish it — had the tear spot."

"That was *his* book; this is yours." An angry light flashed in Jerry-Jo's eyes. He had arranged this surprise with great pains and had used all his savings.

"But it cannot be the same, Jerry-Jo. Thank you — but ——"

"Give us another kiss?" The young fellow begged.

Priscilla drew back and held out the book.

"No." She was ready to relinquish the poems, but she would not buy them.

"Keep the book — it's yours."

Jerry-Jo scowled. And then he shouldered the box and ran up the path. When he came back Priscilla was gone, and the spring day seemed commonplace and dull to Jerry-Jo; the adventure was over. Priscilla had filled her pails and had carried them and the book to the house. Something had happened to her, also. She was out of tune with the sunlight and warmth; she wanted to get close to life again and feel, as she had earlier, the kinship and joy, but the mood had passed.

It was after the dishes of the midday meal were washed that she bethought her of the old shrine back near the woods. It was many a day since she had been there — not since the autumn before — and she felt old and different, but still she had a sudden desire to return to it and try again the mystic rite she had practised when she was a little girl. It was like going back to play, to be sure; all the sacredness was gone, but the interest remained, and her yearning spurred her to her only resource.

At two o'clock Nathaniel was off to a distant field, and Theodora announced that she must walk to the village for a bit of "erranding." She wanted Priscilla to join her, thinking it would please the girl; but Priscilla shook her head and pleaded a weariness that was more mental than physical. At three o'clock, arrayed in a fresh gown, over which hung a red cape, Priscilla stole from the house and made her way to the opening near the woods. As she drew close the power of suggestion overcame the new sense of age and indifference; the witchery of the place held her; the old charm reasserted itself; she was being hypnotized by the Past. Tiptoeing to the niche in the rock she drew away the sheltering boughs and branches she had placed there one golden September day. The leaves had been red and yellow then; they were stiff and brown now. The leering skull confronted her as it had in the past and changed her at once to the devotee.

Before the dead thing the live, lovely creature bowed gravely. After all, had not the image, instead of God, answered her first prayer? Nathaniel's heart had not been softened and school had not been permitted, but there had been lessons given by the master when she told him of her new god. How he had laughed, clapping his knees with his long, thin, white hands! But he had taught her on hillside and woodland path. No one knew this but themselves and the strange idol!

A rapt look spread over Priscilla's face; the look of the worshipper who could lose self in a passion. But this was no dread god that demanded unlovely sacrifice. It was a glad creature that desired laughter, song, and dance. Priscilla had seen to that. A repetition of her father's creed would have been unendurable.

"Skib, skib, skibble — de — de — dosh!"

Again the deep and sweeping courtesy and chanting of the weird words. The final "dosh!" held, in its low, fierce tone, all the significance of abject adoration. With that "dosh" had the child Priscilla wooed the favour and recognition of the god. It was a triumph of appeal.

And then the dance began — the wild, fantastic steps full of grace and joy and the fury and passion of youth. Round and round spun the slight form, with arms over head or spread wide. The red cape floated, rising and falling; the uplifted face changed

with every moment's flitting thought. It was a
beautiful thing, that dance, grotesque, pagan, and
yet divine, and through it all, panting and pulsing,
sounded the strange, incomprehensible words:

"Skib, skib, skibble — de — de — dosh!"

While the rite was at high tide a young fellow,
lying prone under a clump of trees beyond the open
space, looked on, first in amaze mingled with amusement, and then with delight and admiration. He
had never seen anything at once so heathenish and
so exquisite. To one hampered and restricted as
he was in bodily freedom, the absolute grace was
marvellous, but the uncanny words and the girl's
apparent seriousness gave a touch of unreality to
the scene. Presently, from sheer inability to further
control himself, the looker-on gave a laugh that rent
the stillness of the afternoon like a cruel shock.

Priscilla, horrified, paused in the midst of a wild
whirl and listened, her eyes dilating, her nostrils
twitching. She waited for another burst that would
make her understand.

Having given vent to that one peal of mirth,
Richard Travers pulled himself to a sitting position,
and, by so doing, presented his head and shoulders
to the indignant eyes of Priscilla Glenn.

"Oh!" cried she; "how dare you!"

And now Travers got rather painfully upon his
feet, and, with fiddle under one arm and book under
the other, came forward into the open and inclined

his uncovered head. He was twenty then, fair and handsome, and in his gray eyes shone that kindliness that was doomed later on to bring him so much that was both evil and good.

"I beg your pardon. I did not know I was on sacred ground. I just happened here, you see, and I could not help the laugh; it was the only compliment I could pay for anything so lovely — so utterly lovely."

Priscilla melted at once and fear fled. Not for an instant did she connect this handsome fellow with the crooked wrongdoer of the Hill Place. Jerry-Jo's long-ago description had been too vivid to be forgotten, and this stranger was one to charm and win confidence.

"Will you — oh! please do — let me play for you? You dance like a nymph. Do you know what a nymph is?"

Priscilla shook her head.

"Well, it's the only thing that can dance like you; the only thing that should ever be allowed to dance in the woods. Come, now, listen sharp, and as I play, keep step."

Leaning against a strong young hemlock, Dick Travers placed his fiddle and struck into a giddy, tuneful thing as picturesque as the time and occasion. With head bent to one side and eyes and lips smiling, Priscilla listened until something within her caught and responded to the tripping notes. At first she went cautiously, feeling her way after the enchanted music, then she gained courage, and the very heart of her danced and trembled in accord.

"Fine! fine! Now — slower; see it's the nymph stepping this way and that! Forward, so! Now!"

And then, exhausted and laughing madly, Priscilla sank down upon a rock near the musician, who, seeing her worn and panting, played on, without a word, a sweet, sad strain that brought tears to the listener's eyes — tears of absolute enjoyment and content. She had never heard music before in all her bleak, colourless life, and Dick Travers was no mean artist, in his way.

"And now," he said presently, sitting down a few feet from her, "just tell me who you are and what in the world prompts you to worship, so adorably, that hideous brute over there?"

Between fourteen and twenty lies a chasm of age and experience that ensures patronage to one and dependence to the other. Travers felt aged and protecting, but Priscilla grew impish and perverse; besides, she always intuitively shielded her real self until she capitulated entirely. This was a new play, a new comrade, but she must be cautious.

"I — I have no name — he made me!" She nodded toward the grinning skull. "On bright sunny afternoons in spring, when flowers and green things are beginning to live, he lets me dance, once in a great while, so that I can keep alive!"

Priscilla, with this, gave such a beaming and mischievous smile that Travers was bewitched.

"You ——— " But he did not put his thought into words; he merely gave smile for smile, and asked:

"Did he teach you to dance?"

"No. The dance is — is me! That's why he likes me. He's so dead that he likes to see something that is alive."

"The whole world would adore you could it see you as I just have!"

Then Travers, with the artist's eye, wondered how dark hair could possibly hold such golden tints, and how such a dark face could make lovely the blue, richly lashed eyes. He knew she must be from Lonely Farm — Jerry-Jo used to speak of her; lately he had said nothing, to be sure, but this certainly must be the child who had once cried over a book of his. Poor, little, temperamental beggar!

"Come up and deliver!" Travers gave a laugh. "I'm Robin Hood and I want you to explain yourself. Why do you bow down before that brazen and evil-looking brute?"

Priscilla hugged her knees in her clasped hands, and said, on the defence:

"He's the only god that answered my prayer. I tried father's God and — it didn't work! Then I fixed up this one, and — it did!"

"What was it you wanted?"

"I wanted to learn things! I wanted to go to

school. I prayed to have father's heart softened, but it stayed — rocky. Then I began to worship this" — the right hand waved toward the bleached and grinning skull — "and my wish came true. I told the schoolmaster. Do you know Mr. Anton Farwell?"

"I've heard of him."

"I told him I wanted to learn, and after he got through laughing he said he'd been sent by my god to teach me all I wanted to know; but of course he can't do that!"

"Do what?" Travers was fascinated by the child's naïvety.

"Teach me all I want to know. Why, I'm going to suffer and know many things!"

"Good Lord!" ejaculated Travers; "you won't mind if I laugh?"

"I don't think there's anything to laugh at!" Priscilla held him sternly. "Have you ever suffered?"

The laugh died from Travers's face.

"Suffered!" he repeated. "Yes! yes!"

"Well, doesn't it pay — when you get what you want and know things?"

"Why, see here, youngster — it does! You've managed to dig out of your life quite a brilliant philosophy, though I suppose you do not know what that is. It's holding to your ideal, the thing that seems most worth while, and forcing everything else

into line with that. Now, you see I had a bad
handicap — a clutch on me that made me a weak,
sickly fellow, but through it all I kept my ideal."

Priscilla was listening bravely. She was following
this thought as she had the music; something in her
was responding. She did not speak, and Travers went
on talking, more to himself than to her.

"Always before the poor thing I really was, walked
the fine thing I would be. I *thought* myself straight
and strong and clean. Lord! how it hurt sometimes;
but I grew, after a time, into something approaching
the ideal going on before me, thinking high and strong
thoughts, forgetting the meannesses and aches — do
you understand?"

This was a fairy story to the listener. Rigid and
spellbound she replied:

"Yes. And that's what I've been doing — and
nobody knew. I've just been working hard for
that *me* of *me* that I always see. I don't care what
I have to suffer, but —" the throbbing words paused
— "I'm going to know what — it is all about!"

"It?" Again Travers was bewildered and bound.

"Yes. Life and me and what we mean. I'm not
going to stay here; when the lure of the States gets
me I'm — going!"

Things were getting too tense, and Travers yielded
to a nervous impulse to laugh again. This brought
a frown to Priscilla's brow.

"Forgive me!" he pleaded. "And now see here,

little pagan, let us make a compact. Let us keep our ideals; don't let anything take them from us. Is it a go?"

He stretched his hand out, and the small, brown one lay frankly in it.

"And we'll come here and — and worship before that fiend, just you and I? And we won't ever tell?"

Priscilla nodded.

"And now will you dance once more, just once?"

The girl bounded from the rock, and before the bow struck the strings she was poised and ready. Then it was on again, that strange, wild game. The notes rang clear and true, and as true tripped the twinkling feet. With head bent and eyes riveted on the graceful form, Travers urged her on by word and laugh, and he did not heed a shadow which fell across the sunlighted, open space, until Priscilla stopped short, and a deep voice trembling with emotion roared one word:

"You!"

There stood Nathaniel Glenn, his face twitching with anger and something akin to fear. How much he had heard no one could tell, but he had heard and seen enough to arouse alarm and suspicion. In his hand was a long lash whip, and, as Priscilla did not move, he raised it aloft and sent it snapping around the rigid figure.

It did not touch her, but the act called forth all the

resentment and fierce indignation of the young fellow who looked on.

"Stop!" he shouted. Then, because he sought for words to comfort and could think of no others, he said to Priscilla, "Don't let them kill your ideal; hold to it in spite of everything!"

"Yes," the words came slowly, defiantly, "I'm going to!"

"Go!" Nathaniel was losing control. "Go — you!"

Then, as if waking from sleep, the girl turned, and with no backward look, went her way, Nathaniel following.

Travers, exhausted from the excitement, stretched himself once more upon the mossy spot from which Priscilla had roused him. He was sensitive to every impression and quivering in every nerve.

What he had witnessed turned him ill with loathing and contempt. Brutality in any form was horrible to him, and the thought of the pretty, spiritual child under the control of the coarse, stern man was almost more than he could bear. Then memory added fuel to the present. It was that man who had conjured up some kind of opposition to his mother — had made living problems harder for her until she had won the confidence of others. The man must be, Travers concluded, a fanatic and an ignoramus, and to think of him holding power over that sprite of the woods!

He could not quite see how he might help the girl, but, lying there, her dancing image flitting before his pitying eyes, he meant to outwit the rough father in some way, and bring into the child's life a bit of brightness. Then he smiled and his easy good nature returned.

"I'll get her to dance for me, never fear! I'll teach her to love music, and I'll tell her stories. I must get her to explain about the lure of the States. What on earth could the little beggar have meant? It sounded as if she thought America had some sinister clutch on the Dominion. And those infernal-sounding words!"

Travers shook with laughter. "That '*dosh*' was about the most blasphemous thing I ever listened to. In a short space of time that child managed to cram in more new ideas, words, and acts than any one I've ever met before. I shouldn't wonder if she proves a character."

CHAPTER III

THE day of warmth and song and dance changed to a cool evening. There was a glowing sunset which faded into a clear, starry night.

Dick Travers, encased in a heavy sweater, lingered, after the light failed, on the broad piazza facing the still purpled sky, and looked out toward the Georgian Bay, which was hidden from sight by the ridge of hill through which the Fox and Secret Portages cut. The mood of the afternoon had fallen, as had the day, into calmness and restfulness. The fiddle, which was never far from Travers, lay now beside him on the deep porch swing, and every few moments he took it up and began an air that broke off almost at once, either to run into another, or into silence.

"Choppy," muttered Doctor Ledyard as he sat across the hearth from his hostess and looked now at her fair, tranquil face and then at the cheerful fire of hemlock boughs.

"He's always happiest when he's — choppy." Helen Travers smiled. "I wonder why I take your words as I take your pills, without question?"

36

"You know what's good for you."

"And so you really think there is no doubt about Dick? He can enter college this fall?"

"As sure as any man can be. He'll always be a trifle lame probably, though that will be less noticeable when he learns to forget the cane and crutch periods; as for his health — it's ripping, for him!"

"How wonderful you have been; what a miracle you have performed. When I recall ——"

"Don't, Helen! It's poor business retracing a hard road unless you go back to pick something up."

"That's why — I must go back. Doctor Ledyard, I must tell you something! Now that Dick's semi-exile and mine are to end in the common highway, he and — you must know why I have done many things — will you listen?"

From under Ledyard's shaggy brows his keen eyes flashed. There had been a time when he had hoped Helen Travers would love him; he had loved her since her husband's death, but he had never spoken, for he knew intuitively that to do so would be to risk the only thing of which he was, then, sure — her trusting friendship. He had not dared put that to the test even for the greater hope. That was why he had been able to share her lonely life in the Canadian wilds — she had never been disturbed by a doubt of him. And this comradeship, safe and assured, was the one luxury he permitted himself in a world where he was looked upon as a hard, an almost cruel, man.

"I do not want you to tell anything in order to explain your actions now, or ever. I am confident that under all circumstances you would act wisely. You are the most normal woman I ever knew."

"Thank you. But I still must speak — more for Dick than for you. I need your help for him."

Outside, the fiddle was repeating again and again a nocturne that Helen particularly loved.

"Dick is not — my son!" she said quickly and softly from out the shadows. She was rarely abrupt, and her words startled Ledyard into alertness. He got up and drew his chair close to hers.

"What did you say?" he whispered, keeping his eyes upon her lowered face.

"I said — Dick is not my son."

"And — whose is he — may I ask?"

There was a tenseness in the question. Now that he saw the gravity of the confession Ledyard wished beyond all else to cut quick and deep and then bind up the wound.

"He is the child of — my husband, and — another woman."

In the hush that followed, Dick's fiddle, running now through a delicious strain of melody, seemed like a current bearing them on.

"Perhaps you had better — tell me," Ledyard

was saying, and his words blended strangely with the tune. "Yes, I am sure you ought to tell me."

Helen Travers, sitting in her low wicker chair, did not move. Her delicate face was resting on the tips of her clasped hands, and her long, loose, white gown seemed to gather and hold the red glow of the fire.

"I suppose I have done Dick a bitter wrong, but at first, you know, even you thought he could not live and so it would not have mattered, and then I — I learned to love the helpless little chap as women of my sort do who have to make their own lives as best they may. He clung to me so desperately, and, you see, as he grew older I either had to accept his belief in me or — or — take his father from him. They were such close friends, Dick's father and he! And now — I must lay everything low, and I am wondering what will come of it all. He is such a strange fellow; our life apart has left him — well, so different! How will he take it?"

Whatever her own personal sorrow was, Helen Travers made no moan, exacted no sympathy. She had come alone to the parting of the ways, and she had thought only for the boy whom she had mothered tenderly and successfully. Ledyard did not interrupt the gentle flow of her thoughts. There was time; he would not startle or hurry her, although her first statement had shocked and surprised him beyond measure.

"I've always thought of myself as like one of those poor Asiatic hornbills," she was saying. "It seems to me that all my life long some one has walled me up in a nice, safe nest and fed me through my longings and desires. I cannot get to life first hand. I'm not stupid exactly, but I am terribly limited." Helen paused, then went on more rapidly: "First it was my father. He and I travelled after mother's death continually, and alone. He educated me and interpreted life for me; he was a man of the world, I suppose, but he managed to keep me most unworldly wise. Of course I knew, abstractly, the lights and shadows; but I wonder if you will believe me when I tell you that, until after my marriage, I never suspected that — that certain codes of honour and dishonour had place in the lives of those closest to me? The evil of the world was classified and pigeon-holed for me. I even had ambition to get out of my walled-up condition and help some mystical people, detached and far from my safe, clean corner. Father left me more money than was good for any young woman, and my simple impulse was to use it properly."

"You were very young?" Ledyard interrupted.

Helen Travers shook her head.

"Not very. I was twenty-four when I married. I had never had but one intimate friend in my life, and to her I went at my father's death. It was her brother I married — John Travers."

Ledyard nodded his head; he knew of the Traverses — the older generation.

"This thing concerning Dick occurred some three or four years before my marriage. My wedding was a very quiet one; it was not reported, and that accounted for Dick's mother — Elizabeth Thornton — not knowing of it.

"It seems that there had been an alliance between John Travers and — and Dick's mother, and it had been terminated some time before he met me, by mutual consent. There was the child — Dick. The mother took him. There was no question of money: there was enough for them, but she had told John that should anything arise, such as illness or disaster, she would call upon him. They had sworn that to each other.

"Well, my own baby came a year after my marriage and died a month later. When I was least able to bear the shock, the call came from Elizabeth Thornton. John had to tell me. I shall never forget his face as he did it. I realized that his chief concern was for me, and even in all the wreck and ruin I could but honour him for his bravery and sincerity. I think he believed I would understand, but I never did; I never shall. The shock was more surprise than moral resentment. I could not believe at first that such a thing could possibly happen to—one of my own. I felt as if a plague had fallen upon me, and I shrank from every eye, from every touch with the world.

"Doctor Ledyard, you can understand, I hope, but John Travers was not a bad man, and that girl, Dick's mother, was good. Yes; that's the only word to use, strange as it seems to me even after all these years. You see, she was not a hornbill. She came in touch with life at first hand; she took from life what she wanted; she had, what were to me, unheard-of ideas about love and the free gift of self, and yet she never meant to hurt any one; and she had kept herself, amid all the confusion, the gentlest and sweetest of souls.

"When she sent for John she was dying and she did not know what to do about the boy. She had no family — no near friend.

"I went with my husband to see her. There did not seem to be anything else to do. I had no feeling; it was plain duty. Even with the touch of death upon her, Elizabeth Thornton was the most beautiful woman I have ever seen. I cannot describe the sensation she made upon me; but she was like an innocent, pure child who had played with harmful and soiled toys but had come wearily to the day's end, herself unsullied.

"When she knew about me she was broken-hearted. She wept and called to little Dick, who sat in a small chair by her couch:

"'Oh! little son, we could have managed, couldn't we? We would not have hurt any one for the world, would we, sonny?' And the boy got up and soothed

her as a man might have done, and he was only a
little creature. I think I loved him from the moment I saw him shielding that poor, dying mother
from her own folly. 'Course, mummy, course!' he
repeated over and again. Then he looked at me
with the eyes of my own dead baby. Both children
were startlingly like the father. The look pleaded
for mercy from me to them — John, the mother, and
the little fellow himself. And I, who had vaguely
meant to help the world some day, began — with
them! Just for a little time after Elizabeth Thornton's death I became human, or perhaps inhuman. I
resented the wrong that had been done me; I wanted
to fling John and the child away from me; but then a
sense of power rallied me. I had never tasted it
before. I could cast the helpless pair from me, or
— I could save them from the world and the world's
hideous pity for me. I accepted the burden laid upon
me. I think John thought I would forget, would forgive. I cannot explain — my sort of woman is
never understood by — well, John's sort of man.
I am afraid he grew to have a contempt for me, but I
lived on loving them both, but never becoming able
to meet John's hope of me. I knew he was often
lonely — I have pitied him since — but I could not
help being what I was.

"I tried, but it was no use. We lived abroad
for years, and little Dick forgot — I am sure
he forgot — his mother, and when I felt secure

I gave him all, all the passion and devotion of my life.

"John died abroad; I came home with my crippled boy; came home to — you.   That is all!"

Ledyard bent and laid a handful of boughs upon the fire.   The room was cold and cheerless, and the still, white figure in the chair seemed the quiet, chill heart of it all.   And yet — how she had loved and laboured for the boy!   Was she passionless or had her passion been killed while at white heat?

"And — and I suppose Dick must know?"

"Yes.   Dick must know."

There was no sternness, but there was determination in the strong, even voice.   Then:

"Helen, let me do this for you!"

For a moment the uplifted eyes faltered and fell away from the man's face.   Very faintly the words came:

"God bless you!   I could not bear to see — him fail me.   If he must — fail, I cannot see him until — afterward."

The blaze rose higher, and the dark room was a background for that deathlike form before the hearth.

Ledyard left the room silently, and a moment later Helen Travers heard his heavy footfall on the porch outside.   Presently the erratic violin playing ceased and there seemed no sound on the face of the earth.

After what seemed hours, Pine, the guide, en-

tered the room to replenish the fire, and Helen told
him he need not light the lamps.   After his going another aching silence followed through which, at last,
stole the consciousness that she was not alone.
Some one had come into the room from a long
window opening on the piazza.   Helen dared not
look, for if it were Ledyard she would know that
things were very bad indeed.   Then came the slightly
dragging step that she had learned to be so grateful for after the helplessness of crippled childhood.
Still she did not move, nor deeply hope.   The boy
was kind, oh! so tenderly kind, he might only have
come because he must!

The red glow of the fire made the woman's form
by the hearth vividly distinct, and toward that Dick
Travers went as if led by a gleam through a new and
strange experience.   He knelt by her side and, for a
moment, buried his face against her clasped hands;
then he looked up and she saw only intensified love
and trust upon his young face.   She waited for him
to speak, her heart was choking her.

"You thought, dear, that I did not know — that I
had forgotten?   I wonder if any lonely, burdened
little chap could forget — what came before you
lifted the load and taught me to be a — child?   Oh!
she was so sweet; such a playfellow.   I realize it now
even though she has faded into something like a
shadowy dream.   But I recall, too, the loneliness;
the fear that she might leave me alone with no one to

care for me. I can remember her fear, too; always
the fear that one of us might leave the other alone.
The recollection will always stand out in my memory. I shall never forget her nor her sweetness.
Afterward you came and my father. Only lately
have I understood all of — that part of my life and
yours — but I knew he was my father, and I wondered about you, because I could *not* forget — my
mother!

"I learned to love you out of my great need and
out of yours, too, I realize now, and slowly, far too
early, I saw that the happiest thing I could do for
you, who had given me so much, was to seem to forget and rest only on one thought — you were my
mother! Can I make you understand, mother, what
you are in my life — to-night?"

He kissed the cold hands clutching his hot ones,
and with that touch the barrier broke down forever
between them. Travers took her in his arms, but
she did not burden his young strength as the earlier
mother had done. Even in her abandon, they sup-
ported each other bravely.

The days that followed were busy ones. Dick's
tutor came from New York, plans were laid, and
there was small opportunity, just then, for the red-
rock shrine.

"You see," Dick said to Ledyard one afternoon,
"I've never voiced it before — it seemed presump-

tuous — but now that I'm going to have the life of a
fellow, I can choose a fellow's career.   I want, more
than anything else, to be a physician."

Ledyard's eyes flashed, but he lowered his lids.

"It's a devil of a life, boy."

"I think it's the finest of all."

"No hours you can call your own; never daring
to ask for the common things a man cares for.   You
see, women are mostly too jealous and small to
understand a doctor's demands.   They usually raise
hell sooner or later.   I had a friend whose wife used
to look through the keyhole of his consulting-room
door.   A patient tripped over her once and it
nearly cost my friend his practice.   Doctors are only
half human anyway, and women can't go halves
with their husbands."

Dick laughed.

"Between a wife and a profession," he said, "give
me the profession."

"Besides," Ledyard went on; "you get toughened
and brutal; most of us drink, when we don't do
something worse."

"You don't."

"How do you know?"

"I do know, and I'm sure you wouldn't let any
one else say that about your associates; they're the
noblest ever and you know it!"

"Well, we're bound and gagged, and that's a fact.
We're not given much leeway.   We are led up to a

case and forced to carry out the rules.   While we're doctors we can't be men."

Dick recalled that years later with a bitter sense of its truth!

"All the same, if the profession will have me, I'll have it and thank God.   When I think of — well, of the little cuss I was, and of you — why, I tell you, I cannot get too soon into harness.   I'd like to specialize, too.   I've even gone so far as that."

"Good Lord!   In what?"

"Oh, women and children, principally — putting them straight and strong, you know."

"Umph," grunted Ledyard.   "Well, at the first you'll probably be thankful to get any old case that needs tinkering."

Dick Travers did not see Priscilla again that summer.   After a while he went to the rocks, and once he laid sacrilegious hands on the strange god with a longing to smash the hideous skull, but in the end he left it and, after a time, forgot the girl he had played for, even forgot the fantastic dance, for his thoughts were of sterner stuff.

There were guests at the Hill Place, too, for the first time that year, and some entertainment.   There were fishing, and in due season, hunting, at which Ledyard excelled, and the family returned to the States earlier than usual, owing to Dick's affairs.

CHAPTER IV

NATHANIEL GLENN had said some terrible things in Priscilla's presence the evening of the day when he drove her before him while Richard Travers implored her to hold to her ideal. Fortunately, youth spared Priscilla from a full understanding of her father's words, but she caught the drift of his thought. She was convinced that he feared greatly for her here on earth, and had grave doubts as to her soul's ultimate salvation. There was that within her, so he explained, which, unless curbed and corrected, would cast her into eternal damnation! Those were Nathaniel's words.

"She looked a very devil as she danced and smirked at that strange fellow," so had Glenn described the scene; "a man she says she had never laid eyes on before! A daughter of Satan she seemed, with all the witchcraft of her sort." To Nathaniel, that which he could not understand, was wrong.

Theodora spoke not a word. Certain facts from all the evidence stood forth and alarmed her as deeply — though not as bitterly — as they did her husband. There certainly was a daring and brazenness in a young girl carrying on so before a total stranger. In all the conversation the name of the stranger was not mentioned, and oddly enough Priscilla did not even then connect her friend of the music and laughter with the boy of the Hill Place. How could she, when Jerry-Jo's description still stood unchallenged in her mind? Indeed, the stranger did not seem wholly of the earth, earthy. She had accepted him as another phase evolved by the mysterious rite — a new revelation of the strange god.

From all the torrent of misinterpretation Nathaniel gave vent to, one startling impression remained in Priscilla's mind. Sitting in the bare, unlovely kitchen of the farmhouse, with her troubled parents confronting her, a great wave of realization overpowered the girl. She could never make them understand! There was no need to try. She did not really belong to them, or they to her, and she must — get away!

That was it, of course. The lure had caught her. They all felt as she was now feeling — the Hornbys, all the boys and men who left Kenmore. Something always drove them to see they must go, and that was what the lure meant.

Priscilla laughed.

As usual, this angered Nathaniel beyond control.

"You — laugh — you! Why do you laugh?"

Priscilla leaned back in her hard wooden chair.

"The lure's got me!" she panted.

"The — lure?"

"Yes. It means getting away. You have to follow the lure and find your true place. Some people are put in the wrong place — then the lure gets them!"

At this Theodora gave a moan of understanding. They had driven the child too far, been too hard upon her, and the impulse to fly from the love that was seeking to hold her was the one thing to be avoided.

"I'm tired of things. Once I wanted to go to school, but you wouldn't let me." The blazing eyes were fixed upon Nathaniel. "You're always trying to — to hold me back from — from — my life! I want to go away somewhere! I want" — a half-sob shook the fierce, young voice — "I want to be part of — things, and you — you won't let me! I hate this — this place; I'm choking to death!"

And with this Priscilla got up and flung her arms over her head, while she ejaculated fiercely: "I want to be — doshed!"

The effect of this outburst upon the two listeners was tremendous. Theodora recognized with blinding terror that her daughter was no longer a child! The knowledge was like a stroke that left her paralyzed. What could she hope to do with, and for, this new, strange creature in whose young face rising passion and rebellion were suddenly born? Nathaniel was awed, too, but he managed to utter the command: "Leave the room, hussy!"

When the parents were alone they took stock of
the responsibility that was laid upon them.   Helplessly Theodora began to cry.   She could no more
cope with this situation than a baby.   She had never
risen above or beyond the dead level of Kenmore
life, and surely no Kenmore woman had ever borne
so unnatural a child.   She feared hopelessly and trem-
blingly.

With Nathaniel it was different.   He was a hard
man who had forced himself, as he had others, along
the one grim path, but he had the male's inheritance
of understanding of certain traits and emotions.
Had any one suggested to him that his girl had de-
rived from him — not her colourless mother — the
desire for excitement through the senses, he would
have flung the thought madly from him.   Men were
men; women were women!   Even if temptation
came to a girl, only a bad, an evil-natured girl would
recognize it and succumb.   His daughter, Nathaniel
firmly believed, was marked for destruction, and he
was frightened and aroused not only for Priscilla
herself but for his reputation and position.   He had
known similar temptation; had overcome it.   He
understood, or thought he did!

He gave the girl no benefit of doubt; his mind
conceived things that never had occurred.   He believed she had often met the young fellow from the
Hill Place.   God alone knew what had gone before!

"What shall we do?" sobbed Theodora.   "We

cannot make a prisoner of her; we cannot watch her every move — and she's only a bit over fourteen!"

Had the girl died that night Nathaniel would not have mourned her, he would have known only relief and gratitude.

"She was unwelcomed," he muttered to his weeping wife; "and she has become a curse to us. It lies with us to turn the punishment into our souls' good; but what can we do for her?"

Priscilla did not die that night. She slept peacefully and happily with the red, pulsing planet over the hemlock shining faithfully upon her. The next day she reappeared before her parents with a cloudless face and a willingness to make such amends as could be brought about without too much self-abnegation. In the broad light of day the mother could not hold to the horrors of the evening before. She had been nervous and overwrought; it wasn't so bad as they had thought!

"I want you to go erranding," she said to Priscilla soon after the midday meal and by way of propitiation. "It's one by the clock now. Given an hour to go, another to return, and a half hour for the buying, you should be back by four at the latest."

Priscilla looked laughingly up at her mother, "Funny, little mother," she said; "he's made you afraid of me. Hadn't you better tie a string to my foot?" But all the time the girl was thinking.

"An hour for both going and coming will be enough, and that will leave an hour for the schoolmaster."

Aloud she said: "I was fiercely angry last night, mother, for he read me wrong and would not believe me, but it made me feel the *lure;* it really did."

"You must never speak so again, child," Theodora replied, thinking she was impressing the girl; "and, Priscilla, what did you mean by saying you wanted to be — be doshed? That was the most unsanctified word I ever heard. What does it mean? Where did you learn it?"

At this Priscilla doubled over with laughter but managed to say:

"Why, it means just — doshed! Haven't you ever wanted to be doshed, mother, when you were young, and before father took the dosh out of you?"

Theodora was again overcome by former fears, and to confirm her terror Priscilla sprang toward her with outstretched, gripping fingers and wide, eager eyes.

"It means," she breathed, advancing upon her mother's retreating form, "it means skib, skib, skibble — de — de — dosh!"

At this she had her mother by the shoulders and was seeking to kiss the affrighted and appalled face.

Theodora escaped her, and realized that a changeling had indeed entered her home. An unknown element was here. It was as if, having been discovered, Priscilla felt she no longer needed to hide her inner self, but was giving it full sway.

If they could only have known that the spring of imagination and joy had been touched in the girl and merely the madness of youth and the legitimate yearning for expression moved her! But Theodora did not understand and she tried to be stern.

"You are to be back in this house at four!" she cried; "at quarter after at the latest."

So Priscilla started forth. The mother watched her from the doorway. Suspicion was in her heart; she feared the girl would turn toward the woods; she was prepared for that, but instead, the flying figure made for the grassy road leading to Kenmore and was soon lost to sight.

Three miles of level road, much of it smooth, moss-covered rock, was easy travelling for nimble feet and a glad heart. And Priscilla was the gladdest creature afield that day. Impishly she was enjoying the sensation she had created. It appealed to her dramatic sense and animal enjoyment. In some subtle fashion she realized she had balked and de-feated her father — she was rather sorry about her mother — but that could be remedied later on. There was no doubt that she had the whip hand of Nathaniel at last, and the subconscious attitude of defiance she always held toward her father was strengthened by the knowledge that he was unjustly judging her.

There were many things of interest in Kenmore that only limited time prevented Priscilla from investigating. She longed to go to the jail and see if the people had prevailed upon old Jerry McAlpin to discharge himself. She admired Jerry's spirit!

She wanted to call upon Mrs. Hornby and question her about Jamsie, her last boy, who had succumbed to the lure of the States. She longed to know the symptoms of one attacked by the lure. Then there was the White Fish Lodge — she did so want to visit Mrs. McAdam. The annual menace of taking Mrs. McAdams' license from her was man's talk just then, and Mrs. McAdam was so splendid when her rights were threatened. On the village Green she annually defended her position like a born orator. Priscilla had heard her once and had never got over her admiration for the little, thin woman who rallied the men to her support with frantic threats as to her handling of their rights unless they helped her fight her battle against a government bent upon taking the living from a "God-be-praised widow-woman with two sons to support."

It had all been so exactly to Priscilla's dramatic taste that she with difficulty restrained herself from calling at the White Fish.

There was a good hour to her credit when the erranding was finished and the time needed for the home run set aside, so to the little cabin, built beside the schoolhouse, she went with heavily loaded arms and an astonishingly light heart.

Since the day when Anton Farwell had undertaken Priscilla's enlightenment, asserting that he had been ordained to do so by her god, he had had an almost supernatural influence upon her thought. For her, he was endowed with mystery, and, with the subtle poetry of the lonely young, she deafened her ears to any normal explanation of the man.

Reaching the cabin, she pushed gently against the door, knowing that if it opened, Kenmore was free to enter. Farwell was in and, when Priscilla stood near him, seemed to travel back from a far place before he saw her. Farwell was an old-young man; he cultivated the appearance of age, but only the very youthful were deceived. His long, dark hair fell about his thin face lankly, and it was an easy matter, by dropping his head, to hide his features completely.

He was tall and, from much stooping over books or the work of his garden, was round-shouldered. When he looked you fully in the face, which he rarely did, it was noticed that his eyes were at once childishly friendly and deathly sad.

The older people of Kenmore had ceased to wonder about him. Having accepted him, they let matters drop. To the children, to all helpless animals, he was an enduring solace and power. When all else failed they looked to him for solution. For this had Priscilla come.

"To be sure!" cried Farwell at length. "It's Priscilla Glenn. Bad child! It's many a day since we had a lesson. There! there! no excuses. Sit down and — own up!"

While he was speaking Farwell replenished the wood on the fire and brushed the ashes from the hearth. Priscilla, in a chair, sat upright and rather breathlessly wondered how she could manage all she wanted to say and hear in the small space of time that was hers.

Anton's back was toward her when she uttered her first question and the words brought him to an upright position, facing her at once.

"Mr. Farwell, where did you come from — I mean before the wreck?"

For a moment the master looked as if about to spring forward to lock the door and bar the windows. Real alarm was in his eyes.

"Who told you to ask that?" he whispered.

"No one. No one has to tell me questions; I have more of my own than I can ask. I never thought before about you, Mr. Farwell, we're so used to you, but now it's because of *me*. I want to know. Somebody has got to help me — I feel it coming again."

"Feel what coming?" Farwell sat limply down in the chair he had lately occupied.

"Why, the lure. It comes to the boys, Mr. Farwell. They just get it and go off to the States, and it's come to me! I've always known it would. You see, I've got to go away; not just now, but some time. I'm going out through the Secret Portage. I'm going away, away to find my real place. I'm going to do something — out where the States are. I hoped you came from there; could tell me — how to go about it. Do you know, I feel as if I had been dropped in Kenmore just to rest before I went on!"

Farwell looked at the girl and something new and changed about her startled him as it had her parents, but, being wiser, he felt no antagonism. It was an amazing, an interesting thing. The girl had suddenly developed: that was all. She was eager to try her wings at a longer flight than any of her sex in Kenmore had ever before dreamed. It was amusing even if it were serious.

Years before, Farwell had discovered the girl's keen mind and her quaint originality. As much for his own pleasure as her advantage he had taught her as he had some of the other village children, erratically, inconsequently, and here she was now demanding that he fit her out with a chart for deep-sea sailing.

How could he permit her to harbour, even for an idle moment, the idea of leaving her shelter and going away? At this the thin, dark face grew rigid and stern. But too well the man knew the folly of setting up active opposition to any young thing straining against the door of a cage. Better open the door even if a string on the leg or a clipped wing had to be resorted to!

"Did you ever see the States?" The tense voice was imploring.

"Oh, yes. Why do you wish to go there?"

"Why do the boys?"

This was baffling.

"Well, there was Mrs. Hornby's oldest boy, he went to the States, got the worst of it, and came home to die. He did not find them happy places."

"Yes, but all the other Hornbys went just the same, even Jamsie. It's the chance, you know, the chance to try what's in you, even if you *do* come home and die! You never have a chance in Kenmore; and I don't mean to be like my mother — like the other women. You see, Mr. Farwell, I'm willing to suffer, but I *am* going to know all I want to, and I am going to find a place where I fit in, if I can."

So small and ignorant did the girl look, yet so determined and keen, that Farwell grew anxious. Evidently Nathaniel had borne too hard upon her, borne to the snapping point, and she had, in her wild fashion, caught the infection of the last going away — Jamsie Hornby's. It was laughable, but pathetic.

"What could you do?" Farwell leaned forward and gazed into the strange blue eyes fixed upon him.

"Dance.   Have you ever seen me dance?   Do you want to?"   She was prepared to prove herself.

"Good Lord! no, no!"

"Oh!   I can dance.   If some one would play for me — play on — on a fiddle, I could dance all day and night.   Wouldn't people pay for that?"

This was serious business.   By some subtle suggestion Priscilla Glenn had introduced into the bare, cleanly room an atmosphere of danger, a curious sense of unreality and excitement.

"Yes — they do pay," Farwell said slowly; "but where in heaven's name did you get such ideas?"

The girl looked impishly saucy.   She was making a sensation again and, while Anton Farwell was not affected as her parents had been, he was undoubtedly impressed.

"It's this way: You have to sell what you've got until you get something better.   There isn't an earthly thing I can do but dance now; of course I can learn.   Don't you remember the nice story about the old woman who went to market her eggs for to sell?   Master Farwell, I'm like her, and my dancing is my — egg!"

She was laughing now, this unreasoning, unreasonable girl, and she was laughing more at Farwell's perplexity than at her own glibness.   She must soon go, her time was growing short, but she was enjoying herself immensely.

Looking at her, Farwell was suddenly convinced

of one overpowering fact: Priscilla Glenn was destined for — living! Hers was one of those natures that flash now and then upon a commonplace existence, a strange soul from an unknown port, never resting until it finds its way back.

"Poor little girl!" whispered Farwell, and then he talked to her.

Would she let him go to her father and mother?

"What's the use?" questioned Priscilla, and she told him of the experience in the woods. "Father saw only evil when it was the most beautiful thing that ever happened."

Farwell saw a wider stretch and more danger.

"But I will try, and anyway, Priscilla, if I promise to help you get ready, will you promise me to do nothing without consulting me?"

This the girl was ready enough to do. She was restless and defiant under her new emotion, but intuitively she had sought Farwell because he had before aided her and sympathized with her. Yes, she would confide in him.

That night Farwell called at Lonely Farm. Followed by his two lean, ugly sledge dogs he made his way to the barn where Nathaniel was doing the evening's work. While the men talked, the dogs, behind the building, fought silently and ferociously. Farwell had fed one before he left home and a bitter jealousy lay between the animals. It was almost more than one might hope that the master could influence Glenn or change his mind, but Farwell did bring to bear an argument that, because nothing else presented itself, swayed the father.

"You cannot get the same results from all children," Farwell said, looking afar and smiling grimly; "there's no use trying to make an abnormal child into a normal one. Priscilla is like a wild thing of the woods. You may tame her, if you go about it right; you'll never be able to force her. She's kind and affectionate, but she cannot be fettered or caged, without mischief being done. Better let her think she is having her own way, or — she may take it!"

"I'll break her will!" muttered Glenn.

"And if you do — what then?"

"She'll fall into line — women do! Their life takes it out of them. Once I get her on the right track, she'll go straight enough. There's no other way for her sex, thank God!"

"She'd be a poor, despicable thing if she was cowed." Contempt rang in Farwell's voice.

"She'd serve her purpose." Glenn was so angry that he became brutal. "Spirit ain't needed for her job."

"Purpose? Job?" Farwell repeated.

"Yes. Child-bearing; husband-serving. If they take to it naturally they're all the better off; if they have to be brought to terms — well, then ——"

Gradually the truth dawned upon Farwell, and

his thin face flushed, while in his heart he pitied Theodora Glenn and Priscilla.

"I wish I'd kept to my first ideas!" Glenn was saying surlily, "and never let the limb learn of you or another. I gave her her head and here we are!"

"Had she been taught regularly by some one better fitted than I she would have done great credit to you. She has a bright mind and a vivid imagination."

To this Glenn made no response, but the energy with which he applied the brush to his horse caused the animal to rear dangerously.

"Come, come," Farwell continued; "better loosen the rein and let her run herself out — she may settle happily after a bit. If you don't, she may run farther than you know."

"Run? Run where?" Nathaniel, safe from the horse's heels, glared at Farwell.

"To the States.   There is no sex line on the border."

"But there's good, plain law. I'd have her back and well cowed, if she attempted that!"

And then Farwell played his card.

"See here, Mr. Glenn, you do not want to drive this girl of yours to — to hell! Of course there is law and of course you have the whip hand while Priscilla is in your clutch, but with a wit like hers, if she slipped across the border she could lose herself so completely that neither your hate nor legal power could ever find her.   Do you want to drive her to such lengths?"

Some of the truth of what Farwell was saying dashed Glenn's temper with fear.   Hard and cruel as he was, he was not devoid of affection of a clammy sort, and for an instant Priscilla as a helpless girl wandering among strangers replaced Priscilla, the rebellious daughter, and pity moved him.

"Well, what do you suggest?" he asked grudgingly.

"Simply this: You can trust me.   Good Lord you surely can trust me with her!   Let me teach her and bring a little diversion into her life.   What she wants is what all young things want — freedom and fun — pure, simple fun.   Don't let her think you are expecting evil of her; let her alone!"

The extent of Glenn's confusion may be estimated by the fact that he permitted Priscilla thereafter to go, when she chose, to Kenmore and learn of Farwell what Farwell chose to give her, and, for the first time in the girl's life, she felt a glow of appreciation toward her father.

With this new freedom she became happier, less restless, and her admiration for Farwell knew no bounds.

The schoolmaster managed to procure a violin and laboriously practised upon it until an almost forgotten gift was somewhat restored.   He did not play as Travers did — he had only his ear to depend upon; he had never been well taught — but his music sufficed to accompany Priscilla's nimble feet, and it gave Farwell himself an added interest in his dull life.

"She'll marry Jerry-Jo McAlpin some day," the schoolmaster thought at times; "and have a brood of half-breeds — no quarter-breeds — and all this joy and gladness will become a blurred, or blotted-out, background.   Good God!"

CHAPTER V

MRS. McADAM of the White Fish Lodge came out upon the village Green one evening in late August and, in a loud voice, hailed Jerry McAlpin:

"I've heard it said," called she, "that you, you Jerry McAlpin, are not against the taking away of my license; not against the making of Kenmore a teetotal town!"

There was menace in the high-pitched voice; warning in the accusation. But Jerry had not taken a drop to drink since his self-releasement from jail (after an apology from Hornby), and he was uncannily clear headed.

"I've said that same!" he replied, and stopped short in his walk.

Two or three other men, followed by dogs, paused to listen. Then a boat, coming in loaded with fish, tied up to the wharf, and the crew, leaning over the sides, waited for developments.

"And for why?" called Mary, hands on hips and her sharp eyes blazing.

"For this: The drink turns us mad! I'm late finding it out, but I've found it! It sent me to jail with my wits all afire. My boy drank that night, drank like a young beast, and lay on the floor of the cabin, they tell me, after I went away; and he only sixteen, and his dead uncle stark there beside him for company!"

By this time a goodly gathering was on the Green, and Mary was in her element.

"And so," she said calmly, waxing eloquent as her power grew, "you and the like of you would take an honest woman's living from her, and she a God-be-praised widow at that, because you can't control the beast in yourselves and can't train the cubs of your kennels!"

This was going to great lengths, and many a listener who sided with Mary was chilled by her offensive words.

"Come! come!" warned Hornby, the father of the recently lured Jamsie, "them ain't exactly womanly terms, are they?"

But Mary was on her high horse. Availing herself of the safety her sex secured for her, she struck left and right without grace or favour, and her audience gaped while they listened.

"Oh, I know! 'Tis this year a dry town with me ruined, and it's next year a wet town with McAlpin, Hornby, or another creature in trousers taking my place; and after that there will be no more dry town for ever and ever! It's not morals you are after, but a man-controlled tavern. Blast ye!" A sneer marked Mary's thin, dark face. "You want your drinks and your freedom, but you say you fear for your lads. Shame on you! Have I no lads?"

Silence.

"Have I not trained them in the way they should go? Do I fear for them?" A grave silence, and McAlpin glared at Hornby, while an irreverent youth, with a fish dangling from his hands, laughed and muttered:

"Like gorrems!"

"Play a man's part, Jerry McAlpin. 'Tis not for Jerry-Jo you fear; it's my business you'd get from me, and you know it! Teach that lad of yours to be decent, as I've trained mine. I have no fear for my boys! I know what I'm talking about, and I tell you now, if my lads were like yours I'd fling the business over, but I don't see why a decent woman, and her a God-be-praised widow, should lose her living because you can't train your brats in the way they should go. But this is mine! If you don't stand by me and swear to do it here and now, it's not another drink one of you shall get in my place till after things are settled."

This was going farther than Mary McAdam had ever gone before. She had threatened dire restrictions against them who failed to support her cause should her cause be won in spite of them; she had even hinted at cash payments to insure her against want if, possibly, her license was revoked, but this shutting down upon human rights before election came off was upsetting to the last degree. Hornby looked at McAlpin and McAlpin dropped his eyes; there was a muttering and a grumbling, and a general feeling prevailed that every man should be his own keeper and the guardian of his own sons, and it would be a bitter wrong against a God-be-praised widow to let family affairs ruin her business.

In the end Mary McAdam, with a manly following of stern upholders of individual rights and the opportunity for mutual good fellowship, retired to the bar of the White Fish and, waited upon by Mary herself and her two exemplary sons, made merry far into the evening.

Tom and Sandy McAdam, handsome, carefree boys of sixteen and eighteen, passed the drinks with many a jest and often a wink, but never a drop drank they, not until the Lodge had closed its doors on all visitors, and then Tom, the elder, with a final leer at Sandy the younger, drained off a glass of bad whisky with a grace that betokened long practice.

"Hold, there!" cautioned Sandy, filling a glass of beer for himself; "you'll not be able to hide it from the mother, you galoot."

"Oh, the night's long before the day breaks, and it's yourself as must take the turn at house chores the morning."

The following day was cloudy and threatening,

and why Mary McAdam should take that time for suggesting that her boys go over to Wyland Island and buy their winter suits, she herself could not have told.   Perhaps, from the assurance of last night, she felt freer with money; perhaps she thought the boys could not be spared so well later; be that as it might, she insisted, even against Sandy's remark that "a lad couldn't put his mind to a winter outfit with the sweat rolling down his back," that they should set forth by eleven o'clock.

"Make a lark of it," said she generously; "take that scapegoat Jerry-Jo McAlpin with you and have it out with him about being a young beast and worrying the heart out of old Jerry, who means well but ain't got no kind of a headpiece.   Take your lunch along and ——"

Here she pointed her remarks with a lean, commanding finger: "You take that sail off the launch! It's quiet enough now, but it ain't going to last forever, and I couldn't rest with three flighty lads in a boat with a sail *and* an engine."

Mrs. McAdam always expected to be obeyed. Her personality was such that she generally was; but always, when disobedience followed, it was hidden from her immediate attention, and she was never one to show the weakness of watching to see her orders carried out.   That was why she, of all the people in the little village, did not realize that her boys often drank more than was good for them —

always managed, by clever devices, to escape her eye.

"A glass of harmless stuff now and again," she would say with a toss of her head; "what's that but a proof of the lads' self-control? That's what I'm a-telling you: make your lads strong and self-respecting."

Tom did not take the sail from the boat that day, neither did he expect to use it. He furled it close and shipped it carefully, but it was late, and, in the last hurry, he kept his mother's caution in mind, but did not carry out her command. Then Sandy, when they were about to start, did a bold thing. Stealing into the bar, he took a bottle of whisky and a bottle of brandy; these he hid under his reefer, and, with a laugh at his own cunning, put into the empty places on the shelves two partly filled bottles, and ran to the wharf.

Mary McAdam waved them a farewell from the steps. She had packed the hamper and stowed it under the very sail she had ordered off. In the excitement of preparation she overlooked it entirely.

"You, Sandy, see to it that you buy a suit that you won't repent when the winter nips you!" she called.

"And you, Tom, get a quiet colour and *no* checks! When yer last year's suit shrank and the squares got crooked ye looked like a damaged checker-board!"

Jerry-Jo McAlpin from his seat in the stern roared with laughter at this, and just then the sturdy little engine puffed, thudded, and "caught on," and off went the three with loud words of good-bye.

The Channel was as smooth as a summer brook, and the launch shot ahead.

"It's a bit chilly," Sandy said as they neared the mouth opening at Flying Point into the Little Bay.

"Put on your storm coat," cautioned Tom, "and you, too, Jerry-Jo; we'll get the wind when we pass Dreamer's Rock and strike the Big Bay."

The boys got out their coats and put them on, and then Sandy said:

"See what I've got!   Snitched it from under the mother's eye, too!"   He held up the bottles.   Tom laughed, but Jerry-Jo reached out for one.

"A nip will ward off the cold better than a coat," he said.

They all three indulged in this preventive.

Beyond Dreamer's Rock the wind fulfilled Tom's prophecy; it was not a great wind, but it was a steady one, and, perhaps, because the whisky had warmed Tom's blood too hastily and hotly, he grew reckless.

"What do you say, fellows, to eating our lunch and then trying sail and engine together?   We could beat the record and surprise folks by our time in coming and going.   The wind's safe; not a puff! What do you say?"

Jerry-Jo was something of a coward, but by the

time he had eaten his lunch and washed it down with more whisky than he had meant to take, he was ready to handle the sail himself and proceeded to do so.

Little Bear Island was the last one before the entrance to Big Bay, and when the launch passed that, either the wind had changed, or Tom, at the engine and Jerry-Jo at the sail, had lost nerve and head, for the boat became unmanageable. Sandy, keeping to the exact middle of the boat, called to Jerry-Jo to lower the sail, but Jerry-Jo did not hear, or failed to clearly comprehend. The little craft shot ahead like an arrow, but Tom knew that when they went about there would be trouble. They were fully a mile from either rock-bound shore. Wyland Island was a good two miles before them, and home seven miles to the rear.

A biggish sea was rolling and the sky was clouding threateningly. The liquor had done its worst for the boys: it had unnerved them, while at the same time it had given them a mad courage.

"Keep straight ahead," shouted Tom, "until we get near shore, and then pull in that infernal sail!"

What happened just then Jerry-Jo could never tell, and he alone remained at the day's end for the telling!

They were in the water, all three of them! For a moment Jerry-Jo, thoroughly sobered and keener witted than he had ever been before in his life, believed he was the only one of the party ever again to appear in that angry sea.   Then he saw the over-turned boat, heard the last sobbing pants of the engine as it filled with water; then Tom's black head and agonized face appeared; then Sandy's red head. They all made for the boat and the wide sail lying flat in the water!

They reached the launch, chilled and desperate, climbed upon it, and gazed helplessly at each other. Through chattering teeth they tried to speak, but only a moan escaped Tom's blue lips.   The wind was colder; the sun had gone behind a bank of dull storm clouds.   After a long while Sandy, looking over the expanse of ugly choppy waves, shuddered and panted:

"It's going to be dark soon; it can't be more than a half mile to yonder rock — I'm for swimming to it! Once on land we can move about, get our blood going, and perhaps find a sheltered spot — till — morning!"

Tom looked at his brother vaguely; he was suffering keenly:

"Don't be a fool!" he shuddered.   Jerry-Jo, huddled in a wet heap, was sobbing like a baby — gone utterly to pieces.

Another hideous space of silence followed, then Sandy spoke again:

"I'm going to make the try.   I'm dying of cold. It's the only chance for any of us.   Here goes!"

And before any one could interfere he made his

leap and was in the water, a bobbing speck among
the ugly white caps!

"Good God!"

That was all Tom said, but his crazed eyes were
upon that strained, uplifted face. Jerry-Jo ceased
his moaning and — laughed! It was a foolish cackle,
such as a maniac might give, mistaking a death-
struggle for a bit of play.

"He's — a good swimmer!" he gasped, and
laughed again. Tom turned, for an instant, wondering eyes upon him. He may have, in that moment, estimated his own chance, his duty to Jerry-Jo,
and his determination to be with his brother. The
perplexed gaze lasted but the briefest space of time
and then with:

"All right! here goes!" he was making for Sandy
with a strength born of despair and madness.

"Come back!" shrieked Jerry-Jo with the frenzy
of one deserted and too cowardly or helpless to follow: "Come back!"

But neither swimmer heard nor heeded. For a
moment more the black and the red heads bobbed
about, the faces turned toward each other grimly.
Even in that waste and at the bitter last the sense
of companionship held their thought. Jerry-Jo,
rigid and every sense at last alert in an effort for
self-preservation, saw Sandy smile. It was a wonderful smile: it was like a flash of sunlight on that
black sea; then Sandy's lips moved, but no one

was ever to know what he said, and then — Jerry-
Jo was alone in the coming night and the rolling
waves!

"They should," said Mary McAdam, "be home
by seven at the latest. The wind's with them
coming back; it was with them part of the way
going!"

Anton Farwell sat on the steps of the Lodge, his
dogs peacefully lying at his feet. All day, since
hearing of the boys' trip, he had been restless and
anxious. Farwell had his bad hours often, but he
rarely permitted himself companionship at such
times, but to-day, after his noon meal, he had been
unable to keep away from the Lodge.

"Fall's setting in early," Mrs. McAdam went on;
"pickerel come; whitefish go. Beasts and fish and
birds ken a lot, Mr. Farwell."

"They certainly do. The more you live with
dumb creatures, the more you are impressed with
that. Is that Sandy's dog, Mrs. McAdam?"

A yellow, lank dog came sniffing around the side of
the house and lay down, friendly wise, by Farwell.

"Yes, and he's a cute one. Do you believe me,
Mr. Farwell, that there Bounder knows the engine
of our boat! Any other boat can come into the
Channel and he don't take any notice, but let my
boys be out late and Bounder, lying asleep on the
floor, will start up at the chugging of the launch and
make for the dock. He never makes a mistake."

Farwell laughed and bent over to smooth Bounder's back.

"What time is it?" he asked.

"Six-thirty," Mary replied with alarming readiness. "Six-thirty, and the clock's a bit slow at that."

Farwell felt sure it was a good ten minutes slow; but because of that he turned the conversation.

"Jerry McAlpin was telling me to-day," he said in his low, pleasant voice, "of how he and others used to smuggle liquor over the border. Jerry seems repenting of his past."

Mary laughed and shrugged her shoulders.

"My man and Jerry, with old Michael McAlpin, were the freest of smugglers. In them days the McAlpins wasn't pestered with feelings; they was good sports. Jerry marrying that full-breed had it taken out of him somewhat — she was a hifty one. Them Indians never can get off their high heels — not the full-breeds. But I tell you, Mr. Farwell, and you take it for truth, when Jerry begins to maudle about repentance, it's just before a — debauch. I know the signs."

Just then Bounder raised his head and howled.

"None of that! Off with yer!" shouted Mary, making for the dog with nervous energy. "Once," she went on, her lips twitching, "my man and Michael McAlpin had a good one on the officers. They had a big load of the stuff on the cart and were coming down the road back of the Far Hill Place when they sensed the custom men in the bushes. What do they do but cut the traces and lick the horses into a run; then they turned the barrels loose, jumped off, letting them roll down the hill, and they, themselves, made for safety. It was only a bit more trouble to go back in a week's time and gather up the barrels; but those government devils followed the horses like idiots and felt mighty set up when they overtook them! But when they saw they had *only* the horses, oh! good Lord!"

Farwell laughed absently; his eyes were fixed on the water. Even in the Channel it had an angry look. The current was set from the Bay, and the stream rose and fell as if it had an ugly secret in its keeping.

"Mrs. McAdam," he said suddenly, "I'm going out to — to meet the boys!"

"God save ye, Mr. Farwell — for which?"

When Mary fell into that form of speech she was either troubled or infuriated.

"I'm restless; I feel like a fling. Come on, you scamps!" to his dogs, "get home and keep house till I come back."

His dogs leaped to him and then made for the Green. Without another word Farwell walked to his launch at the foot of the wharf steps and prepared for his trip.

A black wave of fear enveloped Mary McAdam.

She was overcome by a certainty of evil, and, when Farwell's boat had disappeared, she strode to the Green and gave vent to her anxiety. There were those who comforted, those who jeered, but the men were largely away on fishing business, and the women and boys were more interested in her excitement than they were in her cause for fear.

It was eight o'clock and very dark when Doctor Ledyard, driving down from Far Hill Place for the mail, paused to listen to Mrs. McAdam's expressions of anxiety. Young Dick Travers was beside him, and Mary's words held him.

"Was Jerry-Jo with your boys, Mrs. McAdam?" he asked.

"He was that! And Jerry-Jo always brings ill-luck on a trip. I should have known better than to let the half-breed scamp go. 'Twas pity as moved me. Jerry-Jo is one as thinks rocking a boat is spirit, and yelling for help, when no help is needed, a rare joke. The young devil!"

Doctor Ledyard and Dick stayed on after getting the mail. A strange, tense feeling was growing in the place. Mary's terror was contagious.

"If the men would only come back," moaned the distracted mother; "I'd send the lot of them out after the young limbs!"

At eight-thirty the storm broke. A dull, thick storm which had used most of its fury out beyond Flying Point, and in the breast of the sullen wind came the sound of an engine panting, panting in the darkness that was shot by flashes of lightning and rent by thunder-claps. Mary McAdam gazed petrified at Bounder, who had followed her to the Green.

"Why don't yer yelp?" she muttered, giving the dog a kick. But Bounder blinked indifferently as the coming boat drew near and nearer.

Every boy, woman, and child, with the old men and lazy young ones, were at the wharf when the launch emerged from the darkness. Some one was standing up guiding the boat, ready to protect it from violent contact; some one was huddled on the floor of the boat — some one who made no cry, did not look up. They two were all! Just then a lurid flash of lightning seemed to photograph the scene forever on the minds of the onlookers.

Ledyard, with Dick, was close to the boat when it touched the dock. By the lurid light of electricity the face of the man in the launch rose sharply against the darkness and for one instant shone as if to attract attention.

Farwell was known by reputation to the doctor; he had probably been seen by him many times, but certainly his face had never made an impression upon him before. But now, in the hour of anguish and excitement, it held Ledyard's thought to the exclusion of everything else.

"Who? where?" The questions ran through his

mind and then, because every sense was alert, he knew!

"Jerry-Jo!" Dick was calling, "where are the others?"

It was a mad question, but the boy, huddling in the launch, replied quiveringly:

"Gone! gone to the bottom off Dreamer's Rock."

Then he began to whimper piteously.

A shuddering cry rang out. It was Mary Mc-Adam, who, followed by her dog, ran wildly, apron over head, toward the White Fish Lodge.

Farwell, casting all reserve aside, worked with Ledyard over the prostrate Jerry-Jo. The recognition was no shock to him; he had always known Ledyard; had cleverly kept from his notice heretofore, but now the one thing he had hoped to escape was upon him, and he grew strangely indifferent to what lay before.

He obeyed every command of the doctor as they sought to restore Jerry-Jo. More than once their eyes met and their hands touched, but the contact did not cause a tremor in either man.

When the inevitable arrives a strength accompanies it. Nature rarely deserts either friend or foe at the critical moment.

CHAPTER VI

THE bay was dragged, various methods being used, but the bodies of Sandy and Tom McAdam were not recovered. Mary McAdam with strained eyes and rigid lips waited at the wharf as each party returned, and when at last hope died in her poor heart, she set about the doing of two things that she felt must be done.

The behaviour of the boys in the boat on the day of the accident had at last reached her ears, for, with such excitement prevailing and Jerry-Jo reduced to periods of nervous babbling as he repeated again and again the story, Mary was certain of overhearing the details. As far as possible she verified every word. That her sons had disobeyed her about the sail there could be no doubt, and when she went to the shelf of the bar and discovered the half-filled bottles which Sandy had put in the places of the brandy and whisky, her heart gave up doubt. She relinquished all that she had prided herself upon in the past. They had defied and deceived her! They had permitted her to be mocked while she prated of her superiority! It was bitter hard, but Mary McAdam made no feeble cry — she prepared for the final act in the little drama.   Beyond that she could not, would not look.

"Dig me two graves," she commanded Big Hornby; "dig them one on either side of my husband's."

"You'll be thinking the bodies will yet be found, poor soul?"   Hornby had a tender nature kept human by his hunger for his absent boys.

"I'm not thinking.   I'm doing my part; let others do the same."

And then Mary went to Anton Farwell.   Farwell, since the night of the tragedy, was waiting, always waiting for the inevitable.   Every knock at his door brought him panting to his feet.   He knew Doctor Ledyard would come; he fervently hoped he would, and soon, but the days dragged on.   There were moments when the man had a wild desire to shoulder his bag and set forth under shadow of the night and the excitement, for one of his long absences, this one, however, to terminate as far from Kenmore as possible.   Once he had even started, but at the edge of the water where his boat lay he halted, deterred by the knowledge that his safer course lay in facing what he must face sooner or later.   Now that he was known to be alive it were easier to deal with one man than with the pack of bloodhounds which that one man might set upon him.   Always the personal element entered in — it was weak hope, but the only one.   He might win Ledyard; he could not win the pack!

When Mary McAdam knocked on Farwell's door he thought the time had come, but the sight of the distracted mother steadied him. Here was something for him to do, something to carry him away from his lonely forebodings.

"Come in, Mrs. McAdam. Rest yourself. You look sorely in need of rest."

It was the early evening of a hot day. It was lighter out of doors than in the cottage, for the shades were drawn at Farwell's windows; he disliked the idea of being watched from without.

"I can't rest, Master Farwell, till I've done my task," said the poor soul, sinking into the nearest chair. "And it's to get your help I've come."

"I'll do what I can," murmured Farwell. "What I'll be permitted to do," he felt would be more true.

"I've said more than once, Mr. Farwell, that were my boys like other boys I'd give up the business of the White Fish. Well, my lads were like others, only they were keener about deceiving me. I thought I'd made them strong and sure, but I did the same hurt to my flesh and blood that I did to others. I put evil too close and easy to them. I prided myself on what I had never done! They'll come back to me no more. Could I have a talk with them, things might be straightened out; but I must do what is to be done alone."

Not a quiver shook the low, severe voice. The very hardness moved Farwell to deep pity.

"It's now, Mr. Farwell, that I'd have you come to the Lodge and help me with my task, and when it's over I want you to stand with me beside those two empty graves and say what you can for them who never had the right mother to teach them. I'm no church woman; the job of priest and minister sickens me, but I know a good man when I see one. You helped the lads while they lived; you risked your life to help them home at the last; and it's you who shall consecrate the empty beds where I'd have my lads lie if the power were mine!"

Farwell got up and paced the room restlessly. Suddenly, with Ledyard's recognition, the poor shell of respectability and self-respect which, during his lonely years, had grown about him, was torn asunder, and he was what he knew the doctor believed him. To such, Mary McAdam's request seemed a cruel jest, a taunt to drive him into the open. And yet he knew that up to the last ditch he must hold to what he had secured for himself — the trust and friendship of these simple people. Hard and distasteful as the effort was he dared not turn himself from it. Full well he knew that Ledyard's magnifying glass was, unseen, being used against him even now. The delay was probably caused by the doctor's silent investigation of his recent life, his daily deeds. He could well imagine the amusement, contempt, and disbelief that would meet the story of his poor, blameless years during which he had played with children, worked in his garden, been friends with the common folk, not from any high motive, but to keep himself from insanity! He had had to use any material at hand, and it had brought about certain results that Ledyard would dissect and toss aside, he would never believe! Still the attempt to live on, as he had lived, must be undertaken. A kind of desperation overcame him.

What did it matter? He might just as well go on until he was stopped. He was no safer, no more comfortable, sitting apart waiting for his summons. He would, as far as in him lay, ignore the menacing thing that hovered near, and play the part of a man while he might.

"I'm ready to go with you, Mrs. McAdam," he said, turning for his hat, "and as we go tell me what you are about to do."

It was no easy telling. The mere statement of fact was so crude that Farwell could not, by any possibility, comprehend the dramatic scene he was soon to witness and partake of.

"I'm going to keep my word," Mary McAdam explained. "I'll not be waiting for the license to be given, or taken away, I'll keep my word."

It was a still, breathless night, with a moon nearly full, and as Mrs. McAdam, accompanied by Farwell, passed over the Green toward the Lodge, the idlers and loiterers followed after at a respectful distance. Mary was the centre of attraction just then, and Farwell always commanded attention, used as the people were to him.

"Come on! come on!" called Mary without turning her head. "Bring others and behold the sight of your lives. Behold a woman keeping her word when the need for the keeping is over!"

A growing excitement was rising in Mary's voice; she was nearing the end of her endurance and was becoming reckless.

By the time the Lodge was reached a goodly crowd was at the steps leading up to the bar. Jerry McAlpin was there with Jerry-Jo beside him. Hornby, just come from the digging of the two graves, stood nearby with the scent of fresh earth clinging to him.

Suddenly Mary McAdam came out of the house, her arms filled with bottles, while behind her followed Farwell rolling a cask.

What occurred then was so surprising and bewildering that those who looked on were never able to clearly describe the scene. Standing with her load, Mary McAdam spoke fierce, hot words. She showed herself no mercy, asked for no pity. She had dealt in a business that threatened the souls of men and boys, made harder the lives of women. She had blinded herself and made herself believe that she and hers were better, stronger than others, and now ——

Mary was magnificent in her abandon and despair. Her words flowed freely, her eyes flashed.

" 'And now,' she cried, 'I'll keep my word to you.   Here!
here! here!'   The bottles went whirling and crashing
on the rocks near the roadway "

"And now," she cried, "I'll keep my word to you. Here! here! here!"

The bottles went whirling and crashing on the rocks near the roadway.

"And you, Master Farwell, break open the keg and set the evil thing free."

This Farwell proceeded to do with energy born of the hour. "And fetch out all that remains!" shrieked Mary. "Here, you! McAlpin, I'll have none of your help! Stay in your place; I'd not trust you inside when all's as free as it is to-night. You have your lad — heaven help you! Keep him and give him a clean chance. Nor you, Hornby! Out with you! It's a wicked waste, is it? Better so than what I suffer. Your lads are above ground, though out of your sight, Hornby, while mine —— Here, Master, more! more! let us water the earth."

The mad scene went on until the last drop of liquor was soaking into the earth or dripping from the rocks.

White-faced and stern, Farwell carried out the mother's commands and heeded not the muttered discontent or the approach of the horse and buggy bearing Doctor Ledyard and Dick Travers. He was one in the drama now and he played his part.

At the close a dull silence rested on the group, then Mary McAdam made her appeal. Her voice broke; her hands trembled. She looked aged and forlorn.

"And now," she said; "who'll come to the grave-yard with me?"

She need not have asked. To the last child they followed mutely. They were overcome by curiosity and fear, and the faces in the dull light of the late day and early night looked ghostly.

As Farwell stood near Mary McAdam by the newly made graves, he raised his eyes and found Ledyard's stern, yet amused, ones on his face. For a moment he quivered, but with the courage of one facing an operation, the outcome of which he could not know, he returned the look steadily. He heard his own voice speaking words of helpfulness, words of memory-haunted scenes. He told of Tom's courage and Sandy's sunshiny nature. 'Twas youth, he pleaded for them, youth with its blindness and lack of foresight. He recalled the last dread act as Jerry-Jo had depicted it. The older brother risking all for the younger. The smile — Sandy's last bequest — the moving lips that doubtless spoke words of affection to the only one who could hear them. Together they had played their pranks, had trod the common path; together they went — Farwell paused, then returned Ledyard's sneering gaze defiantly,— "To God who alone can understand and judge!" This was flung out boldly, recklessly.

With ceremony and the sound of sobbing, the empty graves were refilled, and the strange company turned away.

Then, alone and spent, Farwell returned to his cottage with a sure sense that before he slept he would know his fate, for he acknowledged that his fate lay largely, now, in the hands of the man who no longer had any doubt of his identity.

It was half-past eight when the buggy passed Farwell's window bound for the Hill Place. Young Travers was driving and the seat beside him was empty! Nine o'clock struck; the lights went out in the village, but Farwell rose and trimmed his lamp carefully. Ten o'clock — all Kenmore, excepting Mary McAdam, slept. Still Farwell waited while his clock ticked out the palpitating seconds. The moonlight flooded the Green. Where was he, that waiting man who was to come and give the blow?

It was nearly eleven when Farwell saw him advancing across the Green. He had been down by the water, probably hiding in some anchored boat until he was sure that he would not be seen. As he reached the door of Farwell's house a clear voice called to him:

"Will you come in, or would you prefer to have me come out?"

This took Ledyard rather at a disadvantage. He could hardly have told what he expected, but he certainly did not look for this calm acceptance of him and his errand.

"I'll come in. I see you have a light. Thank

you" — for Farwell had offered a chair near the table — "I hope I'm not disturbing you."

The irony of this was apparently lost upon Farwell. He sat opposite Ledyard, his arms folded on the table, waiting.

"So you're alive!"

"So it seems — at least partly so." Farwell parried the blows as one does even when he sees failure at hand.

"Perhaps you know your death was reported some years ago? There was a full account. You were escaping into Canada. The *La Belle* was the name of the boat. It went down near here?"

"Off Bleak Head," Farwell broke in.

"Thanks. There was even a picture of you in the papers," Ledyard said.

"A very poor one, I recall." Now that he was on the dissecting table, Farwell found himself strangely calm and collected. He saw that his manner irritated Ledyard; felt that it might ruin his chances, but he held to it grimly.

"So you saw — the papers?" The eyes under the shaggy brows looked ugly.

"Oh, yes. I had them all sent to me. It was very interesting reading after I got over the shock of the wreck and had accepted my isolated position."

"I suppose — Boswell keeps in touch with you — damn him!"

"Do you begrudge me — this one friend?"

"Yes. You have put yourself outside the pale of human companionship and friendships."

To this Farwell made no rejoinder. Again he waited.

"What do you think I'm going to do about it, now that I've run you down so unexpectedly?"

"I have supposed you would tell me, once we got together."

"Well, I've come to tell you!"

Ledyard leaned back in his chair and stretched his long legs out before him.

"But first I'm going to ask you a few questions. Your answers won't signify much one way or the other, but I'm curious. Why did you make such a fight — just to live? It must have been a devil of a game."

Farwell leaned against the table and so came nearer to his inquisitor.

"It was," he said quietly, "and I wonder if you can understand why it is that I'm glad to tell — even you about it? I don't expect sympathy, pity, or — even justice, but when a man's been on a desert isle for years it's a relief to speak his own tongue again to any one who can comprehend and who will listen."

"I'm prepared to listen," Ledyard muttered, and shrugged his heavy shoulders; "it will pass the time."

"After the thing was done," Farwell plunged in, "the thing I — had to do — I was dazed; I couldn't

think clear. I'd been driven by drink and — and
other things into a state bordering on delirium.
Afterward, when they had me and I was forced to
live normally, simply, I began to think clearly and
suffer. God! how I suffered! I faced death with
the horror that only an intelligent person can know.
I saw no escape. The trial, the verdict, brought
me closer and closer to the hideous reality. At first
I thought it could *not* happen to me — to me! But
it could! I sat day in and day out, looking at the
electric chair! That was all I could see: it stood
like a symbol of all the torture. I wondered how
I would approach it. Would I falter, or go as most
poor devils do — steadily? I saw myself — afterward — all that was left of me to give back to the
world. Oh! I suffered, I suffered!"

The white, haggard face held Ledyard's fascinated
gaze, but drew no word from him.

Farwell loosened the neck of his shirt — he was
stifling, yet feeling relief as the past dreams of his
lonely life formed themselves into words.

"At night I was haunted by visions," the low,
vibrant voice rushed on. "It was worse at night
when semi-unconsciousness made me helpless. I'd
wake up yelling, not with fright, but pain, actual
pain — the hot, knifing pain of an electric current
trying to find my heart and brain.

"Then they said I was mad. Well, so I was; and
the fight was on! At first there was a gleam — the

chair faded from sight. If I lived — there was hope; but I was mistaken. You know the rest. The legal struggle, the escapes and captures. One friend and much money did what they could; it wasn't much.

"You've seen a cat play with a mouse? The mouse always runs, doesn't it? Well, so did I, though I didn't know where in God's world I was running, nor to what."

For some minutes Farwell had been speaking like a man distraught by fever. He had forgotten the listener across the table; he was remembering *aloud* at last, with no fear of consequences. He did not look at Ledyard, and when he spoke again it was in a calmer tone.

"It was on the last run — that I was supposed to have drowned. Well, I did die; at least something in me died. I lost breath, consciousness, and when I came to I was a poor, broken thing not worth turning the hounds on. I'm done for as far as the past's concerned. I'm a different man — not a reformed one! God knows I never played that rôle. I'm another man. I took what I could to keep me from insanity. I had to do something to occupy my time. That's why I've taught these poor little devils; it wasn't for them, it was for me; and when they grew to like me and trust me — I was grateful. Grateful for even that!"

Ledyard was holding the white, drawn face by

his merciless eyes. So he looked when a particularly interesting subject lay under his knife and he was all surgeon — no man.

"But you're not equal to going back to the States without being hauled there — and taking you medicine?" he asked calmly.

"No. I suppose in the final analysis all that justice demands is that I should be put out of the way — out of the way of harming others? Well, that's accomplished. I don't suppose your infernal ideas of justice claim that a man should be hounded beyond death, and every chance for right living be barred from him? If a poor devil ever can expatiate his sin and try to live a decent life, why shouldn't he be given the opportunity here and now instead of in some mythical place among creatures of one's fancy?"

"You didn't argue that way when you shot Charles Martin down, did you? He was my friend; he had to — take his medicine!" Ledyard almost snarled out these words. "He may have deserved his punishment for the lapses of his life — but you were not the one to deal it. His family demand and should have justice for him — I mean to see that they shall. Martin, for all his folly was a genius, and gave to the world his toll of service. Why should you, who gave nothing, escape at his expense?"

"Martin was no better, no worse, than I. He and

I lived on the same plane then; had the same interests. Had I not killed him, he would have killed
me. He swore that."

"But you took him — at a disadvantage, like the
damned ——" Ledyard paused; he was losing his
self-control. The calm, living face across the table
enraged him.

"I met him in the open; I did not know he was
unarmed. I drew my pistol in full view. A week
before he had done the same; I escaped. No one
believed that when I told it at the trial. I had no
witnesses; he had many when I took my revenge."

"Who could believe you? What was your life compared with his?"

"Exactly. Perhaps that is why I — I kept running. Martin only dipped into such lives as mine
was then; he always scurried back to respectability
and honour; I grovelled in the mire and got stuck!
When you get stuck you get what the world calls —
justice."

"I recall" — Ledyard's face was hardening — "I
recall you always squealed. You were always the
wronged one; society was against you. Bah!"

Farwell sat unmoved under this attack.

"I'm not squealing now," he said quietly; "I am
merely defending myself as I can. That's the pre-
rogative of any human being, isn't it? Why, see
here, Ledyard, there's one thing men like you never
comprehend. On the different stratas of life ex-

actly the same passions, impulses, and emotions exist;
it's the way they're dealt with, how they affect people,
that makes the difference.   Up where you live and
breathe they love and hate and take revenge, don't
they?   That's what happened down where I wal-
lowed and where Martin sometimes came — to enjoy
himself!"

And now Farwell clutched his thin hands on the
table to stay their trembling as he went on:

"I loved — the woman in the case.   That sounds
strange to you, but it's the only thing I warn you
not to laugh at!   I loved her because she was beautiful, fascinating, and as — as bad as I.   I knew the
poor creature had never had half a show.   She was
born in evil and exploited from the cradle up.   Martin knew it, too, and took advantage.   She was
fair game for him and his money.   When he came
down to hell to play, he played with her and defied
me.   But on my plane it was man against man, you
see, and when he flung his plaything aside, she came
to me; that's all!   She told me how he had brought
her where she was — yes, damn him! when she was
innocent!   She paid her toll then, *not* for his money
— though who would believe that? — but for the
chance to be decent and clean.   He told her, when
she was only sixteen, that the one way she could
prove her vows to him was to give herself to him.
If she trusted him so far, he could trust her.   She
trusted, poor child!   Two years later he married

up on his higher plane — your plane — and laughingly offered a second best place to her. It was the only bargain she could make then! The rest was an easy downhill grade.

"Well, I took her. I was all you say, but I meant to do the right thing by her, and she knew it! Yes, she knew it, and later he came back and tried to get her away. After I shot him and went to her with the story — she told me she'd pull herself together and wait for me until — until I came for her. She understood!"

Ledyard moistened his lips and set his jaws harshly. The story had not moved him to pity.

"And — where is she now?" he asked.

"In New York, I suppose. She thinks me dead."

"Boswell tells you that?"

"Yes. And he will never let her know. Unless I —— "

"You expect to go back — some day?"

Farwell gave a dry, mirthless laugh at this, and then replied:

"After I've been dead long enough, when I've been good long enough, perhaps. You know even in a disembodied spirit hope dies hard. Yes — I *had* hoped to go back."

"I — I thought so." Ledyard leaned forward and across the table; his face was not three feet from Farwell's.

"I like to trace diseases down to the last germ,"

he said. "You're a disease, Farwell Maxwell, a mighty, ugly, dangerous one. You oughtn't to be alive; you're a menace while you have breath in your body; you should have died years ago in payment of your debt, just as Martin did, but you escaped, and now some one has got to keep an eye on you; see that you don't skip quarantine. You understand?"

Farwell felt the turning of the screw.

"I'm going to be the eye, Maxwell. You're going to stay right where you are until you pass off this sphere. Remembering what you once were, your pastimes and love of luxury, this seems as hellish a place and existence as even you deserve. When I saw you last night" — and here Ledyard laughed — "it was all I could do to control myself. You play your part well; but you always had a knack for theatricals. I know I'm a hard, unforgiving man, but there is just one phase of human nature that I will not stand for, and that is the refusal to take the medicine prescribed for the disease. What incentive have people for better living and upright thinking if every devil of a fellow who gets through his beast-iality is permitted to come up into the ranks and march shoulder to shoulder with the best? If it's living you want and will lie for, steal for, and beg for — have it; but have it here where the chances are all against your old self. You'll probably never murder any one here or ruin the women; so grovel on!"

As he listened Farwell seemed to shrink and age. In that hour he recognized the fact that through all the years of self-imposed exile he had held to the hope of release in the future: the going back to that which he had once known. But looking at the hard, set face opposite he knew that this hope was futile: he must live forever where he was, or, by departing, bring about him the bloodhounds of justice and vengeance. Ledyard had but to whistle, he knew, and again the pursuit would be keen, and in the end — a long blank lay beyond that!

"You will — stay where you are!" Ledyard was saying.

"Surely. I intend to stay right here."

Then Farwell laughed and leaned back in his chair.

CHAPTER VII

LIFE settled into calm after the storm and subsequent happenings. Mary McAdam, having done what she felt she must do, grimly set her house in order and prepared for a new career. The bar, cleansed and altered, became her private apartment. With the courage and endurance of a martyr she determined to fight her battle out where there would be the least encouragement or comfort.

"I'll drink to the dregs," she said to Mary Terhune, who gave up her profession to share the solitude and fortunes of the White Fish; "but while I'm drinking there's no crime in serving my kind. Come summer I'll open my doors to tourists and keep the kind of house a woman — and a God-be-praised widow one at that — should keep. Time was when the best would not come to me, the bar being against their liking. Well, the best may come now and find peace."

"'Tis a changed woman you are, Mrs. McAdam."

"No, just a stricken one, Mary. When I sit by those empty graves back of the pasture lot I seem to know that I must do the work of my boys as well as my own — and the time's short! I'm over sixty."

"And looking forty, Mrs. McAdam." The manners of her trade clung to Mrs. Terhune.

"The shell doesn't count, Mary, if the heart of you is old and worn."

The people from the Far Hill Place returned early to town that year, and Anton Farwell breathed easier and sunk back into his old life when he knew they were gone.

In resurrecting the man Farwell once was, Ledyard had all but slain the man he had, perforce, become.

Whether former characteristics were dead or not, who could tell? But certainly with temptation removed, with the routine of a bleak, uninteresting existence his only choice, Farwell was a harmless creature. Gradually he had found solace in the commonplaces that surrounded him. Like a person relieved of mortal agony he was grateful for semi-invalidism. Previous to Ledyard's recognition of him he had sunk to a monotonous indifference, waiting, he realized now, for the time when he might safely shake off his disguise and slip away to what was once his own. Now, with his exit from Kenmore barred, he found that he no longer could return to his stupor; he was alert, keen, and restless. In the past he had often forced himself to exercise in order that he might be ready to journey on when the time of release came. His walks to the distant town, his long hours on the water, had all been preparations for the final leave-taking from his living tomb.

But now that he had no need of lashing himself into action, he found himself always on the move. He worked early and late at trifling tasks that occupied his hands while sharpening his wits. With shades drawn at night, he drew, with pencil and paper, plans of escape. He must choose a calm spell after a storm; he would take his launch, with a rowboat behind, to the Fox Portage. He'd set his launch free and shoulder his boat. Once he reached the Little Bay, he'd take his chances for an outgoing steamer. He'd have plenty of money and a glib story of a bad connection. It would go. He must defeat Ledyard.

Then he would tear the sheets of paper in bits, toss them on the coals, and laugh bitterly as he realized that he was imprisoned forever.

Foolish as all this was, it had its effect upon the man. He played with the thought as a child might play with a forbidden toy. Then he decided to test the matter. He would have to buy clothes and provisions for the winter — he always made a pilgrimage about this time. There would be a letter from Boswell, too. There always was one in September. So on a certain morning Farwell turned the key in his lock and quite naturally set forth with a sense of exaltation and freedom he had imagined he would never feel again.

Followed by his dogs, he went to his boat, which happened just then to be tied at the ricketty dock of the White Fish.

"It's off for a tramp you are, maybe?" asked Mrs. McAdam from her doorway. "God keep you, Mr. Farwell, and bring you back safe and sound."

At this Farwell paused.

"I think I'll leave the dogs behind," he said. "I may wish to hurry back, and a brace of dogs, keen on scents and full of spirits, is a handicap on a journey."

"Sure I'll feed and care for the two, and welcome, and if their staying behind brings you quicker home, 'tis a good piece of work I'm doing for Kenmore."

With this Mary McAdam came down to the boat and looked keenly at Farwell.

"Are you well?" she asked with a gentleness new and touching. "'Tis pale you look, and thin, I'm thinking. I'm getting to depend upon you, and the thought of anything happening to you grieves the heart of me. In all Kenmore there's no one as I lean on like you. There be nights when I look out toward your house and see your light a-shining when all else is dark, and say to myself, 'The master and me' over and over, and I'm less lonely."

For a moment Farwell could not speak. Once an inward desire to laugh, to scoff, would have driven him to supernatural gravity; now he merely smiled with grave pleasure, and said:

"A tramp will do me good, Mrs. McAdam.

Thank you. I'll take your words with me for comfort and cheer."

The first night Farwell slept beside his fire, not ten miles from Kenmore. He had revelled in his freedom all day, had played like a boy, often retracing his steps, carefully using the same footprints, and laughing as he imagined the confusion of any one trying to follow him; the vague somebody being always Ledyard.

After a frugal meal, Farwell smoked his pipe, even attempted a snatch of rollicking song, then, rolling himself in a blanket, fell into natural and happy slumber.

At four he awoke with the creeping sensation of unexplainable fear. He first thought some animal was prowling near, and, raising himself on his elbow, looked keenly about. The appearance of the fire puzzled him. It looked as if fresh wood had been laid upon it, but, as no one was in sight he concluded that his own wood had been damp, and, therefore, had burned slower.

He did not sleep again, however, and his excited thoughts trailed back to his past and the one woman who had magically caught and held all the best that was in him. To what point of vantage had she, poor, disabled little soul, drifted? The world was a hard enough place for a woman, God knew, and for her, with her sudden-born determination to rise above the squalor of her early youth, it would be a serious problem. Boswell told him so little. He could count on his fingers the few sharp facts his friend had given him with the promise that if conditions changed he should know, but if all remained well, he might be secure in his faith and hope for the future. The future! Was there any future for him except Kenmore? And if she heard now that he was alive, had only *seemed* dead for her safety and his own, would she come to him and share the dun-coloured life of the In-Place?

She was alive; she was faithful. Boswell was making her comfortable with Farwell's money. She was accepting less and less because she was winning her way to independence in an honourable line. Since no man had entered her life after Farwell's death was reported, Farwell could readily see why.

Over and over, that first night in the woods, Farwell rehearsed these facts for comfort's sake. Suppose he made an escape. Suppose he lost himself in the city's labyrinth — what then?

And then, just at daybreak, a vivid and sharp memory of the woman's face came to him as he had last seen it pressed against the bars of his cell. Behind the squares of metal it shone like an angel's. Fair, pitiful, wonder-filled eyes, and quivering mouth. All day the picture haunted him and seemed to draw him toward it. He walked twenty miles that day and came at sunset to a dense jungle where he made his camp and stretched himself exhaustedly before the fire.

Sleep did not come easily to him; he was too excited and nerve worn. The white face checked by iron bars would not fade, and in the red glow of the flames it began to look wan and haggard, as if the day had tired it and it could find no rest or comfort.

The feeling of suffocation Ledyard had managed to create, returned to him. He grew nervous, ill at ease, and fearful.

Then he fell to moralizing. He was not often given to that, or introspection. Longing and alternate hope and despair had been his comrades and bedfellows, but he rarely indulged in calm consideration. Smoking his pipe, stretched wearily on the moss, he wondered if men knew how much they punished while fulfilling their ideals of justice?

"If only the sense of vindictiveness could be left out," he thought; "the Lord knows they have it all in their power once the key is turned on us. I deserved all they meant to inflict, but no human being deserves all that was given unconsciously."

Then Farwell relived his life, while the wood crumbled to ashes and the moon came up over the hills. A misguided, misspent boyhood; too much money; too little common sense; then the fling in the open with every emotion and desire uncurbed. Well, he had to learn his lesson and God knew he had; but why, in the working of things, shouldn't one be given a chance to prove the well-learned task; an opportunity, while among the living, to settle the question?

However, such fancies were idle, and Farwell shook the ashes from his pipe and gave a humorous shrug.

It would be a fine piece of work to slip from the clutches of the past and make good! This idea caused him to tremble. Surely no one would look for him in the camp of the upright. Walking the paths of the clean and sane he would be more surely secure from detection than anywhere else on earth. That was what his past had done for him. The truth of this sank into the lonely man's soul with sickening finality. And as he realized it, and compared it with the fact of his youth, he groaned. What an infernal fool he had been! What fools all such fellows were who, like him, wasted everything in their determination to make the unreal, real. He did not now desire to be a drivelling repentant; he wanted, God knew he really wanted, a chance to be decent and live; but in order to live he must go on acting a part and cringing and hiding.

These thoughts led nowhere and unfitted him for his journey, so he made the fire safe, lay down beside it, and slept as many a better man would have given much to sleep.

At four he awoke as on the previous night. So quietly, however, did he open his eyes that he took by surprise a man crouching by the fire as if stealing a bit of warmth. Farwell turned over, and the two eyed each other with wide, penetrating gaze.

Tough Pine, the guide, finding himself discovered, grinned sheepishly; he was loathing himself for being taken off guard, and muttered:

"Me share fire? me helped keep it."

Farwell raised himself on his elbow, all the light and courage gone from his face. It was the old story, the dream of freedom and — the prison bars!

"Where are you going?" he asked, though he knew full well.

"Where — you go? There, Pine go! Pine — good friend and good guide."

They questioned each other no more. Farwell finished his errand in dull fashion, bought his goods, found a letter, long waiting him, read all the papers he could lay hands on, and then set his face toward Kenmore. And that winter he devoted himself as he never had before to the simple people who were the means of keeping him sane.

Upon this newly restricted and devastated horizon Priscilla Glenn loomed large and vital. With Nathaniel's loosened rein and Theodora's restored faith, the girl developed wonderfully. Farwell made no more objection to her dancing or her flights of fancy. He fiddled for her and fed the flame of her imagination. She was the sunniest creature he had ever known; the bleak life of Lonely Farm had spurred her to greater lengths of self-defence;

nothing could daunt her. She had an absorbing curiosity about life, out and beyond the Kenmore confines; and more to keep his own memory clear than to satisfy Priscilla, Farwell set himself to the task of educating the girl in ways that would have appalled Nathaniel and reduced Theodora again to tears and apprehension.

The bare room of the master's house was the stage upon which were set, in turn, the scenes of distant city life. Vicariously Priscilla learned the manners of a "real lady" under the most trying circumstances. Farwell told her of plays, operas, and, over his deal table, they chatted in brilliant restaurants. They walked gay streets and stood bewildered before flashing shop windows. It was all dangerous, but fascinating, and in the playing of the game Farwell grew old and drawn, while Priscilla gradually came into her Heart's Desire of delight.

"My Road!" she proudly thought. "My Road!"

The old poem was recalled and was often repeated like a litany, while life became more and more vital and thrilling with dull Kenmore as a background and setting.

Just about this time Jerry-Jo took to wearing his Sunday suit on week days, thus proclaiming his aspirations and awaking the ribald jests of his particular set.

Mary Terhune, now partner of Mrs. McAdam, took note of Jerry-Jo's appearance, and, on a certain afternoon in midwinter, when she, Long Jean, and Mary McAdam sat by the range in the White Fish kitchen, fanned a lively bit of gossip into flame.

"Trade's a bit poor these days, eh, Jean?"

Jean grunted over her cup of green tea.

"Not so many children born as once was, eh? What you make of it, Jean — the woman getting heady or — which?"

Mary McAdam broke in.

"What with poverty and the terrors of losing them, there's enough born to my thinking. Time was when the young 'uns happened; they're thought more on, these days. Women *should* have a say. If there's one thing a man should keep his tongue off it's this matter of families!"

To this outrageous sentiment the listeners replied merely by two audible gulps of tea, and then Mary Terhune found grace to remark:

"You certainly do talk most wonderful things, Mary McAdam. You be an ornament to your sex, but only such women as you can grip them audacious ideas. Let them be sowed broadcast and —— "

"Where would me, and such as me, be?" Long Jean muttered, defending her profession.

Mrs. Terhune tactfully turned the conversation:

"Have you noticed the change in Jerry-Jo Mc-Alpin?" she asked with a mysterious shake of her head.

"Any change for the better would be welcome,"

Mrs. McAdam retorted. "Have another cup, Jean? Strong or weak?"

"Strong. I says often, says I, that unless tea curls your tongue you might just as well take water. When I'm on duty I keep a pot on the back of the stove week in and week out; it do brace me powerful."

Mrs. McAdam poured the tea into the outstretched cup and proceeded to discuss Jerry-Jo.

"Why doesn't the scamp go to the States and find himself instead of worrying old Jerry's very life out of him — the vampire!"

"He may have it in his mind," soothed Mary Terhune, "but the lad's deep and far seeing like his Injun mother — beg pardon, Jean, the term's a compliment, God save me!"

"You've saved your face, Mrs. Terhune. Go on!"

Jean had begun to resent, but the explanation mollified her.

"More tea," she said quietly, "and you might stir the dregs a mite, Mrs. McAdam; it's plain sinful to let the strength go to waste."

"If I was Theodora Glenn," Mary Terhune went on, monotonously stirring the cold liquid in her cup, "I'd have my eye on that girl of hers."

And now the ingredients were prepared for the mixing!

"What's Priscilla Glenn got to do with Jerry-Jo

McAlpin?" Mrs. McAdam asked sharply, fixing her little ferret eyes on the speaker.

Long Jean bridled again and interjected:

"And for why not? Young folks is young folks, and there ain't too many boys for the gels. What with the States and the toll to death, the gels can't be too particular, not casting my flings at Jerry-Jo, either. He's a handsome lad and will get a footing some day. Glenn's girl ain't none too good for him; he'd bring her to her senses. All that dancing and fiddle-scraping at Master Farwell's is not to my liking. The goings-on are evil-looking to my mind. The girl always was a parcel of whimwhams — made up of odds and ends, as it was, of her fore-runners. What *all* the children of the Glenns might have been — Priscilla is!"

"So Jerry-Jo's fixed his bold eyes on the girl?" asked Mary McAdam. "It bodes no good for her. She's a sunny creature and mighty taking in her ways. I wish her no ill, and I hate to think of Jerry-Jo shadowing her life till she forgets to dance and sing. For my part, I wish the master were twenty-five years younger and could play for the lass to dance to the end of their days."

"And a poor outlook for me!" grumbled Jean humorously. "Another cup of the tea, Mary Ter-hune, and make it stronger. I begin to feel the bitter in my toes."

And while this talk and more like it was permeating Kenmore, Jerry-Jo, adorned and uncomfortable, did his own thinking and planned his own plans after the manner of his mixed inheritance. He could not settle to any task or give heed to any temptation from the States until he had made Priscilla secure. The girl's age in no wise daunted McAlpin. His eighteen years were all that were to be considered; he knew what he wanted, what he meant to have. He could wait, he could bide the fulfillment of his hopes, but one big, compelling subject at a time was all he could master.

He secretly and furiously objected to the dancing and visits in Farwell's cottage. He was ashamed to voice this feeling, for Farwell was his friend and had taught him all he knew, but Farwell's age did not in the least blind Jerry-Jo to the fact that he was a man, and he did not enjoy seeing Priscilla so free and easy with any other of the male sex, be he ancient enough to topple into the grave.

"She'll dance for me — for me!" the young fellow ground his teeth. "I'll make her forget to prance and grin unless she does it for me. The master's just training her away from me and putting notions in her head. I'll take her to the States — maybe her dancing will help us both there. I don't mean to drudge as Jamsie Hornby does! Better things for me!"

Sex attraction swayed Jerry-Jo madly in those days and he thought it love, as many a better man had done before him. The blood of his mother controlled him largely and he wished that he might carry the girl off to his wigwam, and, at his leisure, with beads and blankets, or other less tangible methods, win her and conquer her. But present conditions held the boy in check and compelled him to adopt more modern tactics. He stole, when he couldn't beg, from his poor father all the money Jerry wrenched from an occasional day's work. With this he bought books for Priscilla, vaguely realizing that these would most interest her, but his selection often made her laugh. Piqued by her indifference, Jerry-Jo plotted a thing that led, later, to tragic results. Remembering the favour Priscilla had long ago shown for the book from Far Hill Place, he decided to utilize the taste of the absent owner, and the owner himself, for his own ends, not realizing that Priscilla had never connected the cripple Jerry-Jo had described, with the musician of the magic summer afternoon that had set her life in new currents.

It was an easy matter to enter the Far Hill Place, and, where one was not troubled with conscience, a simple thing to select at random, but with economy, books from the well-filled shelves. These gifts presently found their way to Priscilla, cunningly disguised as mail packages. Inadvertently the very book Priscilla had once cried over came to her and touched her strangely.

"Why should he send me these—send me this?" she asked Jerry-Jo, who had brought the package to her.

"He always wanted you to have it. I told you that; he remembers, I suppose, and wants you to have it. He said it was more yours than his." To test her Jerry-Jo was hiding behind Travers.

"I'd walk a hundred miles over the rock on bare feet to thank him," the girl replied, her big eyes shining. And with the words there entered into Jerry-Jo's distorted imagination a concrete and lasting jealousy of poor Dick Travers, who was innocent of any actual memory of Priscilla Glenn. Travers at that time was studying as few college men do, always with the spur of lost years and a big ambition lashing him on.

During that winter the stolen books from the Far Hill Place caused Priscilla much wonderment and some little embarrassment. She had to keep them secret owing to her father's sentiment, and, for some reason, she did not confide in Farwell. This new and unexpected interest in her life was so foreign to anything with which the master had to do that she felt no inclination to share it.

"But I cannot understand," she often said to Jerry-Jo. "I'd like to write to him. Do you think you could find out for me where he is? That he should even remember me! I would not have him think me so ungrateful as I must seem."

She and Jerry-Jo were in the path leading to Lonely Farm from Kenmore as she spoke, and suddenly something the young fellow said brought her to a sharp standstill.

"Oh! I suppose, after your cutting up in the woods that day he wants to make you remember him."

This was an outburst that Jerry-Jo permitted himself without forethought. He was using Travers as an old tribeman might have used torture, to test his own bravery and endurance, but the effect upon Priscilla was so startling and unexpected that he fell back bewildered.

"In — the — the — woods?" she gasped.

"Sure. That time your father drove you home."

For a full moment Priscilla stared helplessly, then she began to see light.

"Do you mean," she gasped, "that he who made me dance — was the boy of the Hill Place?"

"As if you did not know it!" Jerry-Jo grunted.

"But Jerry-Jo you said he — that boy was a poor, twisted thing, ugly past all belief, while he who played and laughed that day was like an angel of light just showing me the way to heaven!"

And now Jerry-Jo's dark face was not pleasant to look upon.

"Can't a twisted thing become straight?" he muttered; "can't a devil trap himself out like an — an angel?"

"Oh! Jerry-Jo, he who played for me in the woods could never have been evil. Why, all his life he had been making himself into something big and fine. He put into words the things I had always thought and dreamed about — an ideal was what he called it! And to think I never knew! And he remembered and wanted to be kind! I shall worship him now while I live. And when he comes back to the Hill Place I will go and thank him, even if my father should kill me. I shall never be happy until I can explain. What a stupid he must think me!"

After that the secret became the sacredest thing in Priscilla's life and the most tormenting in Jerry-Jo's. They were both at ages when such an occurrence would appeal to a girl's sentimentality and a young man's hatred.

The family did not return to the Hill Place for many summers, and only once during the following years did Priscilla's name pass Travers's lips.

Apropos of something they were talking about he said to Helen Travers: "I wonder what has become of that little dancing dervish up in Canada? She wasn't plain, ordinary stuff, but I suppose she'll be knocked into shape. Maybe that half-breed, Jerry-Jo, will get her when she's been reduced to his level. There are not girls enough to go around up there, I fancy. That little thing, though, was too spiritual to be crushed and remodelled. As she danced that day, her scarlet cape flying out in the breeze, she looked like a living flame darting up from the red rock. And those awful words she uttered — poor little pagan! Jerry-Jo told me afterward what the lure of the States meant: it's a provincial expression. Mother, if the lure should ever control that girl of Lonely Farm I wish we might greet her, for safety's sake."

But it was not likely that either of the Traverses for a moment conceived of the reality of Priscilla leaving the In-Place, and in time even the memory of her became blurred to Dick by the eternal verities of his strenuous young life.

Gradually his lameness disappeared until a slight hesitation at times was all that remained. Five years of college, two abroad — one with Helen, one with Doctor Ledyard — and then Richard Thornton Travers (Helen had, when he went to college, insisted for the first time upon the middle name) hung out his modest sign — it looked brazenly glaring to him — under that of Thomas R. Ledyard, and nervously awaited the first call upon him. He was twenty-five when he started life, and Priscilla Glenn, back in forgotten Kenmore, was nearing nineteen, with Jerry-Jo in hot pursuit behind her. As to Anton Farwell, there was no doubt about his age now. Not even the very old called him young, and there was a pathos about him that attracted the attention of those with whom he had lived so long.

"He looks haunted," Mary Terhune ventured; "he starts at times when one speaks sudden, real pitiful like. The look of his eyes, too, has the queer flash of them as sees forward as well as back. Do you mind, Mrs. McAdam, how 'tis said that them as comes nigh to drowning have a glimpse on before as well as the picture of all that has past?"

"I've heard the same," nodded Mary McAdam.

"Belike the master remembers and often looks to the end of his journey. Well, he's been a good harmless sort, as men go. He's kept the children out of trouble far more than one could expect, and he's been a merciful creature to humans and beasts. I wonder what he had in his life before he washed up from the *La Belle?*"

All this seemed to end the discussion.

Mary McAdam was an important personage about that time. The White Fish Lodge had become famous. Without bar or special privilege of any sort, the house was patronized by the best class of tourist. Mary was a born proprietress, and, while she extracted the last penny due her, always gave full value in return. She and Mary Terhune did the cooking; a bevy of clean, young Indian girls from Wyland Island served as waitresses and maids; their quaint, keen reserve was charming, and no better public house could have been found on the Little or Big Bay.

Priscilla drifted to the Lodge as naturally as a flower turns to the sun. The easy-going people, the laughter and merriment appealed strongly to her, and again did she cause Jerry-Jo serious displeasure and arouse her father's lurking suspicions.

"Watch her! watch her!" was his warning, and Theodora returned to her fears and tears.

CHAPTER VIII

ANTON FARWELL had, little by little, accepted the fate of those who, deprived of many blessings, learn to depend on a few. As the remaining senses are sharpened by the loss of one, so in this man's life the cramping process, begun by his own wrongdoing, and prolonged and completed by other conditions, had the effect of focussing all his power on the atoms that went to the making up of the daily record of his days. Had he kept a diary it would have been interesting from its very lack of large interest. And yet, with all this narrowing down, a certain fineness and purpose evolved that were both touching and inspiring. He never complained, not even to himself. After recognizing the power which Ledyard held in his life, he relinquished the one hope that had held him to the past. Then, for a year or two, the light of the doctor's contempt, which had been turned on him, took the zest from the small efforts he had made for better living and caused him to distrust himself. He saw himself what he knew Ledyard thought him — a mean, cowardly creature, and yet, in his better moments, he knew this was not so.

"Men have made friends of mice and insects in prison," he argued; "they have kept their reason by so doing; why, in heaven's name, shouldn't I play with these people here and make life possible?"

But try as he might he found his courage failing, and more and more he dwelt apart and clung to the few — Priscilla Glenn, Mary McAdam, and old Jerry McAlpin — who regarded him in the light of a priest to whom they might confess freely.

Then one of Farwell's dogs died and he was genuinely anxious at the effect this had upon him.

"So this is what I've come to!" he muttered as he buried the poor brute, while the tears fell from his eyes and the other dog whined dolorously beside him — "broken hearted over — a mongrel!" But he got another dog!

For a time Farwell vigorously set himself against depending upon Priscilla Glenn as a support in his narrowing sphere. Many things threatened such a friendship — Nathaniel, Jerry-Jo, and the girl herself — for Priscilla, during the first years of Nathaniel's relaxed severity, was like a bee sipping every flower, and Farwell was not at all confident that anything he had to give would hold even her passing interest for long. Then, too, like a many-wounded creature, he dreaded a new danger, even though for a moment it gave promise of comfort. But finally Priscilla got her bearings and more and more brought all her powers to bear upon one ambition.

The childish madness that prompted her to run away from anything that hurt or angered her, gradually disappeared, and in its place came a staid determination to seek her fortunes, soon, in some place distant from Kenmore.

The tourists opened a new vista to her, but many of them, with stupid ignorance, mistook her position and traditions. She was offered occupations as cook, maid, or laundress. She had sense of humour enough to laugh at these, and often wished she dared repeat them for her father's edification.

"The daughter of the King of Lonely Farm," she said to Farwell one day with her mocking smile and comical courtesy "is bidden to the service of Mrs. Flighty High as skivvy. If this comes to the king's ears, 'twill mean the head of Mrs. Flighty High!"

Farwell joined her in her amusement and felt the charm of her coming womanhood.

"But there is one up at the Lodge," Priscilla went on more gravely, "who is not such a wild fool. She has a sick baby, and for two nights she and I have watched and tended together. She says I have the touch and nature of the true nurse and she has told me how in the States, and England, too, they train young girls in this work. She says we Canadians are in great demand, and the calling is a wonderful one, Master Farwell."

This interested Anton Farwell a good deal and he and Priscilla discussed it often after the woman who had just broached it had departed. It seemed such a normal, natural opening for Priscilla if the time really came for her to go away. The doubt that she would eventually go was slight in Farwell's heart. He, keener than others, saw the closing-in of conditions. He was not blind to Jerry-Jo's primitive attempts to attract the girl's attention, but he was not deceived. When the moment came that Priscilla recognized the half-breed's real thought, Farwell knew her quick impulse would, as of old, be to fly away. She was like a wild bird, he often pondered; she would give to great lengths, flutter close, and love tenderly, but no restraining or harsh touch could do aught but set her to flight.

At twenty-three Jerry-Jo surlily and passionately came to the conclusion that he must in some way capture his prize. Other youths were wearing gaudy ties and imperilling their Sunday bests; he was letting precious time slip. Then, too, by Farwell's advice, old Jerry was growing rigid along financial lines, and at last the *States* took definite shape in Jerry-Jo's mind, but he meant to have Priscilla before he heeded the lure. With all his brazen conceit and daring he intuitively knew that the girl had never thought of him as he thought of her, and he dared not awaken her by legitimate means. Quite in keeping with his unrestrained nature, he plotted, indirectly, to secure what otherwise might escape him. Fully realizing Nathaniel's attitude toward his daughter, counting his distorted conceptions and foolish pride, Jerry-Jo began to construct an obstacle that would shut Priscilla from her father's protection and cause her to accept what others had to offer — others, being always and ever, himself!

Once Lonely Farm was closed to the girl, other houses in the serenely moral In-Place would inevitably slam their doors. The cunning of the half-breed was diabolic in its sureness. Anton Farwell could not assume responsibility for Priscilla if all Kenmore turned its back on her, and in that hour the girl would, of course, come running or crawling — never dancing — to him, Jerry-Jo!

It was all for her own good, the evil fellow thought.

"I'll be kind to her when I get her. I'm only playing her with the hook in her mouth."

But Jerry-Jo was scheming without considering the Lure, which never was long absent from Priscilla's mind at that time.

One early September afternoon Priscilla presented herself at Farwell's cabin in so startling a manner that she roused the man as nothing previously in his association with her had ever done.

He was sitting at the west window of his living-room, his back toward the door leading to the Green.

For a wonder, what he was reading had absorbed him, and he was far and away from the In-Place. He had taken to fine, old literature lately and had found, to his delight, that his mind was capable of appreciating it.

> "Wisdom, slow product of laborious years,
> The only fruit that life's cold winter bears,
>   Thy sacred seeds in vain in youth we lay,
> By the fierce storm of passion torn away;
> Should some remain in rich, gen'rous soil,
> They long lie hid, and must be raised with toil;
> Faintly they struggle with inclement skies,
> No sooner born than the poor planter dies."

With such word-comfort did Farwell dig, from other's experiences, crude guidings for himself! And at that moment a stir outside the open door caused him to turn and confront what, in the excited moment, seemed an apparition from the past, which, for him, was sealed and barred.

"Good Lord!" he ejaculated under his breath and started to his feet. A visitor from the Lodge apparently had descended upon him.

"I beg pardon," he said aloud, and then a laugh, familiar and ringing, brought the colour to his pale, thin face.

The girl came in, threw back the veil from her merry face, and confronted Farwell.

"Miss Priscilla Glenn, sir! Behold her in the

battered finery of the place she is going to — to grace some day!"

Then Priscilla wheeled about lightly and displayed her gown to Farwell's astonished eyes.

"Cast-offs," she explained; "the Honourable Mrs. Jones from the States left them with Mrs. McAlpin for the poor. Just imagine the 'poor' glinting around in this gay silk gown all frayed at the hem and in holes under the arms! The hat and veil, too, go with the smart frock; likewise the scarf of rainbow colours. But, oh! Mr. Farwell, how do I look as a real lady in my damaged outfit?"

Farwell stared without speaking. He had grown so used to the change in the girl since the time when he had prevailed upon Glenn to loosen the rein upon her, that the even stream of their intercourse had been unruffled. He had passed from teacher to friendly guide, from guide to good comrade; but here he was suddenly confronting her — man to woman!

All his misfortune and limitations had but erected a shield of age about him beneath which smouldered dangerously, but unconsciously, all the forbidden and denied passions and sentiments of a male creature of early middle life.

In thinking afterward of the shock Priscilla gave him, Farwell was always glad to remember that his first thought was for her, her danger, her need.

"I declare!" he exclaimed. "I did not know you, Priscilla Glenn."

His tone had a new ring in it, a vibration of defence — the astonished male on guard against the attack of a subtle force whose power he could not estimate.

"And no wonder. I did not know myself when I first saw myself. Do you know, Mr. Farwell, I never thought about my — my face, much, but it is really a — very nice face, isn't it? As faces go, I mean?"

"Yes," Farwell returned, looking at her critically and speaking slowly. "Yes, you are very — beautiful. I had not thought of it before, either."

"Drop me down, now, in the States, Mr. Farwell, and I fancy that with my looks and my dancing I might — well, go! What do you think?"

She was preening herself before a small mirror and did not notice the elderly man, who, under her fascination, was being transformed.

"You're a regular Frankenstein," he muttered, while the consciousness of the blue eyes in the dusky skin, the long slenderness of her body, and the hue of her strange hair grew upon him. "Do you know what a Frankenstein is?"

"No." And now Priscilla, weary of her play and self-contemplation, turned about and took a chair opposite Farwell. "Tell me."

So he told her, but she shook her head.

"You've only helped me to find myself; you did not make me," she said with a little sigh. "Oh, Mr. Farwell, I do — much thinking up at Lonely Farm. The winters are long, and the nights, too. You know there is a queer little plant beside the spring at the foot of our garden; it has roots long enough and thick enough for a thing twice its size. It grew strong and sure underground before it ventured up. It blossomed last summer; an odd flower it had. I think I am like that. You've taught me to — well, know myself. I shall not shame you, Master Farwell. You know we of the lonesome In-Place make friends with strange objects; everything in nature talks to us, if we will but listen. You have taught me to listen, too. Back a piece in the woods are a strong young hemlock and a little white birch. For years I have watched and tended them. When I was a small girl I likened the hemlock to you, sir, and there was I, leaning and huddling close to you, like the ghostly stripling of the woods. Well, I noticed to-day, Mr. Farwell, the birch stands quite securely; it doesn't bend for support on the hemlock, but it is standing friendly all the same. I think" — and here Priscilla clasped her hands close and outstretched them — "I think I am soon going away!"

Her eyes were tear-dimmed, her face very earnest.

"I wish — you would give up the childish folly, Priscilla." A fear rose in Farwell's eyes. "What could you, such an one as you have become, do out —

in the States? It is madness — sheer, brutal madness."

Priscilla shook her head.

"You think it childish folly? Why, I have never lost sight of it for a day. You have not understood me if you have imagined that. I have always known I must go. Lately I have felt the nearness of the going, and it is the *how* to break away and begin that puzzle me. I am ready."

"Priscilla, you are a wild child still, playing with dangerous tools. You cannot comprehend the trouble into which you are willing, in your blindness, to plunge. Why, you are a — a woman; a beautiful one! Do you know what the world does with such, unless they are guarded and protected?"

"What does it do?" The true eyes held Farwell commandingly, and with a sense of dismay he looked back at the only world he really knew: the world of his own ungoverned passions and selfishness. A kind of shame came over him, and he felt he was no safe guide. There were worlds and worlds! He had sold his birthright; this woman, bent upon finding hers, might inherit a fairer kingdom.

"What does it do, Master Farwell?"

"I do not know. It depends upon — you. It is like a great quarry — I have read somewhere something like this — we must all mould and chisel our characters; some of us crush them and chip them. It isn't always the world's fault. God help us!"

Priscilla looked at him with large, shining eyes and the maternal in her rose to the call of his sad recognition of failure where she was to go with such brave courage.

"Do not fear for me," she said gently; "'twould be a poor return if I failed, after all you have done for me."

"I — what have I done?"

"Everything. Have you ever thought what sort I would have been had Lonely Farm been my only training?" she smiled faintly, and her girlish face, in the setting of the faded hat and soiled veil, struck Farwell again by its change, which now seemed to have settled into permanency. Of course it was only the ridiculous fashion of the world he once knew, but he could not free himself of the fancy that Priscilla was more her real self in the shabby trappings than she had ever been in the absurd costumes of the In-Place.

With the acceptance of the fact that the girl really meant to get away and at once, a wave of dreariness swept over him. He thought of the time on ahead when his last vital interest would be taken from him. Then he aroused from his stupor and brought his mind to bear upon the inevitable; the here and now.

"It's a big drop in your ambition, Priscilla," he said; "you used to think you could dance your way to your throne."

"There is no throne now, Master Farwell. I'm just thinking all the time of My Road."

"But there's the Heart's Desire at the end, you know."

"Yes; but I do not think I would want it to be a throne."

"What then?"

"Oh! love — my own life — the giving and giving just where I long to give. It's splendid to tramp along your road, if it *is* your road, and be jolly and friendly with those you care for. It will all be so different from Kenmore, where one has to take what one must."

"I wonder how Jerry-Jo will feel about all this?"

"Jerry-Jo! And what right has he to think at all — about me?"

The girl's eyes flashed with mischief and daring.

"Jerry-Jo!" she laughed with amusement. "Just big, Indian-boy Jerry-Jo! We've played together and quarrelled together, but you're all wrong, Master Farwell, if you think he cares about me! He knows better than that — far, far, better."

But even as she spoke the light and fun left her eyes. She looked older, more thoughtful.

"Isn't it queer?" she said after a pause.

"What, Priscilla?"

"Oh, life and people and the things that go to their making? You're quite wrong about Jerry-Jo. I'm sure you're wrong."

Then suddenly she sprang up.

"I must go," she said abruptly; "go and exchange these rags for my own plain things. I only wanted to surprise you, sir; and how deadly serious we have grown."

She passed out of the cottage without a word more. Farwell watched her across the Green and up to the Lodge. He was disturbed and restless. The old fever of escape overcame him. With the thought of Priscilla's flight into the open, he strained against the trap that Ledyard had caught him in. The guide who, he knew, never permitted him to escape his vigilance, became a new and alarming obstacle, and Farwell set his teeth grimly. Then he muttered:

"Curse him! curse him!" and an emotion which he had believed was long since dead rose hotly in his consciousness. Before the dread spectre, suddenly imbued with vitality, Farwell reeled and covered his face. Murder was in his heart — the old madness of desire to wipe out, by any means, that which barred his way to what he wanted.

"My God!" he moaned; "my God! I — I thought I — was master. I thought it was dead in me."

Farwell ate no evening meal that night. Early he closed and locked his outer door, drew the dark green shades, and lighted his lamp. His hands were clammy and cold, and he could not blot out with book or violin the horror of Charles Martin's face as it looked up at him that night so long ago. Way on toward morning Farwell paced his room trying to forget, but he could not.

But Priscilla, after leaving Farwell, dressed again in her plain serviceable gown and hat, had made her way toward the farm. Her happy, light-hearted mood was past; she felt unaccountably gloomy, and as she walked on she sought to explain herself to herself, and presently Jerry-Jo came into focus and would not stir from her contemplation. Yes, it was Jerry-Jo's personality that disturbed her, and it was Farwell's words that had torn the shield she herself had erected, and set the truth free. Yes, she had played with Jerry-Jo; she had tested her coquetry and charm upon him for lack of better material. In her outbreaks of youthful spirits she had claimed him as prey because the others of his sex were less desirable. Jerry-Jo had that subtle, physical attraction that responded to her youthful allurements, but the young fellow himself, taken seriously, repelled her, and Farwell had taken Jerry-Jo seriously!

That was it! She was no longer a child. She was a woman and must remember it. Undoubtedly Jerry-Jo himself had never given the matter a moment's deep thought. Well, she must take care that he never did. Jerry-Jo in earnest would be unbearable.

And then, just as she reached the pasture bars

separating her father's farm from the red rock highway, Jerry-Jo McAlpin strode in sight from the wood path into which the highway ran. She waited for him and gave him a nervous smile as he came near. His first words startled her out of her dull mood.

"I've been up to the Hill Place. Him and her's there for a few days."

"Him and her!" Priscilla repeated, her face flushing. "Oh, him and her!"

"Sure!" McAlpin was holding her with a hard, fixed gaze.

In the mesh that was closing about Priscilla, strangely enough names were always largely eliminated. They might have altered her course later on, might have held her to the past, but Kenmore dealt briefly with personalities and visualized whatever it could. The name Travers had rarely, if ever, been spoken in Priscilla's presence. "The Hill Place folks" was the title found sufficient for general use.

"And I was remembering," Jerry-Jo went on, "how once you said you wanted to thank him for — for the books. We might take the canoe, come to-morrow, and the day is fine, and pay a visit."

Still Priscilla did not notice the gleam in McAlpin's keen eyes.

"Oh! if I only dared, Jerry-Jo! What an adventure it would be, to be sure. And how good of you to think of it."

"What hinders?"

"Father would never forgive me!"

"And are you always to be at the beck and whistle of your father even in your pleasures?"

Priscilla was in just the attitude of mind to receive this suggestion with appreciation.

"There's no reason why I shouldn't go if I want to," she said with an uplift of her head.

"And — don't you want to?" Jerry-Jo's eyes were taking in the loveliness of the raised face as the setting sun fell upon it.

"Yes, I do want to! I'll go, Jerry-Jo."

Then McAlpin came close to her and said in a low voice:

"Priscilla, give us a kiss for pay."

So taken out of herself was the girl, so overpowered by the excitement of adventure, that before she realized her part in the small drama of passionate youth, she gave a mocking laugh and twisted her lips saucily.

Jerry-Jo had her in his arms on the instant, and the hot kiss he pressed on her mouth roused her to fury.

"If you ever touch me again," she whispered, struggling into freedom, "I'll hate you to the last day of my life!"

So had she spoken to her father years ago; so would she always speak when her reservations were threatened. "I declare I am afraid to go with you to-morrow."

McAlpin fell back in shamed contrition.

"You need not be afraid," he muttered. "I reckon I was bidding you — good-bye. Him and me is different. Once you see him and he sees you, it's good-bye to Jerry-Jo McAlpin."

Something in the words and tone of humility brought Priscilla, with a bound, back to a kindlier mood. After all, it was a tribute that McAlpin was paying her. She must hold him in check, that was all.

They parted with no great change. There had been a flurry, but it had served to clear the atmosphere — for her at least.

But Nathaniel, that evening in the kitchen, managed to arouse in the girl the one state of mind needed to drive her on her course.

"What was the meaning of that scuffling by the bars a time back?" he asked, eyeing Priscilla with the old look of suspicious antagonism. Every nerve in the girl's body twitched with resentment and her spirit flared forth. She shielded herself behind the one flimsy subterfuge that Glenn could never understand or tolerate.

"A kiss you mean. What's a kiss? You call that a scuffle?"

Theodora, who was washing the tea dishes while Priscilla wiped them, took her usual course and began to cry dispiritedly and forlornly.

"What's between you and — McAlpin?" Nathaniel asked, scowling darkly.

"Between us? What need for anything between us?"

Priscilla ceased smiling and looked defiant.

"Maybe you better marry that half-breed and have done with it."

"It's more like — would *he* marry me?"

This was unfortunate.

"And why not?" Nathaniel shook the ashes from his pipe angrily. "A little more such performance as I saw to-day and no decent man will marry you! As for Jerry-Jo, he'll marry you if I say so! You foul my nest, miss, and out you go!"

"Husband! husband!" And with this Theodora dropped a cup, one of Glenn's mother's cups, and somehow this added fire to his fury.

"And when the time comes, wife, you make your choice: Go with her, who you have trained into what she is, or stay with me who has been defied in his own home, by them nearest and closest to him."

Priscilla breathed fast and hard. The tangible wall of misunderstanding between her and her father stifled her to-night as it never had before. Again she realized the finality of something — the breaking of the old ties, the helpless sense of groping for what lay hidden, but none the less real, just on before.

CHAPTER IX

THE next day was gloriously clear and threateningly warm. Such days do not come to Kenmore in September except to lure the unheeding to acts of folly. And at two o'clock in the afternoon Priscilla, from the kitchen door, saw Jerry-Jo paddling his canoe in still, Indian fashion around Lone Tree Island. Theodora was off erranding, and Nathaniel, as far as human knowledge went, was in some distant field; he had started off directly after dinner. Priscilla was ready for her adventure. With the natural desire of youth, she had decked herself out in her modest finery — a stiffly starched white gown of a cheap but pretty design, a fluff of soft lace at throat and wrist, and, over it, the old red cape that years before had added to her appearance as she danced on the rocks. Perhaps remembering that, she had utilized the garment and was thankful that cloth lasted so long in Kenmore!

The coquetry of girlhood rose happily in Priscilla's heart. Jerry-Jo had become again simply a link in her chain of events; he had lost the importance the flash of the evening before had given him; he was not forgiven, but for the time he was, as a human being, forgotten. He was Jerry-Jo who was to paddle her to her Heart's Desire! That was it, and the old words, set to music of her own, were the signals used to attract McAlpin's attention. But the merry call brought Glenn from out the barn just as the canoe touched the rocks lightly, and Priscilla prepared to step in.

"Where you two going?" he shouted in the tone that always roused the worst in Priscilla's nature. Jerry-Jo paused, paddle in air, but his companion whispered:

"Go on!" To Nathaniel she flung back: "We're going to have a bit of fun, and why not, father? I'm tired of staying at home."

This was unfortunate: on the home question Glenn was very clear and decided.

"Come back!" he ordered, but the little canoe had shot out into the Channel. "Hi, there McAlpin, do you hear?"

"Go on!" again whispered Priscilla, and Jerry-Jo heard only her soft command, for his senses were filled with the loveliness of her charming, defiant face set under the broad brim of a hat around which was twined a wreath of natural flowers as blue as the girl's laughing eyes.

Nathaniel, defied and helpless, stood by the barn door and impotently fumed as the canoe rounded Lone Tree Island and was lost to his infuriated sight.

"You'll catch it," Jerry-Jo comforted when pursuit was impossible, and he had the responsibility of the rebel on his hands. "I wouldn't be in your place, and you need not drag me in, for I'd have turned back had you said the word."

A fleeting contempt stirred the beauty of the girl's face for a moment, and then she told him of that which was seething in her heart.

"What does it matter, Jerry-Jo? All my life, ever since I can remember, I have been growing surely to what is now near at hand. I cannot abide my father; nor can he find comfort in me. Why should I darken the lives of my parents and have no life of my own? The lure of the States has always been in my thought and now it calls near and loud."

McAlpin stared helplessly at her, and her beauty, enhanced by her unusual garments, moved him unwholesomely.

"What you mean?" he muttered.

"Only this: It would be no strange thing did a boy start for the States. A little money, a ticket on a steamer, and — pouf! Off the boys and men go to make their lives. Well, then, some day you will — find me gone, Jerry-Jo. Gone to make my life. Will you miss me?"

This question caused McAlpin to stop paddling.

"You won't be — let!" he murmured; "you — a girl!"

"I, a girl!" Priscilla laughed scornfully. "You

will see. This day, after I have thanked him up yonder, I am going to ask his mother to help me get away. Surely a lady such as she could help me. I will not ask much of her, only the guiding hand to a safe place where I can — live! Oh! can you understand how all my life I have been smothered and stifled? I often wonder what sort I will be — out there! I'm willing to suffer while I learn, but Jerry Jo" — and here the excited voice paused — "I have a strange feeling of — myself! I sometimes feel as if there were two of me, the one holding, demanding, and protecting the other. I will not have men always making my life and shielding me; the woman of me will have its way. Men and boys never know this feeling."

And Jerry-Jo could, of course, understand nothing of this, but the thing he had set out to do, more in rude, brutish fun than anything else, assumed graver purpose. A new and ugly look grew in his bold eyes, a sinister smile on his red mouth, which showed the points of his white, fang-like teeth. But Priscilla, too absorbed with her own thoughts, did not notice.

It was four o'clock when the canoe touched the landing spot of Far Hill Place, and Priscilla sprang out.

"I'll bide here; don't be long," said McAlpin.

But Priscilla paused and glanced up at the sky.

"It's darkening," she faltered, a shyness overcoming her. "I smell — thunder. Don't you think you better come up with me Jerry-Jo? Suppose they are not at home?"

"They'll be back soon in that case, and as for a shower, that would hasten them and you would be under shelter. I can turn the canoe over me and be dry as a mouse in a hayrick. I'll not go with you, not I. Do your own part, with them looking on as will enjoy it."

"I believe you are — jealous, Jerry-Jo." This was said idly and more to fill in an awkward pause than for anything else.

"And much good that would do me, after what you've just said. If you're bound for the devil, Priscilla, 'tis little power I have to stay you."

"I'm not — for the devil!" Priscilla flung back, and started sturdily up the hill path toward the house hidden among the trees.

Out of McAlpin's sight, the girl went more slowly, while she sought to arrange her mode of attack. If her host were what he once was, he would make everything easy after she recalled herself to him. As for the mother, Priscilla had only a dim memory of her, but something told her that the call would be a happy and memorable one after the first moment.

A bit of tune cheered the girl; a repeating of the Road Song helped even more, for it resurrected most vividly the young fellow who had introduced music and happiness into her life.

"I'll be doshed!" she cried. The word had not passed her lips for years; it brought a laugh and a complete restoration of poise. So she reached the house. Smoke was issuing from the chimney. A fire had been made even on this hot day, but like enough it was to dry the place after the years of closed doors and windows. Evidently it was a many-houred fire, for the plume of smoke was faint and steady. The broad door was set wide but the windows were still boarded up at the front of the house, though the side ones had escaped that protection.

Priscilla knocked and waited. No reply or sound came in response, and presently a low muttering of distant thunder broke.

"That will bring them in short order," she said, "and surely they will not object if I make myself comfortable until they come."

She went inside. The room had the appearance of one from which the owner had long been absent, that unaccountable, vacant look, although a work-bag hung on the back of a chair by the roaring fire, and a blot of oil lay on the table near the lamp which had evidently been recently filled. Back of these tokens lay a wide sense of desolation.

For a moment Priscilla hesitated before sitting down; her courage failed, but a second thought reconciled conditions with a brief stay after long absence, and she decided to wait.

And while she waited, suddenly and alarmingly, the storm burst! The darkness of the room and the wooded space outside had deceived her: there was no escape now!

She was concerned for the people she had come to see. Jerry-Jo, she knew, would crawl under his boat and be as dry as a tortoise in its shell. But those others!

With this thought she set about, mechanically, making the room comfortable. She piled on fresh wood and noticed that it was so wet that it sputtered dangerously. Presently the wind changed sharply, and a blast of almost icy coldness carried the driving rain halfway across the floor.

It was something of a struggle to close the heavy door, for it opened outward, and Priscilla was drenched by the time it was made secure. Breathing hard, she made her way to the fire and knelt before it. The glow drew her attention from the darkness of the space back and around her.

It was unfortunate and depressing, and she had no choice but to make herself as comfortable as she might, though a sense of painful uneasiness grew momentarily. At first she imagined it was fear of what she must encounter upon her return home; then she felt sure it was her dread of meeting the people for whom she had risked so much. Finally Jerry-Jo loomed in the foreground of her thought and an entirely new terror was born in her soul.

"Jerry-Jo!" she laughed aloud as his name passed her lips. "Jerry-Jo, to be sure. My! how thankful I'd be to see him this instant!"

And with the assertion she turned shudderingly toward the door. The gloom behind her only emphasized her nervousness.

"I'll — I'll have to go!" she whispered suddenly, while the wind and the slashing of sleety rain defied her. "It will be better out of doors, bad as it is!"

The grim loneliness of four walls, compared with the dangers of the open, was worse. But when Priscilla, trembling and panting, reached the door and pushed, she found that the storm was pitting its strength against hers and she could not budge it.

"Oh, well," she half sobbed; "if I must, I must." And she stealthily tiptoed back to the warmth and light as if fearing to arouse something, she knew not what, in the dim place.

There was no way of estimating time. The minutes were like hours and the hours were like minutes while Priscilla sat alone. As a matter of fact, it was after seven when steps, unmistakable steps, sounded on the porch and carried both apprehension and relief to the storm-bound prisoner inside.

"Thank heaven!" breathed she, and sprang to her feet. She was midway in the room when the door opened, and, as if flayed forward by the lashing storm,

Jerry-Jo broke into the shadow and drew the heavy oak door after him. In a black panic of fear Priscilla saw him turn the key in the lock before he spoke a word to her; then he came forward, flung his wet cap toward the hearth, and laughed.

"What's the matter?" he asked quickly as Priscilla's white face confronted him. "Disappointed, I suppose. Do you begrudge me a bit of warmth and shelter? God knows I'm drenched to the bone. The rain came up from the earth as well as down from the clouds. It's a devil's storm and no mistake. What you staring at, Priscilla? Had you forgotten me? Thought me dead, and now you're looking at my ghost? Didn't I wait long enough for you? Where are the — others?"

This seemed to clarify and steady the situation and Priscilla gave a slight laugh:

"To be sure. You did not know. They — they were away. The storm came up suddenly. I had to wait. You are wet through and through, Jerry-Jo. It's good we have such a fire. You'll be comfortable in a moment. I'm glad you came; I was getting — afraid."

"Let's see if there is any oil in the lamp!" Jerry-Jo exclaimed. He was in no mood for darkness himself.

"They must have filled it before they went," Priscilla answered. "See, there is some oil on the table."

McAlpin struck a match and soon the room was

flooded with a new brightness that reached even to the far corners and seemed to set free the real loneliness that held these two together.

"I — I managed to keep this dry," McAlpin spoke huskily. "I always have a bite with me when I take to the woods. Who can ever tell what may happen!"

He pushed a coarse sandwich toward Priscilla and began eating one himself.

"Go on!" he said.

"I'm not hungry, Jerry-Jo, and I want to start back home at once."

Jerry-Jo leered at her over his bread and meat.

"What's your hurry? I want to get warm and dry before I set out again. This is an all-nighter of a storm, if I know anything about it."

"Get dry, of course, Jerry-Jo. It won't take long with this heat; then we must start, storm or no storm."

The old discomfort and unrest returned, and she fixed her eyes on Jerry-Jo.

"There's no great hurry," said he, munching away. "It's warm here and cozy. What's got you, Priscilla? You was mighty keen to come, and you ain't finished your errand yet. What's ailing you? No one could help the storm, and we'd be swamped in the bay if we was there now."

Priscilla got up and walked slowly toward the door, but without any apparent reason Jerry-Jo arose also, and, still chewing his bread and meat,

backed away from the table, keeping himself between the girl and whatever her object was. Noticing this, a real terror seized upon Priscilla and she
darted in the opposite direction, reached the hearth,
and was bending toward a heavy poker which lay
there, before she herself could have explained her
motive. Jerry-Jo was alert. Tossing his food upon
the table as he strode forward, he gripped her wrist.

"None of that!" he muttered. "What ails you,
Priscilla?" They faced each other at close range.

"I — I am afraid of you!"

At this McAlpin threw back his head and roared
with laughter, releasing her at the same time. With
freedom Priscilla gained a bit of courage and a keen
sense of the necessity of calmness. She did not
move away from Jerry-Jo, but fixing him with her
wide eyes she asked:

"Are — are the — family here — here in Kenmore?" Suspicion and anger shook the voice. The
slow, tense words brought things down to fact.

"No! God knows where they are! I don't know
or care."

Brought face to face with great danger, mental or
physical, the majority of people rise to the call.
Priscilla knew now that she was in grave peril —
peril of a deeper kind than even her tormentor could
realize. Every nerve and emotion came to her
defence. She would hold this creature at bay as
hunters hold the wild things of the woods when gun

or club fail. Then, after that, she would have to
deal with what must inevitably confront her at
home. She seemed to be standing alone amid cruel
and unfamiliar foes, but she was calm!

"You lied, then? What for?"

"What do you think?"

"You believe, by shutting me away from everything, every one, you can win what otherwise you
could not get?" It all seemed cruelly plain, now.
She felt she had always known it.

"Something like that, yes. You'll come to me
fast enough, after to-night. Once you come I'll —
I'll do the fair and square thing by you, Priscilla."

The half-pleading caught the girl's thought.

"You mean, by this device you will make me
marry you? You'll blacken my name, bar my
father's house to me, and then you will be generous
and — marry me?"

Jerry-Jo dropped his bold, dark eyes.

"I never cared for you, Jerry-Jo. I hate you, now!"

At this McAlpin raised his head and a fierce red
coloured his face.

"You'll get over that!" he muttered. "Any port
in a storm, you know. You better not drive me
now! I ain't — safe, and I've got you tight for —
to-night!"

Suddenly the pure flame of spirituality flashed into
the soul of Priscilla Glenn. Alone, undefended,
facing a hideous possibility, beyond which lay a

"'You mean, by this device you will make me marry you?
You'll blacken my name, bar my father's house to me,
and then you will be generous and — marry me?'"

black certainty of desolation, she rose supreme to protect something that her rudely aroused womanhood must defend, even by death!

"You — beast!" she cried, and all her shrinking fear fell from her. "Go back! Sit down! I have something to say to you — before ——" She did not finish, but the pause made Jerry-Jo understand that she recognized her position.

"I'll stand here, by God!" he almost shouted, and came close.

The proximity of the rough, coarse body was the one thing the girl felt she could not bear. She smelled the odour of his wet clothing, felt his breath, and she shrank back a step.

"This — this body, Jerry-Jo McAlpin," she whispered, "is all you can touch. That, I will kill tomorrow — the next day — it does not matter. But the soul of me shall haunt you while you live. Night and day it shall torment and clutch you until it brings your sinful spirit to — to God!"

"You — you devil!" cried McAlpin, all the superstitious fear of his mixed blood chilling him. "You ——" And then as if daring the fate she had it in her power to evoke, he rushed toward her and clasped her close in his strong arms. His face was bent over hers, his lips parted from his cruel teeth, but he did not force them upon her.

So here she was — she, Priscilla Glenn, in the jaws of death, she who would have laughed, danced, and sang her way straight into happiness! Here she was, with what on ahead — if she lived?

She waited, she struggled, then she relaxed in the iron hold, and for a moment, only a moment, lost the sense of reality. Presently words that McAlpin was saying came to her in the black stillness of her consciousness.

"I had — to have you! Now that I've shown you my power, I can wait until you come whining to me. I ain't going to hurt you! I want you as you are when you come a-begging of me. I only wanted to prove to you that — I've got you!"

Again Priscilla was aware of the red warmth of the fire, the sickening smell of drying wool, the loosening of the bands of McAlpin's arms.

"You — you who boast that when you hunt, out of season, you shoot one shot in the air in order to give a poor wild thing a chance of escape — you bring me here with a lie; close every hope to me, and — call that — victory! You — you — fiend! What do you mean?"

She was standing free at last! She was so weak that she staggered to a chair, fearing that McAlpin, seeing her need, might again lay hands upon her.

"I mean — that I've fired my shot!" Her words had caught his fancy. "You have your chance to — to get away! But where? Where?"

The dark face leered.

"See! I'm going to leave you. Go out into the

night. You can try for your — your life, but in the end you'll come to me. I don't care what they of Kenmore will say, I'll know you are — what you are, and sympathy will be with me, gal, when I take you. And you'll know, once you come to me, proper and asking, I'll do — I'll do the best any man could do — for — I love you!"

This was flung out desperately, defiantly.

"Yes, I love you as — Jerry-Jo McAlpin knows how to love. It's his way. Remember that!"

Not a word rose to Priscilla's lips. She saw McAlpin turn and stride to the door; she heard him turn the key and — she was alone! But a strange thing happened just at that moment, a thing that did more to unnerve the girl than anything that had gone before. As the heavy oak door slammed after the retreating figure, the jar caused the tall clock, back among the shadows of the far side of the room, to strike! One, two, three! Then followed a whirring that faded into deathly silence. It was like the voice of one, believed to be dead, speaking!

Frightened, but thoroughly roused to her only hope, Priscilla staggered to the door, clutched the key in cold, trembling fingers, and turned it in the lock. Then, sinking upon her knees, she crept back to the fire, keeping close to the wall. If an eye were pressed to a knothole in the shutter it could not follow her.

CHAPTER X

PRISCILLA kept the fire alive. She laid the sticks and logs on cautiously; she turned wide eyes now and again on the tall clock whose white face gleamed pallidly among the shadows like a dead thing that had used its last breath to speak a message. If the clock struck again Priscilla felt that she might go mad.

It was after midnight when Nature laid a commanding and relentless touch upon the girl, and, crouching by the hearth, her head in her arms folded upon a chair, she slept.

Outside the storm sobbed itself into silence; the rain dripped complainingly from the roof of the porch and then ceased. At five o'clock the new day, rosy and full of cheer, made itself felt in the dim room where Priscilla, breathing evenly and softly, still slept. No gleam of brightness made its way through the heavy shutters or curtains, but a consciousness of day at last roused the sleeper. At first the experience through which she had passed made no demand upon her. She got painfully upon her feet and looked about. The fire was but embers, the air was hot and stifling, and then, with the thought of opening a door or window, the grim spectre of the black hours lay warning touch upon her. She shrank back and began again to — wait! Of course McAlpin would return — and what lay before her when he did? Her strength was spent, lack of food —— And here her eyes fell on the broken fragments of stale bread and meat that Jerry-Jo had tossed aside.

She took the morsels and devoured them eagerly; the nerves of the stomach were calling for nutrition, and even the coarse crumbs gave relief.

The moments passed slowly, but presently, with the knowledge that day lay beyond her prison, she gained a new, a more desperate courage. If she must die, she would die in the open, where she at least might test her pitiful strength against Jerry-Jo's did he pursue her. The determination to act gave relief. The dark, damp room she could no longer bear; the lamp had hours before ceased to burn; the smell of stale oil smoke was sickening. No matter what happened she felt she must make a break for freedom. She knew full well that should Jerry-Jo enter now she could not combat him.

Then, for the first time, she wondered why no one had come to seek her through the long, black hours of the night. The men of Kenmore never permitted a wanderer to remain unsought; there was danger. Why, even her father could not be so — so hard as to sleep undisturbed while she was unhoused! And her mother? Oh! surely her mother would have roused the people! And Anton Farwell? Why, he would have started at once, as he had for the McAdam boys. And with that conclusion came a new hope:

"If they are searching it will be on the water!"

Of course. Cheered by this thought, Priscilla made her way silently toward the door. With trembling fingers she turned the key and pushed gently outward. Through the crack the sun poured, and oh, the fresh sweetness of the morning air! Again she pushed, once again, and then with a rush she dashed through and was a hundred feet down the path when a loud laugh stayed her like a shot from a gun.

She turned and braced herself against a tree for support. Jerry-Jo, pressed close to the house and not a foot from the door through which she had come, again shrieked with laughter. Presently he conquered himself, and, without moving, said:

"You're free! The canoe's ready for you, too. Go home — if you want — go home and get what's coming to you! I've been busy. There's a boat stopping at the wharf to-night. I'm leaving for the States. I've told them, as will pass it on, that you and me are going together. I'll stand by it, too, God hears me!"

"My — my father will kill you when he knows of this night!"

Priscilla flung the words back savagely. She knew now that she was free — free for what? Again Jerry-Jo's laugh taunted her, and as she turned to the path her father faded from her hope. Only Anton Farwell seemed to loom high. Just and resourceful, he would help her!

The soggy, mossy path made heavy travelling for weary, nervous feet, but at the foot of the hill Priscilla saw the little canoe bobbing at the side of the dock. Once out upon the sunlit water the soul-horror disappeared and the task before her appeared easy. Now that the real danger was past, her physical demands seemed simple and well within her control. If her father turned her away — and as she drew near to Lonely Farm she felt that he probably would — she would go to Farwell, and from him, with his assistance, go to the States. The time had come — that was all — the time had come! She was as ready as she ever would be. She had herself well in hand before she stepped from the canoe at the foot of her father's garden.

The only signs of anxiety in evidence about the house were Nathaniel's presence in the kitchen at eleven in the morning, and Theodora's red and swollen eyes as she bent over the dishwashing of a belated breakfast.

"Mother! Father!"

They turned and gazed at the pale, dishevelled girl in the doorway. Neither spoke and Priscilla asked.

"May I come in?"

Had she wept, or flung herself upon their mercy, Nathaniel could have understood, but her very calmness and indifference angered him, coming as it did upon his real anxiety. He had not heard the village gossip that Long Jean had already started. He had been out alone most of the night on the water, and the relief of seeing his girl alive and unharmed turned his earlier emotions to bitterness.

"Yes, come in," he said sternly. "Where have you been?"

Had Priscilla been given more time, had she been less physically spent, she would have protected herself from her father's thought; as it was she could only summon enough strength to parry his questions with truthful answers, and until it was too late she did not realize how they damned her.

"Up at — at — Far Hill Place."

"All night?"

"Yes."

"With —— "

"With — with Jerry-Jo McAlpin."

"Oh!" This came like a snake's warning.

"The — the storm was — oh! Father —— "

"The storm!" roared Nathaniel; "the storm! Are you sugar or salt? Have you so little morality that you choose to stay overnight with a man in a lonely house instead of coming wet but clean-charactered to your safe home?"

And then Priscilla understood! She had come into the room and was sitting near the door she had closed behind her. She, on the sudden, seemed to grow old and strong; the ancient distrust and dislike of her father overcame her; she looked at her mother, bent and sobbing over the sink, and only for *her* sake did she continue the useless conversation.

"You — you judge me unheard!" she went on, addressing Nathaniel with an anger, glowing in her eyes, that equalled his own.

"Have you not just incriminated yourself — you!"

"Stop! Do you think that is all? Do you think I would have stayed there — if — if ——" Here the memory of what she had endured choked her.

"A woman who puts herself in a man's power as you have can expect no mercy." Nathaniel stormed.

"Why?"

"Because it is God's law. All decent women know it. That is what I've feared for you always, but I'll still stand by you if you show reason. I'll do it for your mother's sake and my good name. He shall marry you, by God! Say the word and I'll bring him here."

Priscilla's upper lip twitched. This was a trick her nerves had of warning her, but she heeded not.

"You — you would *force* me to marry Jerry-Jo even against his will? You would make that little hell for me without even knowing what has happened? You'd fling me in it to — to save your name?"

"You've made your own hell! No matter what has happened, there is only one way out for you. If you refuse that —— " And here Nathaniel flung his big arms wide, as if pushing his child out — out!

With white face but blazing eyes Priscilla got up and went over to her mother. She drew the bowed and quivering form toward her and looked straight into the tear-flooded eyes.

"Mother, tell me, do you believe me — dishonoured?"

The contact of the dear, strong young body gave Theodora power to say:

"Oh! my dear, my dear, I cannot, I will not believe evil of you. But you must do what your father thinks best; it is the only way. You have been so heedless, my child, my poor child."

"You — side with her?" thundered Nathaniel, feeling himself defied. "Then heed me! If she refuses, out you go with her! No longer will I live with my family divided against me. The world with her, or the home with me!"

Then suddenly and quite clearly Priscilla saw the only way open to her, the only way that led to even the poor peace she yearned to leave to the sad, little, clinging, broken creature looking piteously up at her.

"My child, my child, your father knows best."

"There! there mother. Now listen!"

Still holding Theodora, she looked over the gray head at her father's cruel face.

"I have only to tell you," she said slowly and with deadly hardness, "you will not have to force Jerry-Jo McAlpin to marry me; he's eager enough to do it. He leaves to-night for the States; he has arranged for me to go with him." She paused, then went on, speaking now to her mother:

"As God hears me, I am not dishonoured, little mother. I will never bring dishonour upon you. I could have explained to you — you would have understood, but father — never! I am going to the States. Good-bye."

"My child! oh! my girl!"

"Good-bye, dear mother."

"Oh, Priscilla! Do not leave us so!"

"This is the only way."

"But, you — you are not yet wedded."

Priscilla smiled.

"You must leave that to Jerry-Jo and me. And now a kiss — and the dear cheek against mine. So!"

"But you will come back —— " Theodora sank gently to the floor. She had fainted quite away!

Priscilla bent with her, she lifted the white head to her knee, and again addressed her father.

"You are satisfied?" she asked. The shield was

down between them. Man and woman, they stared, understandingly, in each other's eyes.

"Leave her to me!" commanded Nathaniel, and strode toward the prostrate form.

"You've lied first and last. Neither McAlpin nor any other honest man will have you! Go!"

"I will go and — my hate I leave with you!"

And when Theodora opened her eyes she was lying on the rough couch in the sunny kitchen, and Nathaniel was bathing her face with cool water.

"The child?" faltered the mother, looking pleadingly around. And then Nathaniel showed mercy, the only mercy in his power.

"She's gone to McAlpin. They leave for the States to-night. It's you and I alone now to the end of the way."

"Husband, husband! We've been hard on her; we've driven her to —— "

"Hush, you! foolish one. Would you defy God? Each one of us walks the path our feet are set upon. 'Twas fore-ordained and her being ours makes no difference. Every light woman was — some one's, God knows — and with Him there be no respecter of persons."

"Oh! but if you had only been kinder. It seems as if we haven't gone beside her on her path. Couldn't we have drawn her from it — if we had expected different of her? Oh! I shall miss her sore. The loneliness, the loneliness with her out of the days and the long nights."

Theodora was weeping again desolately.

"Be grateful, woman, that worse has not come to us."

Now that the deathlike faint was over, Nathaniel's softening was passing.

"And she went from our door hungry, the poor dear! We wouldn't have treated a beggar so."

"Had she come as a suppliant, all would have been different."

Then Theodora sat up, and a kind of frenzy drove her to speak.

"She had something to tell! You did not let her say her say. *What* kept her away all night? Jerry-Jo McAlpin has the devil blood in him when he's up to — to pranks. Suppose —— " A sort of horror shook the thin, livid face. Nathaniel, in spite of himself, had a bad moment; then his hard common sense steadied him.

"Would she go to him, if what you fear was true?"

"Has she gone to him?"

"Where else then — and all Kenmore not know? Wait till to-morrow before you leap to the doing of that which you may regret. Calm yourself and wait until to-morrow."

And Theodora waited — many, many morrows.

CHAPTER XI

"AND you see, Master Farwell, I cannot go back to my father's house."

It was after nine of the evening of the day Priscilla Glenn had left home. She had reached Farwell's shack without being seen. By keeping to the woods and watching her opportunity, she had gained the rear of the schoolhouse, entered while Farwell was absent, and breathed freely only after securing the door.

The master had returned an hour later and, the gossip of the Green ringing in his ears, confronted the white, silent girl with no questions, but merely a glad smile of relief. He had insisted upon her taking food, drink, and rest before explaining anything, and Priscilla had gratefully obeyed.

"I'll gather all the news that is floating about," Farwell had comforted her. "Sleep, Priscilla. You are quite safe." Then he went out again.

So she had eaten ravenously and slept far into the early evening while Anton Farwell went about listening to all who talked. It was a great day for Kenmore!

"She and him were together all the night," panted

Long Jean, about noon, in the kitchen of the White Fish.

"What's that?" called Mary McAdam from the closet. Jean repeated her choice morsel, and Mary Terhune, preparing the midday meal, thrilled.

"I was at her borning," Jean remarked, "and I minded then and spoke it open, that she was made of the odds and ends of them who went before her. I've a notion that the good and evil that might have thinned out over all the Glenn girls must work out thick in Priscilla."

"I'm thinking," Mary Terhune broke in, "that the mingling with such as visits at the Lodge has upset the young miss. Her airs and graces! Lord of heaven! how she has flouted the rest of the young uns! Aye, but they are mouthing about her this day! 'Me and her,' said Jerry-Jo to me this early morning, 'me and her got caught up in the woods, and, understanding one another, we chose the dry to the wet, and brought things to a point. Her and me will make tracks for the States. It's all evened up.' And I do say," Mary went on, "that all considering, Jerry-Jo is doing the handsome thing. I ain't picking flaws in her — maybe she's as clean as the cleanest, but there's them who wouldn't believe it, as you both very well know."

This last was to include Mrs. McAdam, who had issued from the closet with an ugly look on her thin, dark face.

"You old harpies!" she cried, striding to the middle of the big room and getting into position for an oratorical outburst. "You two blighted old midwives as ought, heaven knows, to have mercy on women; you who see the tortures of women! You would take a girl's name from her on the word of that half-breed, who would sooner lie than steal — and both are easy to the whelp. That girl is the straightest girl that ever walked, and no evil has come to her from my house. A word more like that, Mary Terhune, and you'll never share my home again, and as for you, Jean, you who helped the lass into life, what kind of a snake-heart have you?"

Mary McAdam had both women trembling before her.

"I'll go up to Lonely Farm myself," screamed she, "and if Glenn and his poor little slave-wife are doing the low trick by their girl, as God hears me, I'll take her for my own, and turn you both back to the trade you dishonour!"

Anton Farwell, passing near the window, heard this and went his way.

Later old Jerry McAlpin came to him on the wharf where the men were gathered to meet the incoming steamer.

"Lordy! Master Farwell," quavered Jerry; "while I was out on the bay this early morning, my lad, what all the town is humming about, goes to

my home and takes everything — everything of any
vally and leaves this —— "

McAlpin passed a dirty piece of paper to Farwell.

"I'm going to get out on the steamer. Going to the
States, and had to have the stuff to get away with. *I —
ain't — alone!* I'm going down the Channel to board the
steamer where it stops for gasoline. *Don't* follow me for
God's sake. I'll pay you back and more."

Farwell read the words twice, then said:
"Well?"
"Shall I — stop him, Master Farwell?"
"Can you spare what he has taken?"
" 'Tain't that, sir."
"Then let him go! Let him have his fling."
"They do say — Long Jean, she do say — it's
Glenn's girl. My lad's been crazy for her. I'm
afraid of Glenn."
"Let things alone, McAlpin. This is your time to
lie low and hold your tongue."

Farwell tore the paper in shreds and cast them to
the wind.

The steamer came in at eight. At nine-thirty it
left the wharf, and, a mile down the Channel, stopped
at the little safety station to take on oil and gasoline.
Tom Bluff, a half-breed, had the place in charge, and
later that evening he put the finishing touch to the
day's gossip.

" 'Twas Jerry-Jo, as you live, who jumped aboard,

taking the last can I was hauling up with him. So in a hurry was he that he nigh pushed some one down who was in front of him.

"'Where going?' calls I. 'To the States,' he says back, and picks up the young person he nigh knocked down."

Long Jean, to whom Tom was confiding this, drew near.

"Who was the young person?" whispered she, with the fear of Mary McAdam still upon her.

"Her face? I did not see her face."

"'Twas Glenn's girl," panted Long Jean; "Priscilla!"

"Ugh!" grunted Tom as his ancestors had often grunted in the past. "Ugh!"

That was all for the day, and behind closed doors and windows Kenmore slept. The storm of the previous night had been followed by a cold wave, and upon Farwell's hearth a fire crackled cheerily.

"And so, you see, I cannot go back to my father's house."

Farwell bent his head over his folded arms.

"But Mrs. McAdam will take you in, Priscilla. After things calm down and the truth is accepted, your people will forgive and forget. You poor child!"

Priscilla closed her lips sharply. Her eyes were very luminous, very tender, as they rested upon Farwell, but her heart knew no pity for her father.

"How old one grows, Master Farwell, in — a night," she said with a quiver in her voice. "I went happily away with Jerry-Jo, quite, quite a girl, only yesterday. I had the feeling of a child trying to make believe I was a woman. I wanted to show my father he could no longer control me as he always had before. I — I wanted to have my way, and then my way brought me to — those black hours of horror when something in me died forever and something new was born. And how strange, Master Farwell, that when I could think at all clear — you stood out as my only friend. I seemed to know how it would be with my father and my poor mother. My father has always expected evil of me, and something in me seemed ever to work against the good of me, to give him cause for believing me wrong. But you saw the good, my friend, and to you I come — a woman, now. I do not know the language of what I feel here" — she pressed her hands to her heart — "but I feel sure you will understand. I cannot stay in Kenmore! I do not want to. Always I have wanted to have a bigger place, a larger opportunity, and even if Kenmore would take me, I will not have Kenmore! Somehow I feel as if I had never belonged here, really. You do not belong here. Oh, Master Farwell, can you not come, too?"

As she spoke, the old, weary look passed for an instant from her eyes; she was a child, daring, yet fearful! Ready to go forward into the dark, but pleading for a trusted hand to hold. And Farwell, who, could she have known, was clinging more to her than she to him, almost groaned the one word:

"No!"

"Why, oh, why, Mr. Farwell? Like father and daughter we could make our way. I think I have never known what a father might be, but you would show me now in my great need."

"Hush!" Farwell's eyes held hers commandingly, entreatingly. "You must hear what I have to say. Why do you think I have stayed in Kenmore? Why I *must* stay? Have you thought?"

"No." And for the first time in her life Priscilla wondered. Before, the man had been but part of her life; now she wondered about him, with the woman-mind that had come so suddenly and tragically to her.

"No, Master Farwell, why?"

"Because — well, because Kenmore is my grave — must always be my grave. I'm dead. Good people, just people said I was dead. I am dead. Alive, I would be a menace, a curse. Dead, I am safe. I've paid my debt, and you, you, the people of my grave, since you do not know, have given me a chance, and I've been a friend among friends! Why, I've even come to a consciousness that — perhaps it is best for me to be dead, for back there, back among the living, the thing I once was might assert itself again."

The bitterness, the pitiful truthfulness, of Farwell's voice and words sank deep into Priscilla's heart. Out of them she instantly accepted one great, vital fact: he was in Kenmore as a refugee; he had been — had done — wrong! With the acceptance of this, a strange thing happened. Curiosity, even interest, departed. For no reason that she could have classified, Priscilla Glenn fiercely desired to — keep Farwell! If she knew what he seemed bent upon telling, he might take away her faith — her only support. She would keep and hold to what she believed him, what he had been since he came to the In-Place. It was childish, blind perhaps, but her words were those of a determined woman.

"Master Farwell, I will not listen to you. If you are dead, and are safe, dead, I will not look into the grave. All my life you have been good to me, been my only friend; you shall not take yourself from me! And I — please let me do this one little thing for you — let me prove that I can love and honour you without — explanation!"

Farwell's face twitched. He struggled to speak, and finally said unsteadily:

"I have been — good, as you say, because I had to be. At any moment I might have been what I once was. Why, girl, without knowing it, Kenmore — all of you — had it in your power to fling me to the dogs had you known, so you see —— "

But Priscilla shook her head.

"You did not have to risk your life as you did for the McAdam boys. Perhaps you do not know how you have — grown in your grave, Master Farwell. Trust and liking come hard to us in Kenmore, yet not one of us doubts you. No, no, lie quiet. I do not want to see you as you remember yourself; you are better as you are. I will not hear; I will not have it in my thought when I am far away."

The hardness passed from Farwell's face. Something like relief replaced it, and he said slowly:

"My God! what a woman you will make if they do not harry you to death.'

"They will not!" The white, tired face seemed illumined from within. "Last night made me so sure — of myself. It showed me how weak I was, and how strong. Do you know" — and here a flush, not of ignorance, but of strange understanding, struck across Priscilla's face like a flame — "women like my mother, all the women here in Kenmore, do not understand? They just let people take from them what no one has a right to take, what only they should give! It's when this something is taken that they become like my poor mother — afraid and crushed. If I live and die alone and lonely, I shall keep what is my own until I — I give it gladly and because I trust. I am not afraid! But if I had married Jerry-Jo because of — of — what he and my father thought, then I would have been lost, like my mother, don't you see? I — I can — live alone, but I will not be lost."

"But, great heavens! you are a woman!"

"Is it so sad a thing to be a — woman? Why?"

To this Farwell made no reply. Shading his gloomy eyes with his thin hand, he turned from the courageous, uplifted face and sighed. Finally he spoke as if the fight had all gone from him.

"Stay here. The thing you want isn't worth the struggle. There is no use arguing, but I urge you to stay. The In-Place is safer for you. What is it that you must have?"

Priscilla laughed — a wild, dreary little sound it was, but it dashed hope from Farwell's mind.

"I want my chance, a woman's chance, and I cannot have it here. I'm not going to hide under Mrs. McAdam's wing, or even yours, Master Farwell. I've left all the comfort with my poor mother that I can. Never let her know the truth, now I am going — going to start on My Road! I do not care where it leads, it is mine, and I am not afraid."

In her ignorance and defiance she was splendid and stirred the dead embers of Farwell's imagination to something like life. If she were bent upon her course, if his hand could not rest upon the tiller of her untested craft when she put out to sea, what could he do for her? To whom turn?

"Is there not one, Master Farwell, just one, out

beyond the In-Place, who, for your sake, would help me at first until I learned the way?"

The question chimed in with Farwell's thought.

He leaned across the table separating him from Priscilla Glenn and asked suddenly:

"Can you keep a secret?"

Promptly, emphatically, the answer came. "Yes, I can."

"Then listen! You must stay here, hide yourself, keep yourself as best you may, while I go to — make arrangements. I will be no longer than I can help, but it will take time. The house is well stocked; make yourself comfortable. There are days when no one knows whether I am here or elsewhere. Protect yourself until I return. And when" — Farwell paused and moistened his lips — "when you are over the border, in the whirlpool, the past, this life, must be forgotten. Raise up a high wall, Priscilla, that no one can scale. Begin your new life from the hour you reach the States. The one who will befriend you need know no more than I tell him; others must take you on faith. At any moment your father, or some one like Jerry-Jo, might hound you unless you live behind a shield. You understand?"

He did not plead for his own safety, and he was, at that moment, humanly thinking of hers alone.

"If you get the worst of it, come back; but leave the gate open only for — yourself."

"Yes, yes." And now Priscilla's eyes were

shining like stars. " I will do all that you say; I feel so brave and strong and sure. I want the test, and I will leave the door to Kenmore ajar until the day when I can push it wide and enter as I will, taking or bringing my dear friends with me. I see" — she paused and her eyes grew misty — "I see My Road, stretching on and on, and it ends — oh, Master Farwell, it ends in my Heart's Desire!" She was childishly elated and excited.

Farwell was fascinated.

"Your Heart's Desire?" he muttered; "and what is that?"

"Who knows until — she sees it? Hurry! hurry! Master Farwell, I long to set forth."

Forgotten was her recent experience of horror; fading already was Kenmore from her sight. Danger by the way did not daunt her; the man bowed before her was but a blurred speck upon her vanishing horizon; then suddenly a sound caught her ear.

"You — you — are" — she arose and stood beside Farwell, her hand upon his bent shoulder — "you are crying; and for why?"

"Loneliness, remorse, and fear for *you*, poor child."

And then Priscilla came back to the grim room and the cowering form.

"I will bring happiness to you," she whispered; "this I swear. In some way you shall be happy."

But Farwell shook his head.

"To bed," he said suddenly; "to bed, girl, and to

sleep. I'll take a nap out here on the couch. Before you awake I'll be on my way. Keep the shades drawn; it's my way of saying I do not wish to be disturbed. Good night, and God bless you, Priscilla."

CHAPTER XII

ABOUT two in the morning Farwell set out upon his business for Priscilla. He left a safe and roaring fire upon the hearth; the window shades he did not raise, and well he knew that with that signal of desire for privacy his house would be passed by without apparent notice. The smoke might curl from the chimney, the dogs might, or might not, materialize, but with those close-drawn shades the simple courtesy of Kenmore would protect the master.

Priscilla was sleeping when Farwell silently closed the door after him, and, followed by his dogs, provided with food and blankets, he noiselessly took to the shadowy woods. It was a starry, still hour, lying between night and morning, and it partook of both. Dark it was, but with that silvery luminosity which a couple of hours later would be changed to pink glow. The stars shone, and the one great, pulsing planet that hung over the sleeping village seemed more gloriously near than Farwell had ever before noticed it. All nature was waiting for the magic touch of day; soon action and colour and sound would stir; just then the hush and breathlessness were a strange setting for the lonely man moving forward into the deeper shadows followed close by his faithful dogs. This man who, in the mad passion of his blighted youth, had taken life as if it were but one of the many things over which he claimed supremacy, with bowed head and slow steps, was going on an errand of mercy; he was going to claim, for a helpless human creature, assistance from the only man in all God's world upon whom he could call with hope of success.

The program, the next few days, was as clear in Farwell's mind as if he had already followed it from start to finish. By eight Pine would be on his tracks; by noon they would be together, the dogs grumbling and fighting at their heels. Two nights by the fire, smoking in a dull silence, broken now and then, in sheer desperation, by Farwell himself.

In Ledyard's plan there had evidently been but one stipulation: the constant guardianship with explicit reports. Beyond that there seemed to be no exactions. Farwell had tried to make Pine drink more than was good for him on various occasions in order to test the metal of the restraint, but the Indian displayed a wonderful self-control. He knew when and where to begin and stop in any self-indulgence, but having fulfilled his part he showed no interest or curiosity in his companion. Once the trading station was reached, Farwell might buy or seek pleasure as he chose; he might write or receive letters; might sleep or wake. So long as the tangible Farwell was where the guide could locate him at a moment's notice, he was free to think and act to his own satisfaction.

As he plodded on Farwell contemplated, as he never had before, his relations with the Indian; in fact, the Indian himself. A superficial friendliness had sprung up between the two. How deep was it? how much to be depended upon? If Ledyard could buy the fellow, might not a higher price secure his allegiance? This, strange to say, was a new thought to Farwell. Perhaps he had accepted the situation too doggedly; it was his way to cease struggling when the tide turned against him. It was weakness, it was folly, and, after Priscilla went, after the girl opened the doors again into that old life, how could he endure the loneliness, the tugging of her hold upon him from the place he once had called his?

The day came late to the deep woods beyond Kenmore, and Farwell seemed going toward the night instead of facing the morning. At five he paused to feed his dogs and take a bite himself, and, as he sat upon a fallen tree, the mystic stirrings of life thrilled him as they often had before. It was more a sense of rustle and awakening than actual sound. Hidden under the silence of the forest lay the quivering promises, as the rosy light lay just on the border of the woodland. Both were pressing warm and comfortingly close to the lonely man with his patient dogs at his feet. Farwell was a better man, a finer man, than he knew, but only subconsciously did this support him.

It was three of the afternoon before he heard the quick, measured steps on the trail behind him. He did not turn his head, but he called back a genial "Hello!" which was answered by a grunt not devoid of friendliness.

The evening meal was eaten together, and the two arranged their blankets near the fire for the night's rest. Farwell's two dogs and Pine's one faithful henchman lay down in peace a short distance away. It was as it had been for a time back, except that the Indian had become, suddenly, either an obstacle to be overcome or a friend to assist. Not realizing his new importance, the guide grunted a good night and fell into that sleep of his that never seemed to capture his senses entirely.

At the small town, which was reached late the following day, Farwell engaged two rooms at the ramshackle tavern and informed Pine that he was to share the luxuries.

This was unusual. In the past a day at the station sufficed for business transactions, and night found them in the woods again. Pine was confused but alert. However, things progressed comfortably enough. The expected mail was awaiting Farwell, and he greedily bought all the newspapers he could get. His purchases at the store did not interest the

Indian and he was not even aware that several garments for a woman were included in Farwell's list. A telegram sent, and another received, did perturb the fellow a good deal, but when Farwell tore the one he got into shreds, the simple mind of the guide concluded that the matter was unimportant, and he forgot it before they reached Kenmore. He could not burden his poor intellect with unnecessary rubbish, and the whole business was getting on to what stood for nerves in the Indian's anatomy.

What really had occurred was this: Farwell had reached across the desolate stretches that divided him from his one friend and got a response. He had impressed upon John Boswell that he could not come in person to Kenmore, but he could meet a certain needy young person and convey her to safety in the States. And he had asked a question that for months had never risen to the surface — he had been too crushed to give it place.

"Is Joan Moss still alive?"

Boswell was ready to aid him in any way, would even deny himself the longing of seeing his old friend face to face, since that seemed desirable. He would meet the young woman at a place called Little Corners and would do what he could for her.

"Joan Moss is still alive."

A strong light and a new hope came into Farwell's sad eyes. He had a hold on the future! With the possibility of supplanting Ledyard in Pine's ideas of loyalty and economics what might not happen?

And so they started back.

It was midnight, four days after Farwell had left home, that he entered his own door again. The return trip had been rushed, much to Pine's approbation. Priscilla was quietly sewing at the table when Farwell, having loudly bidden the Indian good night, came into the living-room.

The girl's alarmed glance turned to one of relieved welcome when she saw Farwell. She had some food ready for him — every night she had been prepared — and he ate it ravenously. She noted how white and weary he looked, but the triumphant expression in his sad eyes did not escape her, either.

"You have good news?" she asked as soon as Farwell had rested a bit by his fireside.

"Yes. And you?"

"Oh! I have done famously. Only two knocks at the door, and I was well hidden. Once it was Mrs. McAdam and once old Jerry. They did not try to enter."

"They would not. And there was food and fuel enough?"

"Food — yes; I went out three times for wood, and I took one wild, mad walk. I ran, while all the world slept, to Lonely Farm. I looked in at my father's window; he was dozing by the fire, and — my mother —— "

"Well, Priscilla?"

"My mother — was crying! I shall always remember her — crying. I did not know there were so many tears in the world!"

"You — you still insist upon going away?"

"Yes. There is no other way for me. Already I seem a stranger, a passerby. Not even for my mother can I stay; it could work no good for her or me. Perhaps, by and by —— " Priscilla paused. Now that she was about to turn her back on all that was familiar to her, she became serious and intense, but she knew no shadow of wavering.

Then Farwell told her the arrangements he had made.

"I have a hundred dollars for you, Priscilla. I wish it were more. My friend Boswell will meet you at Little Corners. This is Friday; he will be there on Sunday and will wait for you at the inn; there is only one. Ask for it and go straight to it. From here to Little Corners is the hardest part. I will go as far as I dare with you; the rest you must make alone. Halfway, there is a deserted shanty near the old factory; there you can make yourself comfortable for the night. Are you afraid?"

Priscilla was white and intent, but she answered:

"No, I shall not be afraid."

"You ought to cover the distance in a couple of days and a night; the walking is not hard, and the woods are fairly well cleared. Once you reach Boswell you are safe. He will not question you, but you can trust him. He's a strange man — younger than I; he stands, has always stood, for all that is noble and good in my life. I have told him that you are some one in whom I am interested."

The feeling of adventure closed in and clutched the girl. Now that the hour had actually come, the hour up to which all her preparations tended, she quivered with excitement tinged with sadness.

"This way of leaving Kenmore is safer," Farwell was saying. "If any one were to see you and know you, your father would find you out and bring you back. No one will know you at Little Corners. That's a place which most honest people let alone. You'll like Boswell — every one does — after the first. He'll put you in the way of helping yourself, and your people may still hold their belief about you and Jerry-Jo, since it makes things easier for them."

"Yes; they must believe that until —— " But Priscilla did not finish the sentence.

The two sat silent for a few minutes while the tired dogs upon the hearth breathed loud and evenly. Then at last Priscilla asked:

"When do we start, Master Farwell?"

"Start? Oh, to be sure. I had forgotten." Farwell roused himself from his lethargy. "We start at once; in an hour or two at the latest. I will nap here on the couch; you must rest as best you can. There's a long coat and a hat in yonder bundle.

They must serve you until you meet Boswell. He'll rig you out in some town before you reach civilization. Here's the money; take wallet and all. Hide it somewhere, Priscilla." Farwell was on his feet and active once more.

"Go in an hour or two?" gasped Priscilla absent-mindedly, following Farwell's words and accepting the money with a long, tender look of gratitude. "In an hour or two? Why, you've only just come in, Master Farwell!"

"What matters? After to-morrow I shall have time to rest and sleep to my fill."

"You will — miss me, Master Farwell?" Priscilla's eyes were dim. "I would like to have some one — miss me!"

"I shall, indeed, miss you! You can never understand what you have meant to me, Priscilla. I cannot make you understand; I shall not try; but in helping you I have perhaps helped myself. I cannot walk out of the In-Place beside you, as I would like to do — not now. Maybe a long time hence, some day, I may follow!"

Farwell's excitement showed in his eyes and voice and wiped out the weariness of his face.

"You mean that, Master Farwell? You are not trying to comfort me?"

"No; I am comforting myself!"

Then, forgetful of the need for sleep, he went on rapidly:

"Out where you are going, Priscilla, there is a — a woman I love; she once loved me. This must seem queer to you who have only known me as — as I now seem. I will seem different to you when you have wakened up — seen other kinds of men and women."

"Is she young — pretty?"

The senseless words escaped Priscilla's lips because quivering interest and a strange embarrassment held her thought.

"I — I do not know — how she is now. She *was* pretty. Good God! how pretty she was, and young, and kind, too. It was the kindness that mattered most. You see, she thinks me dead; it was best so. I — I had to be dead for a while and then I meant to go to her myself. But — something happened. I was obliged to stay on here, and she might not have understood. I'd like —— " Farwell paused and looked pleadingly at the white girl-face across the rude table, where the fragments of food still lay: "I'd like you to go and see her. Boswell could take you. He's done everything for her, God bless him! I'd — I'd like to have you tell her gently, kindly, that I am alive. You might say it so as to spare her shock; you might, better than any one else!"

The longing in the man's eyes was almost more than Priscilla could endure. Crude as she was, wrong and sinful as the man near her may at one time have been, she knew intuitively that the love for that woman in the States had been his consuming and uplifting passion. If he had sinned for her, he had also died for her, and now he pleaded for resurrection in her life.

"I will do anything in all the world for you, Master Farwell; anything!"

And Priscilla stretched her hands out impulsively. Farwell took them in his cold, thin ones and clung to her grimly.

"I'd like to know she'd welcome me!" he whispered. "Unless she could, I'd rather stay — dead!"

Another silence fell between the man and girl while he relived the past and she sought to enter the future.

The clock struck the half-hour of one and Farwell sprang up.

"Get ready!" he said. "No time for napping now. It is — it is Saturday morning! We must be off! I'll go with you as far as I can. For the rest —— "
He stopped suddenly and looked blankly at Priscilla.

A little after two they started away from the small, darkened house. It was a cloudy morning; day would be long in coming, and the two made the most of the darkness. They were well in the deep woods by six o'clock; at seven they ate some food Farwell had hurriedly prepared, and were on their way again by eight. They did not talk much. Priscilla found that she needed all her strength, now that she

must soon depend upon herself, and Farwell had
nothing more to say but — good-bye!

Anton Farwell had got ahead of his spy for once!
Not even so indefatigable an Indian as Pine could be
expected to watch a man who had just returned
from a long tramp. But Farwell knew full well that
by high noon his guard would have sensed danger
and be uncommonly active, so he pushed the march
to Priscilla's utmost limit.

At four o'clock they reached the deserted hut near
the old factory. A fire was made upon the hearth
and a broken-down settle drawn close.

"I'd rest until early morning," advised Farwell in
a hard, constrained voice. "Good Lord, Priscilla,
it's a cruel place to leave you — alone!"

"I shall not mind, Master Farwell." All that was
brave and unselfish in the girl rose now to the fore.
She recognized that Farwell, even more than she,
needed comfort.

"I shall never forget you," she said, holding her
hands out to him; "never forget you or cease to —
love you!"

The last words made him wince.

"Good-bye, Priscilla."

"Good-bye, Master Farwell."

When the door closed upon the man, for a moment
Priscilla stood with horrified glance following him.
The sense of high adventure perished at his going.
Alone in the woods, in the ghostly hut, the night to

face, and the blank future stretching beyond! It was more than she could bear, and a cry escaped her parted lips. But Farwell did not hear, and the paroxysm passed.

Priscilla slept that night, slept well and safely, and the early light of Sunday morning found her refreshed and full of courage. She never knew that two hours after leaving her Farwell met Pine and found in him — a friend!

They had come face to face on a side trail.

"Here I am!" said Farwell cheerfully; then he took his place in front of the guide. That had always been the unspoken understanding.

"See here, Pine, we've never said much to each other about what — all this means, but I want to say something now. I won't give you much trouble in the future. I shall not go often for my mail, or necessaries. In return, forget *this* journey. I went to let a — a poor little devil of a creature out of a trap. That is all. I just couldn't — leave it to suffer — and I hadn't time to call you up after our long tramp of yesterday."

"Ugh!" came from behind.

"Pine, can you trust me?"

"Ugh!" But the grunt was affirmative.

"Smoke on it, Tough?"

And they smoked while they plodded wearily back into bondage.

CHAPTER XIII

LITTLE CORNERS, lying on the borderland of Canada and the States, stretched like a hand, the thumb and small finger of which belonged to the Dominion, the three digits, in between, to the sister country. Of course it was comparatively easy to bring merchandise, and what not, by way of the thumb and little finger and send the same forth by the three exits, known to Timothy Goodale as "furrin parts." Timothy was excessively British, as so many Canadians are, but he was a broad-minded man in his sympathies, and a friend to all — when it paid. He was a man of keen perceptions, of conveniently short memory, and had the capacity for giving a lie all the virtuous appearance of truth and frankness. Goodale had no family, and, as far as possible, served his guests himself. A half-breed cooked for him; a half-witted French-Canadian girl did unimportant tasks about the bedchambers, but the host himself took his patrons into his own safekeeping and their secrets along with them.

Little Corners was not a town of savoury reputation. Law-abiding folks gave it a wide berth;

tourists found nothing interesting there, and new-comers, of a permanent type, were discouraged. For these reasons it was the place of all places for Mr. John Boswell to enter, by way of the long, middle finger, and meet Priscilla Glenn, who advanced via the thumb. No one would know them; no one would remember them an hour after they departed.

Timothy was bustling about on a certain Sunday morning, ruminating on the thanklessness of the task of getting ready for people who might never appear, when, to his delight, he saw a team of weary horses advancing. He had time only to put his features in order for business when a man entered the room.

No one but Goodale could have taken the shock of the traveller's personality in just the way he did. The smile froze on his face, his eyes beamed, and his stiff, red hair seemed bristling with welcome. "Advance agent of a circus," he thought; "sort of advertising guy."

The man who had entered was about three feet tall, horribly twisted as to legs, and humped as to back and chest. The long, thin arms reached below the bent knees, and large, white hands dangled from them as if attached by wires. The big head, set low on the shoulders, seemed to have no connecting link of neck. It was a great, shaggy head with deep-set, wonderful eyes, sensitive mouth and chin, and a handsome nose.

"Ah, sir, delighted," said Goodale. "Shall I tell your driver to go to the stables?"

"I'm my own driver, but I'd like your man to see to the horses. I'm John Boswell from New York, though you'll probably forget that an hour after I leave."

Goodale nodded. This was quite in his line, and he suddenly became aware of the exquisite texture and quality of the stranger's clothing; the fineness of the piping voice. All sorts came to the inn, but this last comer was a gentleman, for all his defects.

"I'm expecting a young woman, a distant relative, from farther back in Canada. I shall await her here. My stay is uncertain. Make me as comfortable as you can; I like to be comfortable."

"You — you are alone, sir?"

"Until the young lady comes, yes. She is to return to the States with me. It depends upon her how soon we travel back."

This did away with the show business, but it added romance to the adventure.

Goodale made Boswell extremely comfortable, surprisingly so. Two bedrooms were got in order as if by magic; a little sitting-room emerged from behind closed doors; an apartment quite detached and cozy, with a generous fireplace and accommodations for private meals.

After a good dinner Boswell went for a stroll,

telling his host to make the young lady welcome upon her arrival.

At half-past four Priscilla Glenn walked into the office of the inn. She was tired and worn, rather unkempt as to appearance, but she stepped erect and with some dignity.

"Is — is Mr. Boswell here?" she asked.

"He is, and then again he ain't," smiled Timothy, who was always playful with women when he wasn't brutal. None knew better than he the use and abuse of chivalry.

"You are to make yourself at home, Miss; then I'll serve tea in the sitting parlour; all quite your own and no fear of intrusion. I'm host and servant to my guests. I never trust them to — to menials."

"Where's my room?" Priscilla broke in abruptly. She was near the breaking-point and she longed for privacy and shelter before she collapsed. Her tone and manner antagonized Goodale. He understood and recognized only two classes of women, and this girl's attitude did not fit either class. In silence he showed her to her bedchamber, and once the door separated him from her his smile departed and he relieved his feelings by muttering a name not complimentary to Mr. Boswell's relative.

The sense of safety, warmth, and creature comforts speedily brought about courage and hope to Priscilla; a childish curiosity consumed her; she was disappointed that Boswell did not present himself, but his absence gave her time for rallying her forces. She found her way to the little sitting-room by six o'clock, and, to her delight, saw that tea things were on a table by the hearth and a kettle was boiling over the fire.

"And so — this is Miss Priscilla Glenn?"

So noiselessly had the man entered the room through the open door, so kind and gentle his voice, that, though the girl started, she felt no fear until her eyes fell upon the speaker. Boswell waited. He knew what must follow. Readjustment always took time. In this case the time might be longer because of the crudity of the girl.

"Ah!" The shuddering word escaped the trembling lips and the tightly clasped hands that had instinctively gone to the face. "Ah!"

The man by the door sent forth a pitiful appeal for mercy and acceptance in so sweet and rare a smile that for very shame Priscilla stood up and smiled back wanly and apologetically.

Boswell liked the attempt and ready willingness; they showed character.

"Now that that is over," he said in his strange, fine voice, "we may sit down and be friends. May we not?"

"I will make fresh tea for you — please let me!" for Boswell was waving aside the suggestion.

"Very well! Weak — just flavoured water. Now, then!"

The sidling form edged to the deep chair beside the hearth and scrambled up, using both hands as a child does. Priscilla kept her eyes upon her task and struggled for composure.

"I — I suppose Max — I mean Farwell — did not describe me?"

"No, sir."

"It was mistaken kindness. My friends have a habit of doing that. They think to spare me; it only makes it harder. Try to forget, as soon as you can, my ugly shell; I am commonplace beneath."

The pathos of this almost brought tears to Priscilla Glenn's eyes. Her warm, sympathetic nature responded generously.

"I — I am very sorry I gave you pain, sir. Forgive me!"

"We will not mention it again. If you can think of me as — a man, a friend who wishes to help you for another friend's sake, you will honour me and make easier your own position. You see, you are no stranger to me; I have the advantage of you. Farwell has kept me in touch with you from your childhood up. You have amused him, helped him to bear many things that would have been harder for him without you. I thank you for this. I am Farwell's friend. Why, do you know" — and now the deep eyes glowed kindly — "he has even told me of that original religion you evolved from your needs;

he pictured the strange god you worshipped. I've laughed over that many times."

"Your tea is getting cold, sir."

Priscilla was gaining control of her emotions, and John Boswell's evident determination to place her in a comfortable position won her gratitude and admiration.

"I like cold tea; the colder and weaker the better. Thank you. Let the cup stand on the table; I will help myself presently. I sincerely hope we, you and I, are going to be friends. It would hurt Farwell so if we were not."

"How good you are!"

"Yes. Goodness is — my profession." The drollery in the voice was more touching than amusing. "I call myself the Property Man. I help people artistically, when I can. It is my one pleasure, and I find it most exciting. You will learn, now that you have taken your place on the stage of life, that the Property Man is very important."

In this light talk, half serious, half playful, he reassured Priscilla and claimed for himself what his deformity often retarded.

"Already you seem my friend. Mr. Farwell said you would be."

Priscilla's eyes did not shrink now. The soul of the man had, in some subtle fashion, transformed him. She began to succumb to that power of Boswell's that had held many men and women even against their wills.

"Farwell was always a dramatic fellow," the weak voice continued. "When he sent me word, I wanted to go direct to Kenmore; I wanted to see him after all these years. But he had made his own plans in his own way. There were — reasons."

Priscilla looked bravely in the thin, kindly face. She remembered that Farwell had said that she need tell nothing more than she cared to, but an overpowering desire was growing upon her to confide everything to this friend of an hour. His deep, true eyes, fixed upon her, were challenging every doubt, every reserve.

"Farwell says you dance like a sprite."

At this Priscilla started as if from sleep.

"Ah! a childish bit of play," she said. "I — I have almost forgotten how to dance."

"I hope you will never forget. To dance and sing and laugh should be the heritage of all young things. You must forget to be serious, past the safety point! That's where danger lies. It does not pay to take our parts ponderously. I learned that long ago."

"I shall be — happy after a while." And now, quite simply and frankly, Priscilla cast away her anchors of caution and timidity and spoke openly:

"I — I have been so troubled. Things have happened to me that should not have happened if — if my mother and father could have trusted in me.

They believed — wrong of me when really they should have pitied me. You trust me?"

"Absolutely."

"Master Farwell trusted me. As things were, the only comfort I could give my poor parents was to let them think I left Kenmore with — with a young man. Something had occurred that — looked wrong. It was only a terrible experience. No one helped me but Master Farwell. My — my people turned from me."

"It was Farwell's way: to help where he had faith," murmured Boswell.

The deep eyes were so perilously kind that Priscilla had to struggle to keep back her tears. A sense of security and peace flooded her heart, but the past strain had left its mark.

"My father would have been glad to have me marry the — the man. I would rather have died after what happened! They — my father and mother — must believe I have gone with him. It will at least make them feel I have not disgraced them. Now — you can understand!"

"Perfectly."

"I want to go into training. I want to be a nurse. I am sure I can succeed."

So very humble and modest was the ambition that it quite took Boswell by surprise. Priscilla did not notice the uplifting of the shaggy brows. She went on eagerly, thoughtfully:

"You see, I have only such education as Master Farwell has given me, but I have a ready mind, he says. I am sure I could watch and tend the sick. A lady staying in Kenmore at one time told me I had the — the touch of a skilled hand. I want — to help the world, somehow, and this seems the only way open to a girl like me. I am strong; I never tire. Yes; I want to be a nurse, the best one I can be."

Boswell understood the deeper truth. This girl, original, artistic, was foregoing much in accepting this safe, humble course. She expected no charity, nothing but a helpful interest. It was unusual and delightful.

"I have a hundred dollars that Master Farwell gave me. It will help, and I can repay it by and by. I know it will be years before I can do so, but he understands. While I am studying there will be little expense, the lady told me. And oh!" — here Priscilla interrupted herself suddenly — "I have an errand to do for Master Farwell as soon as I get to New York. He told me you — would help me."

"An errand?"

"Yes. There is a — woman he once — loved; loves still. She thinks he — is dead. It was best so in the past. There was a reason for letting her believe so; but now he wants her — to know!"

Boswell sprang up in his chair as if he were on a strong spring.

"Wants you to go and tell her — that he still lives?"

"Yes. It will be hard, but I will do it for him."

Boswell settled back in his seat.

"I thought he only meant her to know — when he could go himself," he said quietly.

"He made me promise."

Boswell leaned forward and drew the cup from the table, and in one long draught drank the cold, weak tea. When he spoke again the conversation was set in a different channel.

"I hardly know what I expected to find you, Miss Glenn," he said with his rare, sweet smile. "You evidently seemed more a child to Farwell than you do to me. That was natural. Now that we have become acquainted I hope you will accept my help and hospitality until your own plans are formed. I can make you very comfortable in my town home. I am sure I can place you in the best training school in the city; I have some influence there. But before you settle to your hard work you will let me play host, as Farwell would in my place? This would be a great pleasure to me."

What there was in the words and tone Priscilla could never tell, but at once the future seemed secure, and the present placed on a sound foundation. Every disturbing element was eliminated and the whole situation put upon a perfectly commonplace basis. By a quick transition the unreality was swept aside.

"Indeed, I will be glad to accept."

They smiled quite frankly and happily at each other.

"An odd story occurs to me." Boswell pressed back in his chair and his face was in shadow. "You must get used to my stories and plays. The Property Man must have his sport. There was once a garden, very beautiful, very desirable, but full of traps to the unwary. Quite unexpectedly, one day, a particularly fine butterfly found herself poised on the branch of a tree with a soaring ambition in her heart, but a blind sense of danger, also. It was a wise butterfly, by way of change. While it hesitated, a beetle crawled along and offered its services as guide. The pretty, bright thing was sane enough to accept. Do you follow?"

Priscilla started. She had been caught in the mesh of the story, and now with a sudden realization of its underlying thought she flushed and laughed.

"I still have my childish delight in stories, you see," she said. Then, "I — I do see what you mean. Again I repeat, I am so glad to accept your — your kindness."

"Middle life has its disadvantages." The voice from out the shadows sounded weary. "It has none of the blindness of youth and none of the assurance of old age. If I were twenty, you and I could play together in the Garden; if I were ninety I could tuck you safely away in my nest and feed you on dainties, and no one could say a word. As it is — well, we'll do the best we can, and, after you are in your training, you'll be glad enough to have my nest to fly to for a change of air and an opportunity to chat with me. The Property Man will come in handy. Hark! the wind is rising. How it blows!"

The ashes were flying about on the hearth and the trees outside beat their branches against the windows.

"It never roars like that in the In-Place," whispered Priscilla, awed by the sound and fury that were rapidly gaining power.

"The In-Place?" Boswell sighed. "What a blessed name! To think of any one fluttering about in the dangerous Garden when he or she might remain in the In-Place!"

There was a tap on the door, and in reply to Boswell's "Come!" Goodale entered.

"Shall I serve supper now, sir?"

"Yes."

"In here?"

"No; in the dining-room." Then, "How far is it to the railway station?"

"Twenty-six miles, sir."

"It seemed like a hundred. Can the team make it to-morrow if the storm ceases?"

"They look capable, sir."

"Then we will start to-morrow for the States."

CHAPTER XIV

PRISCILLA GLENN always looked back on the next four weeks of her life as a transition stage between one incarnation and another. Kenmore, and that which had gone to the making of her life previous to her meeting with John Boswell, seemed to have accomplished their purpose and left her detached and finished, up to a certain point, for the next period of her existence. In the severing of all the ties of the past, even affection, gratitude, and memory, for the time being, were held in abeyance. This was a merciful state, for, had ordinary emotions and sentiments held her, she would have been unfitted for the difficult task of readjustment which she gradually achieved, simply because of her dulled mental and spiritual sensations.

The noise and flash of the big city bewildered and dazzled the girl from the In-Place and encrusted her with an unreality that spared her many a pang of loss, and also fear for the future. Boswell's apartment, high above the street and overlooking the Hudson River and Palisades, became a veritable sanctuary from which she dreaded to emerge and to which she clung in a passion of self-preservation.

The gray wall of stone across the sparkling stream grew to be, in her vivid fancy, the barrier between the past and future. Against it, unseen, faint, but persistent, beat what once had been — her grim father, her weak, tearful mother, lonely, kindly Master Farwell, and all the lesser folk of Kenmore. Pressing close and straining to hold her, these dim, shadowy memories clustered, but she no longer appeared a part of them, like them, or in any way connected with them. On the other hand, below the eyrie dwelling in which she was temporarily sheltered, lay the whirlpool of sound and motion into which, sooner or later, she must plunge.

With keen appreciation and understanding of this phase of her development, John Boswell kept conversation and life upon the surface, and rarely permitted a letting-down of thought. Cautiously, and not too often, he took his guest on tours of inspection and watched her while she underwent new ordeals or experienced pain from unknown thrills. He had never been more interested or amused in his life, and, in his enthusiasm, exaggerated Priscilla's capabilities. He revelled in her frankness and her confidence; he learned from her more of Farwell than he could have learned in any other way, and his faithful heart throbbed in pity, pride, and affection for the lonely master of the In-Place, who, little heeding his own progress, had triumphed over his old and lesser self at last.

The home of Boswell was a large and sunny apartment high up in the huge building. Only one servant, a marvellously silent and efficient Japanese, ran the economic machinery, awesomely defended Boswell's library when the master retired to perform his mystic rites, and in all relations was exemplary. Poor Boswell's rites comprised a devouring appetite for reading and a rather happy talent for turning off a short story as unique and human as he was himself.

After Priscilla Glenn arrived, Toky, as the servant was called, was tested to the uttermost. Never before had Boswell introduced a woman into the sphere sacred to Man. Toky disapproved, was utterly disgusted; he lost his implicit faith in his master's wisdom, but he adopted a manner at once so magnanimous and charming that Boswell set to work and planned future gifts of appreciation for his servant.

No other woman came to the apartment; Boswell shrank from them, not bitterly or resentfully, but sensitively. Men took him more or less for granted when he touched their lives; women overdid the determination, on their parts, to set him at ease. Long since he had turned his poor, misshapen back upon the very natural and legitimate desire for the happy mingling of both sexes, but after Priscilla Glenn became his guest he recognized the need of women friends in a sharp and painful manner. They could have helped him so much; could have solved so many problems for him and the girl; but as it was he had to do the best he could alone.

The hundred dollars, still to be repaid to Farwell, worked wonders in the week following the arrival of the Beetle and the Butterfly, as Boswell insisted upon calling himself and Priscilla. Having no power at court, Boswell cast himself on the mercy of lesser folks and managed, by way of secret nods and whispers, to gain the coöperation of sympathetic-looking shop girls in order to array Priscilla in garments that would secure her and him from impudent stares and offensive leers. The evenings following these shopping expeditions were devoted to "casting up accounts." Priscilla was absolutely lacking in worldly wisdom, but she had a sense of accuracy that drove Boswell to the outer edge of veracity. Never having bought an article of clothing for herself, Priscilla attacked this new problem with perfectly blank faith. Prices often surprised and startled her by their smallness, but the results obtained were gloriously gratifying.

"I can better understand the lure of the States now, Mr. Boswell," she said one evening as the two sat in the library with the wind howling down Boswell's exaggerations and the fire illuminating the girl's face. "Kenmore prices were impossible, but one can go wild here for so little. Just fancy! That whole beautiful suit for two dollars and eighty-seven —— "

"Eighty-nine!" Boswell severely broke in, shaking

his pencil at her as he sat perched, like a benign gargoyle, by his study table. "I'll not have Farwell defrauded while he cannot protect his own interests."

"Two eighty-nine," Priscilla agreed, with a laugh so merry and carefree that the listener dropped his tired eyes. "And how much does that leave of the hundred, Mr. Boswell? I tremble when I think of the silk gown so soft and pretty, the slippers and stockings to match, and the storm coat, umbrella, heavy shoes, and — and — other things."

Boswell referred to his notes and long lines of figures.

"All told, and in round numbers, there are forty-seven dollars and three cents left."

"It's marvellous! wonderful!" Priscilla exclaimed. "You are sure, Mr. Boswell?"

"Do you doubt me?"

"Sometimes I do, you are so kind, so generous, and under ordinary circumstances it would seem impossible to buy things so cheap. You must select your shops carefully."

"One has to on a moderate allowance."

Then quite suddenly Priscilla Glenn spoke quickly and breathlessly:

"Mr. Boswell, I — I must begin my training. Have you made any arrangements? And, when I go, will they pay me from the start?"

Boswell grew grave as he thought of the knowledge that would come concerning dollars and cents later on.

"I have started operations," he replied; "in a short time you will be able to begin your studies, and I hear they will pay you the princely sum of ten dollars a month from the day you are accepted. Canadians are greatly in demand."

"Ten dollars!" gasped Priscilla, "Ten dollars a month! when I think what this hundred has done, and the twelve months in each year, it — it dazzles me!"

Boswell gave an uncomfortable laugh. In the light of nearby disillusionment his practical joke looked mean and ghastly.

Then, with another abrupt change of thought, Priscilla brought Boswell again at bay.

"Before I go into training," she said, "I must go and see Master Farwell's friend — his old friend, you know. I feel very guilty and ungrateful, but it has all been so strange and bewildering, I have seemed dead and done for and then born again, I could not help myself; but I can now. Please tell me all about her, Mr. Boswell, and how I can find her."

Boswell dropped the pencil upon the mahogany desk and looked blankly at Priscilla.

"Let us sit by the fire," he said presently, "I am cold and — tired. Turn down the lights."

They took their positions near the hearth: the dwarf in his low, deep leather chair with its wide "wings" that hid him so mercifully; Priscilla in the small rocker that from the first had seemed to meet every curve and line of her long, young body with restful welcome.

"And now," Priscilla urged, "please tell me. I feel, to-night, like myself once more. I am adjusted to the new life, I hope, ready to do my part."

When John Boswell cast aside his whimsical phase he was a very simple and direct man. He, too, was becoming adjusted to Priscilla's presence in his home and her rightful demands upon him.

"Yes, I will tell you," he said slowly, wearily.

"Perhaps you are too tired to-night, Mr. Boswell? To-morrow will do."

"No. I never sleep when the wind howls; it gets into my imagination. I'd rather talk. The thing I have to tell you — is what I shall tell Farwell if I ever see him again. It's rather a bungling thing I've done. I'll receive my reward, doubtlessly, but I would do the same, were I placed in the same position, over and over again.

"Farwell Maxwell, known to you as Anton Farwell, has been part, the biggest part, of my life since we were young boys. We were about as pitiful a contrast as can be imagined, and for that reason met each other's needs more completely. We had only one thing in common — money. He was a straight, handsome fellow, while I was — what you see before you — a crooked, distorted creature, but one in whose heart and soul dwelt all the cravings and aspirations of youth and intelligence. I was alone in the world. My father died before my birth, and I cost my mother — her life. Farwell had, until he was twenty, an adoring though foolish mother, who laid undue emphasis upon his rights and privileges. She, and an older brother, died when he was twenty-one — died before the trouble came, but not before they had done all they could to train him for it. At twenty-one he was a selfish, hot-headed fellow with a fortune at his command, a confused sense of right and wrong, an ungoverned, artistic nature swayed by impulse, and, yes, honest affection and generous flashes. And I? Well, I found I could buy with my money what otherwise I must have gone without, but the shadow never counted for the substance with me. The fawning favour, which held its sneer in check, filled me with disgust, and I would have been a bitter, lonely fellow but — for Farwell.

"I never could quite understand him; I do not to-day, but he, from the beginning, did not seem to recognize or admit my limitations. Through preparatory school and college we went side by side. He called me by the frank and brutal names that boys and men only use to equals. I wonder if you can understand when I say that to hear him address me as an infernal coward, when I shrank from certain things, was about the highest compliment I knew?"

"Yes," murmured Priscilla, "I can understand that." She could not see Boswell; the low, impassioned words came from out the shadows like thoughts. "Yes, I can quite understand how you felt."

"I am glad that you can, for then you will see — why I have done — what I could for Farwell — when he needed me. Back in those old days he was not content to shame me into playing my part; by that power of his, that worked both good and evil, he compelled others, in accepting him, to accept me on equal terms. There was a seat for me at the tables to which he was invited; he discovered my poor talent for telling a story, and somehow hypnotized others into considering me a wit! A wit!"

A silence fell between the two by the fire. Priscilla's throat was hard and dry, her heart aching with pity.

"And then," Boswell continued drearily, "the crash came when he was only twenty-five! I suppose he was savagely primitive. That was why externals did not count so much with him. He could not brook opposition, especially if injustice marked it; he was never able to estimate or eliminate. He was like a child when an obstacle presented itself. If he could not get around it, he attacked it with blind passion.

"It was part of his nature to espouse the cause of the weak and needy; that was what held him, unconsciously, to me; it was what attracted him to Joan Moss."

The name fell upon Priscilla's mind like a shock. The story was nearing the crisis.

"She was outwardly beautiful; inwardly she was as deformed — as I! But in neither case was he ever able to get the right slant. He loved us both in his splendid, uncritical way. His love brought me to his feet in abject devotion: it lured the woman to accomplish his destruction. Something, some one, menaced her! He tried to sweep the evil aside, but —— "

"Yes, yes, please go on!" Priscilla was breathless.

"Well, he couldn't sweep it aside; so he committed — murder."

"Oh! Mr. Boswell! "

The shuddering cry drew Boswell to the present. He remembered that his listener knew Farwell only as a friend and gentle comrade. Her shock was natural.

"You — you never guessed? Why do you think he, that brilliant fellow, stayed hidden like a dead thing all these years?" — there was a quiver in Boswell's voice — "hidden so deep that — not even I dared to go to him for fear I would be followed and he again trapped! Oh! 'twas an ugly thing he did; but he was driven to insanity — even his judges believed that — at the last; but his victim was too big a man to go unavenged, so they hunted Farwell down, caught him in a trap, and tried to finish him, but he got away and they thought him — dead."

"Yes, yes," moaned Priscilla, "yes, I know. And the woman — did her heart break?"

At this Boswell leaned forward, and, in the fire's glow, Priscilla saw his face grow cruel and hard.

"Her heart break? No, she went promptly to the devil, once she was sure she had lost Farwell and his money. Down to the last hope she made him believe in her. How she acted! But when he was reported dead, well!" — and Boswell gave a harsh laugh — "her heart did not break!"

A sound brought Boswell back to the dim room.

"You are — crying?" he said slowly; "crying for him?"

"For him, yes, and for you!"

"For me?" — a wonderful tenderness stole into the man's voice — "for me? I do not think any one before — ever cried for me. Thank you. You understand what all this meant to me? What a — woman you will be — if —— "

Priscilla raised her tear-stained face and her lips quivered as she recalled that Farwell had said almost exactly the same words to her back there in the In-Place. She understood because she had been lonely and known the suffering of the lonely. She must never forget, never fail those who needed her! But Boswell was talking on again with a new note of feeling in his voice.

"While I thought him dead I sank back into my shell, sank lower than I had ever been before. I wanted to die; wanted it so truly that I planned it; grew interested in arranging my affairs. Preparing to die became my excitement, and when everything was ready, Farwell spoke to me — from his grave! That letter from your In-Place worked a miracle upon me. While he lived there would always be something for me to do. He had made a place in the world for me; I could keep his place ready for him. It was a small return, but it meant life — for me.

"There were years when Farwell felt he was coming back. I heard from him spring and autumn, and there were hope and promise each time. When people forgot, he would return, and he wanted to go to — to Joan Moss himself with his story. So long as he knew that she was alive and faithful it was enough, and, besides, he realized that had she or I gone to him just then it might have been fatal. He believed that if she knew where he was she would hasten to him!

"Well, just at first I thought that he might come at any time and might rescue — Joan Moss. I was even willing for him to have her if it could add any happiness to him. Then there was the money — his money. I kept his belief in that, too. Everything of his went at the time of the trial, but mine was his, so that was a small matter. I suppose all the sentiment and passion that most men spread over their entire lives were, in me, concentrated on Farwell. When I thought of him caged and alone, in the wilds, I found lying to him about the only thing I could do. So I kept his belief in Joan Moss and his fortune. Then something happened to him. I never knew what it was, but it seemed to take all the hope and courage from him. He wanted me to see that Joan Moss was well taken care of, and in case of his death she must have all that he died possessed of. Just at that time Joan Moss came to me, a wreck! She lived only six months, but for his sake I saw that she had all that he would have had for her. She thought that he gave it to her, too, or at least she thought his money gave it, since it was in his will that she should have it. His name was on her lips when the end came. I will tell him that some day. It will help him to forgive me. After that I wrote and wrote to him, making frantic efforts to secure to him, until he were free, what existed no longer on earth! That is all."

The fire had died down and become ashy; the wind no longer howled; the night had fallen into peace at last.

Priscilla got up stiffly, for she was cold and nerve-worn. She walked unsteadily to Boswell, her tear-stained face twitching with emotion, her hands outstretched. In her eyes was the look that only once or twice in his life had Boswell ever seen directed toward him by any human being — the look that claimed the hidden and best in him, forgetting the deformities that limited him.

"I think you are the best man on earth, the noblest friend. Oh! what can we do for Master Farwell?"

Quite simply Boswell took the hands in his. Her eyes made him brave and strong, and her "we" throbbed in his thoughts like a warm and tender caress.

"You must leave that to me," he said gently, giving his kindly smile. "I cannot share this burden with you. So long have I borne it that it has become sacred to me. It means only making the story a little longer, a little stronger. Some day he will have to know — some day; but not now! not now!"

Just then a distant church bell struck the midnight hour. Solemnly, insistently, the twelve strokes rose and fell.

"The wind has passed," whispered Boswell.

"Yes, and the fire is dead. You are very, very tired, I am sure," Priscilla murmured.

Something new and maternal had entered into her thought and voice. While life lasted she was always to see in the crippled man a brave and patient soul who played with sternest problems because he had no other toys with which to while away his dreary years; no other offerings for them he loved.

"Yes. The play is over for — to-night. The Property Man can take his rest until — to-morrow. Turn on the lights, Priscilla Glenn. You and I must find our way out of the darkness."

"Let me help you, Mr. Boswell."

"Help me? That sounds very kind. I will make believe that I am ninety! Yes, you may help me. Thank you! And now good night. You need not write of — Joan Moss to Farwell. I am grateful because you understand and appreciate my — my attempt. I can bring the tale to a close in great style. I was a bit discouraged, but it seems clear and convincing now. That is often the way in my trade of story-maker. We come against a blank wall, only to find there a gateway that opens to our touch."

CHAPTER XV

AFTER Boswell's confidence concerning Anton Farwell, Priscilla's relation to the man who had befriended her, to life itself, became more vital and normal. The superficial conditions were dissipated by the knowledge that Boswell, in speaking so frankly to her, considered her a woman, not a child, and expected a woman's acceptance of duties and responsibilities. Besides this, Boswell himself took on new proportions. His whimsical oddities had been, for an hour, set aside. For a time he had permitted her to see and know him — the simple, good man he really was. In short, Priscilla could no longer play, could no longer make a defence of her shyness and ignorance; she realized that she must plunge into the whirlpool for which she had left the In-Place and she must do so at once.

Boswell might fantastically play at being ninety and permit her to lend her strength and youth to his use, but she never again could be deceived. He was assisting her for Farwell's sake. He liked her, found her entertaining, but intuitively she knew that in order to retain his respect and confidence she must fulfil her part.

For a week or so longer he and she went to operas and theatres together while final arrangements were being completed for her immediate admittance, on trial, to the finest private hospital in the city, to which was attached a training school of high repute.

Priscilla was both right and wrong about Boswell. He did appreciate and admire her insistence to begin her career. It was the only course for her to take; but he looked forward to the lonely, empty days without her with real concern.

He had, to a certain extent, grown used to the detachment and colourlessness of his life since Farwell had left it; but here, quite unexpectedly, a young and vital personality had entered in and had given him, in a crude, friendly way, to be sure, what his absent friend had given — the assurance that his deformity could not exclude him from the sweet humanity that was keen enough to recognize the soul of him. Sensitive, shrinking from suffering and publicity, the man found in Priscilla's companionship and confiding friendliness the deepest joy he had known since his great loss. He wished that he was ninety, indeed, and that his infirmity and wealth might secure for him this new interest that had taken him out of himself and caused his sluggish senses to revive. But he was not yet fifty. For all his handicaps he was still in fair health, and the best that he could hope for was that Priscilla, among her new duties, would remember him, come back to him, make his lonely home a retreat and comfort when her arduous duties permitted.

Those last few days of freedom and companionship were beautiful to them both. With pride and a certain complacency, Boswell saw that he had somewhat formed and developed Priscilla's tastes and judgment. She was no longer the ignorant girl she once had been. Music did not now move her to tears and a kind of dumb suffering. She began to understand, to control her emotions, and gain, through them, pleasure without pain.

"She laughs," Boswell thought, "more intelligently and discriminately when she sees a good farce."

All this was satisfying to them, but on a certain late-winter day it came to an end, and Priscilla, thrilling with a sense of achievement, entered St. Albans on probation.

What the weeks of doubt and preparation meant, no one, not even Boswell, ever knew. The old childish determination to suffer, in order to know, held true and unfaltering. The tortured nerves, after the first shocks, regained their poise and strength; the heavy work and strict discipline left the sturdy body like fine steel, although weariness often tested it sorely.

" 'Tis not to dance, Priscilla Glenn," she often warned herself; "it is to suffer and know!"

Then she grimly set her strong, white teeth. With

all the getting and relinquishing, however, she never forgot to laugh, and her courageous cheerfulness won for her more than she realized while she was learning the curves of her Road.

And then she was accepted. No one but herself had ever doubted her triumph, but when she first learned the verdict she was wild with delight and could hardly wait for her "hours off" to tell Boswell all about it.

She was "capped" at last. No hard-won crown was ever appreciated more than that white trifle which rested like a bit of snow upon the "rusty hair" of Priscilla Glenn.

Before the little mirror in her own bedchamber, on that first victorious day, she posed and confided to her appreciative reflection.

"So this is Priscilla Glenn of the In-Place?" she whispered. "I simply can't believe it! No one else would believe it either; and you are not the same. You never will be again what you once were."

The flush of excitement showed plainer now than of yore, for the clear, dark skin had taken on the delicacy of the city's tint. The eyes were deep and grave, for already they had witnessed the mystery of life and death. They had smiled down at pain-racked motherhood; had held, in calm courage, many an outgoing soul. Priscilla had a closer vision than she once had had when she dreamed her dreams of what lay beyond the Secret Portage and the Big Bay.

The reflection nodded acknowledgment to all that the excited brain affirmed. Then suddenly:

"Why, Priscilla Glenn, you are crying! And for — which?"

The quaint expression brought a smile.

"You are homesick, Priscilla Glenn, homesick for what you have never had! That's the matter with you. You want some one to go to and tell about this, but in all the world there isn't any one who could understand. You poor, poor dear! What would your father and mother think of you? There, now, never mind. You are only a — blue and white nurse. Even Master Farwell and Mr. Boswell could not understand; but a woman could. Some woman! She would know what it means to be free at last and have something, quite your own, with which to hew and cut your own road; yes, your own road, right along to — to the end, just as old Pine used to cut the new trails. It's the standing up straight at last on your own roots like the dear little white birch in the Place Beyond the Winds. A woman could understand, but no one else."

By some subtle power Priscilla had thought and talked her fancy far and away from the plain room of St. Albans. Her longing, her quaint "for which?" the memory of the Indian guide and the little white birch had performed a miracle. Through the excitement and elation stole the fantastic power of childhood. She was on her Road, bound for her Heart's

Desire! No doubt, no misgiving, assailed the moment of joy. Forward, just a little beyond, success awaited her. The possibility of defeat was over forever. From now on, through weariness, toil, and perhaps suffering, she was going to her own. She had never realized the tense mental and physical strain through which she had passed; she did not realize it now, but with the relaxation came an almost dangerous exhilaration. The present, only so far as it verified the past, had no hold upon her; she let herself go.

Back again was she in Kenmore. It was springtime, and the red rocks and hemlocks shone and the water sparkled; she heard it lapping against the tiny islands, so glad was it to be free of the winter's grasp. Some one was dancing to the Spring's Call — a small, graceful thing with a bright red cape flying on the wind, the soft wind of the In-Place. There was music, too! Oh! how clearly it came rising and falling; and then, in the bare hospital room, the blue-clad nurse tripped this way and that, while memory held true to note and step!

Oh! It was on again, on again, that dear old dance. It dried the tears in the tender eyes and held the smile on the joyous lips. Then, as suddenly as it had begun, the dance ceased, a flushed face confronted the reflection in the glass, and a low curtsey followed, while a reverent voice repeated as if in prayer:

"Skib, skib, skibble — de — de — dosh!"

The words came of their own volition; they were part and kin to the mood that held and swayed her. They were a pagan plea for guidance and protection in the opening life where wind and fury would beset her.

Suddenly words of everyday life found their way to her detached consciousness and recalled her to the present with almost cruel force.

"It's the little Canuck he wants! Just fancy! I heard him say so to — to Mrs. Thomas. Such injustice! But there the old Grenadier comes now. Hustle!"

Priscilla heard the scampering feet, then, after a moment's pause, the dignified advance of the superintendent. There was a tap on the door. The doors of some rooms, owing to discipline, were never tapped by Mrs. Thomas, but the reason that compelled her to show this courtesy to Priscilla also caused her to wish this young Canadian was a less serious person; one more prone to frivol in her "hours off," and not have, for her most intimate companion, the strange dwarf. She could have forgiven Priscilla Glenn if, having overdone her "late leave," she had crawled into a back window to escape punishment. It would have made her more understandable. As it was, Mrs. Thomas tapped!

"Come in, please," said Priscilla, and the large, handsome superintendent entered and sat down.

"I thought I would come and tell you," she said,

trying to keep her professional expression while her maternal heart warmed to the girl, "that you have been highly honoured. There is to be a very important operation to-morrow at three o'clock. Doctor Ledyard is to perform it, assisted by his young partner. He has asked for several nurses, and he named *you* — singled you out. He has observed you; wishes to — use you. It's a great compliment, Miss Glynn." So often had Priscilla corrected, to no avail, the wrong pronouncing of her name, that she now accepted it without further demur. Flushing and trembling, she went close to Mrs. Thomas and held her hands out impulsively.

"All my glory is coming at once!" she faltered.

"Glory? Well, you are a queer girl. To stand for hours under that man's eye! You call it glory? Why, it is an honour because it is *that man, that eye;* but as to glory! My dear Miss Glynn, I must insist that you go off this afternoon and play — somewhere. Then come back and get a good night's rest. The life of the richest man in New York will hang in the balance to-morrow, and not even the glorified nurse can afford to have a trembling hand when she passes up an instrument or wipes the perspiration from the surgeon's brow."

"Thank you, oh! thank you, Mrs. Thomas! Of course, if I were not so stupid I could make you understand how I feel. I seem to have found the right way, and everything is conspiring to tell me so. You see, I might not have qualified; some girls do not. No one might have noticed me; you might not have been so kind. Often I am rather lonely and ungrateful; but you must try to believe that I am — very happy now."

"I suppose" — Mrs. Thomas was holding the radiant young face with her clear, calm eyes — "I suppose you are one of those natures that craves success; cannot brook defeat. Life will deal harshly with you."

"I am willing to suffer. It is the learning I must have. It is the chance to learn that makes me so glad," Priscilla burst in, "and it's this sure feeling that I am on the right trail."

"There is a difference. But somehow the career of a nurse is so — well — difficult, and — hard," Mrs. Thomas went on. "I wonder how you can approach it with your enthusiasm undaunted after months of service."

"I do not know, but it seems my road to what is mine. It gets me so near people — when they most need me — are so glad to have me! There seems to be nothing between me — and them. I love it, oh! I love it, Mrs. Thomas!"

"See here, Miss Glynn, where are you going this afternoon?"

"I do not know; just — going."

"I wish — dear me! I do wish you could go somewhere; do something shockingly frivolous."

"No, I couldn't to-day. I feel like praying — or dancing. There's the most wonderful, singing feeling inside of me. That's why I do not need — fun as much as most of the girls do. You are very kind; I think I will go to your big, fine park and walk and walk. I'd like to see the sun set and the stars —— "

"Now, Miss Glynn, unless you promise me to get under shelter before the stars come out I'll call the police. Some day you will learn that New York is not your Canadian hamlet."

Priscilla laughed gayly.

"Very well. I will take my walk and then go to my dear old friend. He'll be looking for me from his high window. He always stands there late afternoons, on the chance of my coming. He says it's a pleasure to feel you have something that *may* come, even if you know it isn't coming just then."

Priscilla changed her clothing and set forth a half hour later for her walk and to meet with an adventure that changed the current of her thought materially. From that afternoon she was pressed and forced up her Road by a power that had taken her into control with definite purpose.

She went into the park at the lower entrance and walked rapidly to a high place that was a favourite with her. So peaceful and detached it was that she could generally think her thoughts, sing aloud a little song, and feel safe from intrusion. Being high and open, the sunlight rested longer there than it did below and misled one as to time.

There was a glorious sunset that evening, a golden, deep one, against which the bare trees, towers, and house roofs stood outlined black and sharp. It was like a burnished shield. It was a still day, with a gentle crispness in the air that stimulated while it did not chill.

"Everything is waiting. What for? what for?" Priscilla whispered sociably to herself. She was young, full of health and success. Of course she was waiting as the young do. And then something touched her cheek softly, and, looking down, she saw that her dark suit was covered with feathery snowflakes. So silently had they escaped a passing cloud that she was startled. She arose at once and was surprised to find, in the hollow below, that the paths were crusted and the electric lights gleamed yellow through a fluttering mist of flying snow. It was very beautiful, but it warned one to hasten, and besides it had grown quite dark.

There was a path, Priscilla knew it well, that led straight across the park to an entrance near Boswell's home, and she took it now at a rapid pace.

The beauty of the walk did not escape her, the exhilaration of the air acted like a cordial upon her, she seemed hardly to touch the ground as she ran on; and once she paused before setting her foot upon the lovely whiteness. As she hesitated some one stepped from the shadow of a clump of bushes and confronted her under the electric light.

"Can you tell me how to find the nearest way out? I'm lost."

Priscilla's heart gave one hard throb and stood still, it seemed for an hour, while an almost forgotten terror seized and held her. She was looking full upon Jerry-Jo McAlpin! A soiled and haggard shadow he was of what he once had been, but it was Jerry-Jo and no other.

"I — I did not mean to frighten you. Forgive me. I ain't going to hurt you, Miss. I —— "

But Priscilla was gone before the sentence was finished. Gone before she knew whether the speaker had recognized her or not. Gone before — and then she stood still. She could not leave him to wander alone at night in that big, strange place. No matter what happened, she must treat him humanly, she, who knew the danger. She went back, her blood running like ice through her body; but Jerry-Jo McAlpin was not there. Priscilla waited, and once she spoke vague directions to the empty space, but no answering voice replied. Presently she controlled herself, and took to the path again, and reached John Boswell's house before he had left his window.

She did not tell of the encounter; she felt she must wait, but in her heart she knew that Jerry-Jo McAlpin was as surely on her trail as she was herself.

Such things as that meeting did not happen to them of the In-Place unless for a purpose.

She had a wonderful evening with Boswell. They did not go out, and after dinner he read her some manuscript stories. Boswell had never before so intimately permitted her to come close to his work. She had seen stories of his in print, had heard plans for others, but before the fire in his study that night he read, among other things, "The Butterfly and the Beetle." So beautifully, so touchingly, had he pictured the little romance, of which Priscilla herself was part, that the tears fell from the girl's eyes while her lips were smiling at the tender humour. The undercurrent of meaning threw new light on the lonely life of the rich, but wretched man. The joy depicted in simple, friendly intercourse, the aspiration of the Beetle, the grateful appreciation for the plain, common happenings that in most lives were taken for granted, but which in his rose to monumental importance, endeared him to her anew. It brought back to her what Boswell had told her of his relations with Farwell Maxwell, her Anton Farwell. She could now, with her broader, more mature reason, understand the devotion the cripple had given the one man who, in the empty years, had taken him without reservation, had ignored his limitations, and had been his friend and comrade.

Suddenly she asked:

"Have you heard from — from Master Farwell lately?" The question startled Boswell.

"Yes. I had a letter yesterday. He has been ill. That squaw woman, Long Jean, took care of him. The letter sounded restless. There'll be trouble with Farwell before we get through. My letters are evidently lacking power, and your silence baffles him."

"Poor Master Farwell!"

"I fancy he thought Joan Moss would go to him. It has been hard work to build a barrier between him and her that could satisfy, now that he believes you have told her of his being among the living."

"What have you said to him all this time?"

Boswell shifted his position, and Priscilla saw the haggard, careworn look spread over his face. By sudden insight she realized that he looked old, pitiful, and far from well, and her heart filled with sympathy. The half-mystical life was telling upon him, becoming a burden.

"Oh, at first I said the surprise of knowing he lived had made her, made Joan Moss, ill. It took nearly six months to cover that, and I did some good writing during that period. Then I told him there were things to settle; then, fear for his safety overpowered her: dread of being tracked. And since then — well, since then there has been silence. Can you not understand? His pride has asserted itself at last. If she will not communicate with him herself, he will have none of me; none of you. Has he ever said a word about her to — you?"

"Never," Priscilla answered.

"But," Boswell went on, "I notice a change in him; an almost feverish impatience. I fear he doubts me — after all these years!"

"And when he knows?"

The man by the fire shrank deeper in his chair.

"When he knows?" he repeated. "Why, then he will have an opportunity to understand my life-long devotion, my gratitude, my love! That is all."

CHAPTER XXI

F OR real emergencies," Doctor Ledyard once
remarked to Helen Travers, "give me the
nervous, high-strung women. They come
through shock and danger better, they hold to a
climax more steadily. Your phlegmatic woman goes
to pieces because she hasn't imagination and vision
enough to carry her over the present."

This reasoning caused him to select Priscilla
Glenn for one of the most critical operations he had
ever performed. Among the blue and white nurses
of his knowledge this girl with the strange, uplifted
expression of face; this girl who was actually on the
lookout for experience and practice, and who seriously loved her profession, stood in a class by herself. He had long had his eye upon her, had
meant to single her out. And now the opportunity
had come.

Perhaps the most important man in business circles, certainly one of the richest men in the city, had
come to that period of his life's career when he must
pay toll for the things he had done and left undone
in his past. The broad, common gateway gaped wide
for him, and only one chance presented itself as a

possible means of holding him back from the long journey he so shudderingly contemplated.

"One chance in ten?" he questioned.

"One — in —— " Ledyard had hesitated.

"A hundred?"

"A thousand."

A breathless pause followed. Then:

"And if I do not take it, how long?"

"A week, a month; not longer."

"I'll take it."

"I'll have my partner —— Would you care for any one else?" Ledyard asked.

"No. Since it must be, I put myself in your hands. I trust you above any one I know. Do your best for me, and in case I slip through your fingers I thank you now, and — good-bye."

Before any great event, or operation, Ledyard was supersensitive, highly wrought, and nervous. When he heard the announcement that day of the operation: "All is ready, sir!" he stepped, gowned and masked, into the operating-room, and was aware of a senseless inclination to ask some one — he did not know whom — to make less noise and to lower the shades. Then his eye fell, not on the dignified and serene head nurse, not on the other ghostly young forms in their places near the table, not on the anesthetist, nor young Travers, his partner, but on the nurse who stood a little apart, the girl he had selected in order to test her on a really great case. So radiant and inspired was Priscilla Glenn's face that it fairly shone in that grim place and positively had the effect of bringing Ledyard to the calmness that characterized his action once the necessity demanded.

"How is your patient, Doctor Sloan?" he asked the anesthetist.

"Fine, Doctor Ledyard. I'm ready when you are."

Then tense silence followed, broken only by the click of instruments and the curt, crisp commands. The minutes, weighted with concentration, ran into the hour. Not a body in that room was aware of fatigue or anxiety. A life was at stake, and every one knew it. It did not matter that the man upon the table was important and useful: had he been the meanest of the mean and in the same critical state, that steady hand, which guided the knife so scientifically and powerfully, would have worked the same.

The sun beat down upon the glass roof of that high room; the perspiration started to Ledyard's forehead and a nurse wiped it away.

From her place Priscilla Glenn watched breathlessly the scene before her. It seemed to her that she had never seen an operation before; had never comprehended what one could be. She realized the odds against which those two great men were battling, and her gaze rested finally, not on the head surgeon, but on his partner. Once, as if by some subtle attraction, he raised his eyes and met hers. Above the mask his glance showed kindly and encouragingly. He knew that some nurses lost their nerve when a thing stretched on as this did; he never could quite overlook the fact that nurses were women, as well, and he hated to see one go under. But this young nurse was showing no weakness. Travers saw that, after a moment, and dropped his eyes. But that glance had fixed Priscilla's face in his memory, and when, after the great man had been carried to his room with hope following him, when he could be left with safety to his private nurse, Travers came upon the girl standing by a deep window in the upper hall. He remembered her at once and stopped to say a pleasant word.

This was not the strictly proper thing to do, and Travers knew it. Ledyard was always challenging his undignified tendencies.

"Unless doctors and nurses can leave their sex outside their profession," was a pet epigram of Ledyard's, "they had better choose another."

But Travers had never been able to fulfil his partner's ideal.

"It was a wonderful operation," he said. "I hope it did not overtire you. You will get hardened after a while."

"I am not at all tired. Yes, it was — wonderful! I did not know any operation could be like that — I mean in the way that it was done. I have always been afraid of Doctor Ledyard before; all of us are; I shall never be again."

"May I ask why?"

Travers, being young and vital, was forgetting, for the moment, his professional air to a dangerous extent. He was noticing the strange coloured hair under the snowy cap, the poise of the head, the deep violet eyes in the richly tinted face.

"It was that — well, the look on his face after he had done all that he could — done it so wonderfully. That look was — a prayer! I shall never forget."

Travers gave a light laugh.

"It would be like Doctor Ledyard," he said with a peculiarly boyish ring in his voice, "to do his part first and pray afterward."

"But no one could ever be afraid of him again having once seen that look!"

"Miss Glynn," Travers replied; "they could! and yet the *look* holds the fear in check."

Priscilla went early to bed that night. She had planned a visit to Boswell when her enthusiasm was at its height, but at the day's end she found herself so exhausted that she sought her room in a state bordering on collapse.

Sounds outside caught and held her attention; every sense was quiveringly alert and receptive; she was at the mercy of her subconscious self.

"Extry! extry!" bellowed a boy just below her window; "turribul accident on — de — extry! extry! Latest bulletin — Gordan Moffatt — big fin — cier — extry! extry!"

Priscilla sat up in bed and listened. So intimate had the insistent boy in the street become that she was drawn to him by a common bond of sympathy.

Slowly a luxurious sense of weariness overcame her and again she leaned back on her pillow and sank into a semiconscious sleep. Balanced between life and the oblivion, into which reason enters blindfolded, she made no resistance, but was swayed by every passing wave of thought, memory, and vision.

The voice outside merged presently into Jerry-Jo McAlpin's. So naturally did it do so that the girl upon the bed, rigid and pale, accepted the change with no surprise.

Jerry-Jo was asking her the way out! He was lost — lost. He wanted to get out of the darkness and the noise; he wanted to find his way back to the In-Place.

Yes, she would show him! There was no fear of him; no repulsion. She was very safe and strong, and she knew that it was wiser for Jerry-Jo to go back home.

Then suddenly she and he were transported from the bewildering city, talking in its sleep, to the sweet, fresh dimness of the Kenmore Green, where the steamer had left them. It was early, very early morning, not more than four o'clock, and the stars were bright and the hemlocks black, and the red rocks looked soft in the shadows, like pillows. And over the Green, loping and inquisitive, came Sandy McAdam's dog, Bounder. How natural and restful the scene was! Then it was Jerry-Jo, not Priscilla, who was leading. The half-breed with a gesture of friendliness was beckoning her on toward the mossy wood path leading to Lonely Farm. There was a definiteness about the slouching figure that forbade any pause at the White Fish Lodge or the master's dark and silent house. Priscilla longed to stop, but she hastened on, feeling a need for hurry.

Presently she saw the little house, her father's house, and there was a light shining from the kitchen window. Jerry-Jo, still preceding her, tapped on the outer door, but when the door fell open Jerry-Jo was gone! Alone, Priscilla confronted her father, and saw with surprise that he evidently expected her. While the look of hatred and doubt still rested in his eyes, there was also a look of dumb pity. No word was spoken. Nathaniel merely stepped aside and closed the door behind her. Then she began a strange, breathless hunt for something which, at first, she could not call by name; it evaded and eluded her. Something was missing; something she wanted desperately; but the rooms were horribly dark and lonely, and the stillness hurt her more and more.

At last she came back to her father and the warm, lighted kitchen.

"I cannot find — my mother," she said, and the reality set her trembling.

"Your — mother? I — I cannot find her, either. I thought she — followed you!"

Cold and shivering, Priscilla sat up in bed. Her teeth chattered and there were tears on her cheeks. They did not seem like her own tears. It was as if some one, bending over her, had let them fall from eyes seeking to find her in the dark.

"Mother!" moaned Priscilla, and with the word a yearning and craving for her mother filled every sense. By a magic that the divine only controls, poor Theodora Glenn in that moment was transformed and radiantly crowned with the motherhood she had so impotently striven to achieve in her narrowed, blighted life. The suffering of maternity, its denials and relinquishings she had experienced, but never its joy of realization, unless, as her spirit passed from the Place Beyond the Winds to its Home, it paused beside the little, narrow, white bed upon which Priscilla lay, and caught that name "Mother!" spoken with a sudden inspiration of understanding.

And that night, with only her grim husband and Long Jean beside her, Theodora escaped the bondage of life.

After the strange dream, Priscilla, awed and trembling, walked to the wide open window of her room. For some moments she stood there breathing fast and hard while the cruel clutch of superstition hurt and held her.

"Something has happened," she faltered, leaning upon the casement and looking down into the silent street, for the restless city had at last fallen to sleep. "Something in Kenmore!"

A red, pulsing planet, shining high over a nearby church tower, caught her eye and brought a throb of comfort to her — a tender thought of home.

"To-morrow, perhaps, a letter will come from Master Farwell; if not, I will write to him. I must know."

CHAPTER XVII

FOR two or three days things fell into such commonplace routine that the excitement of the big operation and the disturbing dream of the night lost their sharp, clear lines; became blurred and part of the web and woof of the hospital régime. There was little time for introspection or romancing and even the chance meeting with Jerry-Jo was relegated to the non-essentials. Of course he was in the city, but so were the Hornby boys and others from the In-Place. The whirlpool was a big and rushing thing, and if they who had once been neighbours caught a glimpse of each other from dizzy eddies, what did it matter? The possibility of second meetings was rare.

John Boswell had been sympathetic, to a certain degree, with Priscilla concerning the operation and her very evident pride in the part she had been permitted to take in it. With the instinctive horror that many have concerning sickness and suffering, he always made an effort to appear sympathetic when Priscilla grew graphic. Often this caused her to laugh, but she never doubted Boswell's sincere interest in her, personally. That she had overcome

244

and achieved was a thing of real gratification to the lonely man; that she came to him naturally and eagerly, during her hours of freedom, was the only unalloyed joy of his present existence. Even Toky hailed her appearances now with frank pleasure, for she, and she alone, brought the rare, sweet smile to the master's face and gave a meaning to the artistic meals that were planned.

"I think, my Butterfly," Boswell often said to her, "that you have soared to glory through suffering and gore! But it is the soaring and the glory that matter, after all. Do not lay it up against your poor Beetle if he makes a wry face now and then. You are desperately dramatic, you know, but even in my shudders I do not lose sight of the fact that you are a very triumphant Butterfly."

Priscilla beamed upon him; the new light of well-poised serenity did not escape him.

"If I could only explain!" she once said to him as they sat facing each other across the table that Toky had laid so artistically. "When I feel the deepest my words seem shut in a cage; only a few get through the bars. I really believe people all feel the same about their little victories. It isn't the kind of victory; it is the sure realization that you are doing your work — the work you can do best. Why, sometimes I feel as if I were the big All Mother, and the sad, helpless, suffering folk were my dear children just looking to me — to me! And then I try to take the pain and fear from their faces by all the arts my profession has taught me and all the — the *something* that is in me, and — I tell you —— "

Priscilla paused, while the shining light in her big eyes was brightened, rather than lessened, by the tears that gathered, then retreated.

"And for all this," Boswell broke in, "you are to get twenty-five per, or for a particular case, thirty-five per?"

They smiled broadly at each other, for their one huge, compelling joke loomed close.

"Well, sir, when one considers what two intelligent people, like you and me, did with Master Farwell's one hundred dollars, the future looks wonderfully rich! I shall soon be able to repay the loan with interest."

And then they talked a bit of Master Farwell and the In-Place, always skirting the depths gracefully, for Boswell never permitted certain subjects to escape his control. It was the half-playful, but wholly kind dignity that had won for him Priscilla's faith and dependence.

For a week or two after Gordon Moffatt's operation things went calmly and prosaically at the hospital. The rich man recovered so rapidly and satisfactorily that even the outside world took things for granted, and any items of news concerning him were to be found on the inside pages of the newspapers. During his convalescence Priscilla met Doctor Ledyard and Doctor Travers many times. Once, by some mysterious arrangement, she was assigned charge, in the rich man's room, while his own nurse was absent. For three days and nights she obeyed his impatient commands and reasoned with him when he confused his dependent condition with his usual domineering position.

"Damn me!" he once complained to Travers when he thought Priscilla was out of hearing; "that young woman you've given charge over me ought to have a bigger field for her accomplishments. She's a natural-born tyrant. I tried to escape her this morning; had got as far as one foot out of bed when she bore down upon me, calmly, devilishly calmly, pointed to my offending foot, and said: "Back, sir!" Then we argued a bit — I'm afraid I was a trifle testy — and finally she laid hands upon my ankle in the most scientific manner and had me on my back before I could think of the proper adjectives to apply to her impudence."

Travers laughed and looked beyond the sick man's bed to the bowed head of Priscilla as she bent over some preparation she was compounding in an anteroom. From a high window the sunlight was streaming down on the wonderful rusty-coloured hair. The girl's attitude of detachment and concentration held the physician's approving glance, but the wave of hair under the white cap and against the smooth, clear skin lingered in the memory of the *man* long after he forgot Moffatt's amusing anecdote.

And then, because things were closing in upon Priscilla Glenn's little stage, something happened so commonplace in its character that its effect upon the girl was out of all proportion.

After a rather strenuous day she was sleeping heavily in her little white room when a sharp knock on her door brought her well-trained senses into action at once.

"There's been an accident, Miss Glynn." It was the superintendent who spoke. "Please report on Ward Five as soon as possible."

It was an insignificant accident; such a one as occurs shockingly often in our big cities. A large touring car, with seven passengers, rushing up a broad avenue with a conscientious man at the wheel, had overhauled a poor derelict with apparently no fixed purpose in his befuddled brain. In order to spare the fellow, the chauffeur had wheeled his car madly to one side, and, by so doing, had hit an electric-light pole, with the result that every one was more or less injured, the forlorn creature who had caused the excitement, most of all, for the overturned machine had included him in its crushing destruction.

Four men and three women were carried to St. Albans and now occupied private rooms, while the torn and broken body of the unknown stranger lay in Ward Five, quite unconscious. He was breathing faintly, and, since they had made him clean and de-

cent, he looked very young and wan as he rested upon
the narrow, white bed.

Priscilla stood at the foot of the cot and read the
chart which a former nurse had hurriedly made out;
then she came around to the side and looked down
upon — Jerry-Jo McAlpin!

She knew him at once. The deathlike repose had
wiped away much that recent years had engraven
on his face. He looked as Priscilla remembered him,
standing in his father's boat, proudly playing the
man.

For a moment the quiet girl grew rigid with superstitious fear. That deathlike creature before her
filled her with unreasoning alarm. She almost expected him to open his black eyes and laughingly
announce that he had found her at last! She longed
to flee from the room before he had a chance to gain
control of her. She breathed fast and hard, as she
had that morning when his ringing jeer had stayed
her feet as she ran from the Far Hill Place after the
night of terror. Then sanity came to her relief
and she knew, with a pitying certainty born of her
training, that Jerry-Jo McAlpin could never harm
her again. That he was a link between the past and
the future she realized with strange sureness. He
had always been that. He had made things happen;
been the factor in bringing experiences to her. She,
in self-preservation, would not claim any knowledge
of him now; she would care for him and wait — wait

until she understood just what part he was to play in her present experience. He might threaten all that she had gained for herself — her peace and security. Her only safeguard now was to ignore the personality before her and respond to the appeal of the "case."

Jerry-Jo was destined to become interesting before he slipped away. Known only as a number, since he had not been identified or claimed, he rapidly rose to importance. After three days of unconsciousness he still persisted, and while his soul wandered on the horizon, his body responded to the care given it and grew in strength. One doctor after another watched and commented on his chances, and in due time Doctor Travers, hearing of the case, stopped to examine it, and, in the interest of science, suggested an operation that might possibly return the poor fellow to a world that had evidently no place for him.

"It's worth trying," Travers said as he and Priscilla stood beside the bed. "We haven't found out anything concerning him, have we?"

Priscilla shook her head.

"Suppose he — well, suppose he had any claim upon you, would you take the chance of the operation for him?"

The deep, friendly eyes were fixed upon the girl. She coloured sharply, then went quite pale. There was a most unaccountable struggle, and Travers smiled as he thought how conscientious she was to feel any deep responsibility in a question he had asked, more in idle desire to make talk than for any other reason.

"Yes," she replied suddenly, as her head was lifted; "yes, I'd give him every chance."

Just then, in one of those marvellous flashes of regained consciousness, the man upon the bed opened his eyes and looked, first at Travers, then at Priscilla. Again his gaze shifted, gaining strength and meaning. From the far place where he had fared for days his mind, lighted by reason, was abnormally clear and almost painfully reinforced by memory. Then he laughed — laughed a long, shuddering laugh that drew the thin lips back from the white, fang-like teeth. Before the sound was finished the light faded from the black eyes and the grim silence shut in close upon the last quivering note.

"We'll take the chance," said Travers. And late that very afternoon they took it.

A week later Priscilla sat beside the man's bed, her right hand upon his pulse, her watch in her left. So intent was she upon the weak movement under her slim fingers that she had forgotten all else until a voice from a far, far distance seemingly, whispered hoarsely:

"So — so this is — you? I'm not dreaming? I wasn't dreaming before when — when he and you came?"

They had all been expecting this. The operation had been very successful, though it was not to give the patient back to life. They all knew that, too.

"Yes, Jerry-Jo, it's I."

There was no tremor in the low voice, only a determination to keep the world from knowing. Jerry-Jo was past hurting any one.

"The — lure got you, too?"

"Yes, the lure got me."

"I knew you that night in the dark — that night in the park — you ran from me. I was lost and — and starving!"

"I came back, Jerry-Jo. I did indeed."

"Have I been here — long?"

"Not very. Do not talk any more. You must rest. There is to-morrow, you know."

The poor fellow was too weak to laugh, but the long teeth showed for a moment.

"I must talk. Listen! Do they know here — about me? know my name?"

"No."

"Don't tell them. Don't tell any one. I have done something for you! They think, back there in Kenmore, that you are with me. I've written that — and schoolmaster hasn't let on. I haven't gone to the Hornbys here, because I stood by you. No one must know. See?"

"Yes, Jerry-Jo, I see. Please lie still now. It shall be as you wish. You have been — very good — for my sake!"

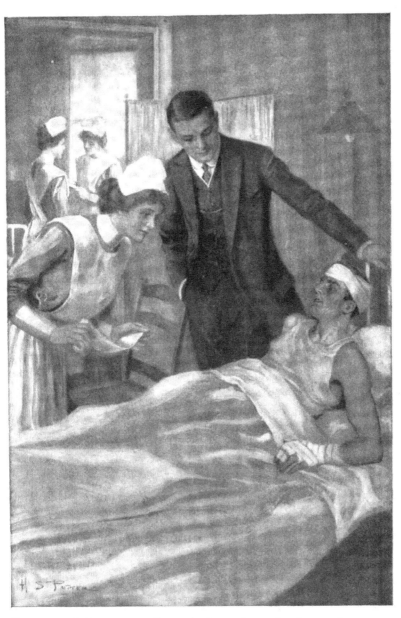

" In one of those marvellous flashes of regained consciousness,
the man upon the bed opened his eyes and looked,
first at Travers, then at Priscilla "

"I've starved and slept in dark holes — for you, and now you and him — have got to take care of me — or — I'll tell! I'll tell, as sure as God hears me!"

"We will take care of you, Jerry-Jo. There! there! I promise; and you know we of the In-Place stand by each other."

He was comforted at last, and fell into the deep sleep of exhaustion. Occasionally, in the days following, he opened his tired eyes and gave evidence of consciousness. He was drifting out calmly and painlessly, and all the coarseness and degeneracy of the half-breed seemed dropping by the way. Sometimes his glance rested on Doctor Travers's face, for the young physician was deeply interested in the case and was touched by the lonely, unclaimed fellow who had served science, but could derive no benefit in return. Often Jerry-Jo's dark eyes fell upon the pitying face of Priscilla Glenn with ever-growing understanding and kindliness. Sometimes in the long nights he clung to her like a child, for she was very good to him; very, very devoted.

One night, when all the world seemed sleeping, he whispered to her:

"You — you don't know, really?"

Priscilla thought he was wandering, and said gently:

"No, Jerry-Jo, really I do not know."

"What will you give me — if I tell you the biggest secret in the world?"

254 THE PLACE BEYOND THE WINDS

She had his head in the hollow of her arm; he was resting more calmly so. He had been feverish all day.

"What — can I give you, Jerry-Jo?"

The old, pleading look was in the dark eyes, but low passion had vanished forever.

"Could you — would you give me a kiss for the secret?"

"Yes, Jerry-Jo," and the kiss fell upon the white brow.

Could John Boswell have been there then he would have understood.

"You — you are crying! I feel a tear with the kiss!"

The quivering, broken smile smote Priscilla to the heart. The ward was deathly quiet; only the deep breathing of men closer to life than Jerry-Jo Mc-Alpin broke the stillness.

"Why — do you cry?"

"You know, it's a bad habit of mine, Jerry-Jo."

"Yes. You — you cried on his book, you remember?"

"I remember."

"Do — you know where he is — now?"

"No. Do you?"

The head upon the strong, young arm moved restlessly.

"Yes — I know — and I'm — going to tell you! It's the biggest joke I ever knew. Just to think —

that you don't know, and he doesn't know, and — and I do!"

A rattling, husky laugh shook the thin form dangerously. Every instinct of the nurse rose in alarm and defence.

"You must not talk any more, Jerry-Jo. Lie still. Come, let us think of the In-Place."

Priscilla slipped her arm from under the dark head, and took the wandering hands in hers. Her random words had power to hold and chain the weak mind.

"I'm going to tell you — where he is — but we'll go back to the In-Place. I want to tell you there, and — he'll come and find you. I'd like to do you both a good turn — for what you've done for me."

Then, after a pause and a gasping breath:

"It's growing dark, but there's Dreamer's Rock and Bleak Head!"

"And, Jerry-Jo," whispered Priscilla, "there's Lone Tree Island, don't you see? Your boat is coming around into the Channel. Please tell me — where he is, Jerry-Jo —— "

Priscilla realized he was going fast, and the secret suddenly gripped her with strange power. She must have it; she must know!

"Please, Jerry-Jo, tell me where he is. I have wanted so to know! Listen! Can you not hear — the dear old sounds, the pattering of the soft little waves that the ice has let go free? There's the farm, the woods —— " But Jerry-Jo was struggling to rise; his black eyes wide and straining, his thin arms outstretched.

"No!" he moaned hoarsely, and already he seemed far away. "I can't make the Channel. I'm headed for the Secret Portage and the Big Bay."

"Jerry-Jo! oh! tell me, where is he? Where is he?"

But Priscilla knew it was too late. She bent and listened at the still breast that was holding the secret close from her. Then, with a sense of having been baffled, defeated, and cruelly cheated, she dropped her wet face in her hands for a moment before she went to do her last duty for Jerry-Jo.

CHAPTER XVIII

THE following June Priscilla Glenn graduated. She and John Boswell grew quite merry over the event.

"I really can't let you spend anything on me," she said laughingly; "nothing more than the cost of a few flowers. I have the awful weight of debt upon me at the beginning of my career. One hundred dollars to Master Farwell, and ——"

"The funeral expenses of that poor waif you were so interested in! My dear child, you are as niggardly with your philanthropies as you are with your favours. Why not be generous with me? And, by the way, can you tell me just why that young fellow appealed to you so? I daresay other 'unknowns' drift into St. Albans."

"He looked — you will think me foolish, Mr. Boswell — but he looked like some one I once knew in Kenmore."

The warm June day drifted sunnily into Boswell's study window. There was a fragrance of flowers and the note of birds. Priscilla, in her plain white linen dress, was sitting on the broad window seat, and Boswell, from his winged chair, looked at her with a tightening of the throat. There were times when she made him feel as he felt when Farwell Maxwell used to look at him before the shadow fell between them — the shadow that darkened both their lives.

"And that was why you had a — a Kenmore name graven on the stone?"

"Yes, Mr. Boswell, Jerry-Jo McAlpin. Jerry-Jo is dead, too, you know. They name living people after dead ones. Why not dead people?"

"Why, indeed? It's quite an idea. Quite an original idea. But as to my spending money on your graduation, a little more added to what you already owe me will not count, and, besides, there is that trifle left from Farwell's loan still to your credit."

"Now, Mr. Boswell, don't press me too close! I was a sad innocent when I came from the In-Place, and a joke is a joke, but you mustn't bank on it."

The bright head nodded cheerfully at the small, crumpled figure in the deep chair.

"After you live in New York three years, Mr. Boswell, you never mistake a shilling for a dollar, sir. But just because it is such a heavenly day — and between you and me, how much of that magic fund is left?"

"I've mislaid my account," Boswell replied, the look that Toky watched for stealing over his thin face; "but, roughly speaking, I should say that, with the interest added, about fifty dollars, perhaps a trifle more."

Priscilla threw back her head and laughed merrily.

"I can understand why people say your style is so absorbing," she said presently; "you make even the absurd seem probable."

"Who have you heard comment on my style?" Boswell leaned forward. He was as sensitive as a child about his work.

"Oh, one of the doctors at St. Albans told me that, to him, you were the Hans Christian Andersen of grown-ups. He always reads you after a long strain."

A flush touched the sallow cheeks, and the long, white fingers tapped the chair arms nervously.

"Well!" with a satisfied laugh, "I can prove the amount to your credit in this case without resorting to my style. Would you mind going into your old room and looking at the box that you will find on the couch?"

Priscilla ran lightly from the study, her eyes and cheeks telling the story of her delight.

The box was uncovered. Some sympathetic hand, as fine as a woman's, had bared the secret for her. No mother could possibly have thought out detail and perfection more minutely. There it lay, the gift of a generous man to a lonely girl, everything for her graduating night! The filmy gown with its touch of colour in embroidered thistle flowers; the slippers and gloves; even the lace scarf, cloud-like and alluring; the long gloves and silken hose.

Down beside the couch Priscilla knelt and pressed her head against the sacred gift. She did not cry nor laugh, but the rapt look that used to mark her hours before the shrine in Kenmore grew and grew upon her face.

"You will accept? You think I did well in my — shopping?"

Boswell stood in the doorway, just where a long path of late June sunlight struck across the room. For the girl, looking mutely at him with shining eyes, he was transfigured, translated. Only the great, tender soul was visible to her; the unasking, the kind spirit. Moved by a sudden impulse, Priscilla rose to her feet and walked to him with outstretched hands; when she reached him he took her hands in his and smiled up at her.

"I — I accept," she whispered with a break in her voice. "You have made me — happier than I have ever been in my life!"

Boswell drew her hands to his lips and kissed them.

"And you will come and see me in them" — Priscilla turned her eyes to the box — "when I — dance?"

"You are to dance?"

"We are all to dance."

"I have not seen you dance for many a day. If you dance as you once did there will be only you dancing. Yes, I will come."

And Boswell went. The exercises were held in the little chapel. From his far corner he watched the young women, in uniforms of spotless white, file to the platform for their diplomas. They all merged, for him, into one — a tall, lithe creature with burnished hair, coppery and fine, and an exalted face. Later, from behind the mass of palms and ferns in the dancing hall, he saw only one girl — a girl in white with the tints of the thistle flower matching the deep eyes.

And Priscilla danced. Some one, a young doctor, asked her, and fortunately for him he was a master hand at following. After a moment of surprise, tinged with excited determination, he found himself, with his brilliant partner, the centre of attraction.

"Look! oh, do look at the little Canuck!" cried a classmate.

"I never saw any one dance as she does" — it was Doctor Travers who spoke from the doorway beside Mrs. Thomas — "but once before. It's quite primeval, an instinct. No one can teach or acquire such grace as that."

Then, suddenly, and apropos of nothing, apparently:

"By the way, Mrs. Thomas, Miss Moffatt has been ordered abroad by Doctor Ledyard. He spoke to-day about securing a companion-nurse for her. She's not really ill, but in rather a curious nervous condition. I was wondering if ——" His eyes followed Priscilla, who was nearing the cluster of palms behind which Boswell sat.

"Of course!" Mrs. Thomas smiled broadly; "Miss Glynn, of course! She's made to order. The girl has her way to make. She's been rather overdoing lately. I don't like the look in her eyes at times. She never asks for sympathy or consideration, you understand, but she makes every woman, and man, too, judging by that rich cripple, Mr. Boswell, yearn over her. She'd be the merriest soul on earth, with half a chance, and she's the most capable girl I have: ready for an emergency; never weary. Why, of course, Miss Glynn!"

"I'll speak to Doctor Ledyard to-night," said Travers.

Then, strangely enough, Travers realized that he was very tired. He excused himself, and, walking back through the dim city streets to the Ledyard home, he thought of Kenmore and the old lodge as he had not for years.

"I believe I'll run up there this summer," he muttered half aloud. "I'll take mother and urge Doctor Ledyard to join us. I would like to see how far I've travelled from the In-Place in — why it's years and years! All the way from boyhood to manhood."

But Ledyard changed the current of his desire. The older man was sitting in his library when Travers entered, and Helen Travers was in the deep window opening to the little garden space behind the house.

Time had dealt so gently with Helen that now, in her thin white gown, she looked even younger than in the Kenmore days, when her dress had been more severe.

"You're late," said Ledyard, looking keenly at him.

"Very late," echoed Helen, smiling. "I had dinner here and am waiting to be escorted home."

"She's refused my company. Where have you been, Dick?"

"I had to give out the diplomas, you know, at St. Albans."

"It's after eleven now, Dickie." Helen's gaze was full of gentle pride.

"I stopped for an hour to see those little girls play."

"The nurses?" Ledyard frowned. "Girls and nurses are not one and the same thing, to a doctor."

"Oh, come, come, dear friend!" Helen Travers went close to the two who were dearest to her in the world. "Do not be unmerciful. Being a woman, I must stand up for my sex. Did they play prettily, Dick? I'm sure they did not look as dear as they do in their uniforms."

"One did. She was — well, to put it concisely, she was a — dance!"

"Umph! That ruddy-headed one, I bet!" Ledyard turned on another electric light. "See here, Dick, do you think that girl could go abroad with Gordon Moffatt's daughter? Moffatt spoke about her. She rather impressed him while he was in St.

Albans. She stood up against him. He never forgets that sort; he swears at it, but he trusts it. The old housekeeper is going along to keep the party in order, but a trained hand ought to go, too. The Moffatt girl has the new microbe — Unrest. It's playing the devil with her nerves. She's got to be jogged into shape."

"I think we could prevail upon Miss Glynn to go. She has her way to make. She's been rather ——" Travers stopped short; he was quoting Mrs. Thomas too minutely.

"Rather what, Dick?" Helen had her head against her boy's shoulder.

"Hunting a job," he lied manfully. "Most of those girls are up against it once the training is over."

"And Dick," Helen raised her eyes, "Doctor Ledyard and I were talking of a trip abroad this summer for — ourselves. Will you come? We want the off-the-track places. Little by-products, you know. I'm hungry for — well, for detachment; but with those I love."

"Just the thing, little mother, just the thing!" The In-Place faded from sight. In its stead rose a lonely mountain peak that caught the first touch of day and held it longest. A little lake lay at its foot, and there was the old house where he and Helen had spent so much of the summer while he and she were abroad!

"Where does Miss Moffatt intend to go?" asked Travers.

"That's it. Her ideas at present are typical of her condition. 'Snip the cord that holds me,' she said to me to-day; 'beg father to give me a handful of blank checks and old Mousey' — that's what she calls the housekeeper — 'buy a nice nurse for me in case I need one — a nice un-nurse-like nurse,' she stipulated — 'and let me play around the world for a few months to see if I can find my real self hiding in some cranny; then I'll come back and be good!' The girl's a fool, but most girls are when they've been brought up as she has been. Moffatt is at his wits' end. Young Clyde Huntter is on the carpet just now. Think of that match! think of what it would mean to Moffatt! There are times when I regret the club and cliff-dwelling age where women are concerned."

"Now, now, my dear friend, please remember my sex."

Helen ran from Richard to Ledyard. "We're all fagged, and the June night is sultry. After all, girls, even women, should be allowed a mind of their own! Take me home, Dick, I'm deeply offended." She smiled and held out her hands.

"If they were all as sane as you, Helen," Ledyard's glance softened. "You are exceptional."

"Every woman is an exceptional something, good friend, if only an exceptional fool. I'm rather proud of Margaret Moffatt's determination to have her way, and that idea of finding herself in some cranny of the old world is simply beautiful. I wonder ——"

"What, Helen?"

"I wonder if an old lady like me, a lady with hair turning frosty, might, by any possibility, find *her* real self left back there — oh! ages, ages before — well, before things happened which she never understood?"

Ledyard's eyes grew moist, but he made no reply.

It was three days later that Priscilla Glenn received a note from Margaret Moffatt, but she had already been prepared for it by Doctor Ledyard and Mrs. Thomas.

"Since they think I need a nurse," the note ran, "will you call at eleven to-morrow and see if you consider me sufficiently damaged to require your care? From what father says, I am prepared to succumb to you at once. Both father and I like strong oppositions!"

The June weather had turned chilly after the brief spell of heat, and when Priscilla was ushered into Margaret Moffatt's private library she found a bright cannel coal fire in the little grate, beside which sat a tall, handsome girl in house gown of creamy white.

"And so you are — Miss Glynn?"

As a professional accepts a non de plume, Priscilla had accepted her name.

"Yes. And you are — Miss Moffatt?"

"Please sit down — no, not way off there! Won't you take this chair beside me? I'm rather an uncanny person, I warn you. If I do not like to have you close to me now, we could never get on — across the water! What belongs to me, and what I ought to have, is mine from the first. Besides, I want you to know the worst of me — for your own sake. Would you mind taking off your hat? You have the most cheerful hair I ever saw."

Priscilla laid her broad-brimmed hat aside and laughed lightly. She was as uncanny as Margaret Moffatt, but she could not have described the charm that drew her to the girl across the hearth.

"I'm rather a hopelessly cheerful person," she said, settling herself comfortably; "it's probably my chief virtue — or shortcoming."

"You know I am not a bit sick — bodily, Miss Glynn. It's positively ridiculous to have a nurse for me, but if I am to get my way with my father I must humour him. A dear old family servant is going with me. Father did want a private cook and guide, but we've compromised on — you! I do hope you'll undertake the contract. I'm not half bad when I have my way. Do you think, now that you have seen me for fifteen minutes, that you could — tolerate me; take the chance?"

"I should be very glad to be with you." Priscilla beamed.

"Your eyes are — blue, I declare! Miss Glynn,

by all the laws of nature you should have eyes as dark as mine."

"Yes; an old nurse back in my Canadian home used to say I was made of the odds and ends of all the children my mother had and lost."

"What a quaint idea! I believe she was right, too. That will make you adaptable. Miss Glynn, let me tell you something, just enough to begin on, about myself—as a case. I'm tired to death of everything that has gone before; I do not fit in anywhere. I believe I'm quite a different person from what every one else believes; I've never had a chance to know myself; I've been interpreted by — by generations, traditions, and those who love me. I want to get far enough away to — get acquainted with myself, and then if I am what I hope I am, I will return like a happy queen and triumphantly enter my kingdom. If I am not worthy — well, we will not talk about that! Something, I may tell you some day, has suddenly awakened me. I'm rather blinded and deafened. I must have time. Can you bear with me?"

Margaret Moffatt leaned forward in her chair. Priscilla saw that her large brown eyes were tear-filled; the strong, white, outstretched hands trembling. A wave of sympathy, understanding, and great liking overwhelmed Priscilla, and she rose suddenly and stood beside the girl.

"I — think I was meant — to help you," she

said so simply that she could not be misunderstood. "When do we — go?"

"Go? Oh! you mean on the hunt for myself?"

"Yes."

"Father has the refusal of staterooms on two steamers. Could you start in — a week? Or shall we say three weeks?"

"It will not take me a day to get ready. My uniforms —— "

"Please, Miss Glynn, leave them behind. I'm sure you're just a nice girl besides being a splendid nurse. I want the nice girl with me."

"Very well. That may take two days longer."

"We'll sail, then, in a week. And will you — will you — will you accept something in advance, since time is so short?"

"Something —— ?"

"Yes. Your — your salary, you know."

"Oh, you mean money? I had forgot. I shall be glad to have some. I am very poor."

Again the simple, frank dignity touched Margaret Moffatt with pleasurable liking.

"It's to be a hundred and fifty dollars a month and all expenses paid, Miss Glynn."

"A hundred and fifty? Oh! I cannot —— "

"Doctor Ledyard arranged it with my father. You see, they know what you are to undergo. I rather incline to the belief that they consider they are making quite a bargain. I hate to see you cover your hair. Somehow you seem to be dimming the sunshine. Good-bye until —— ”

“Day after to-morrow.”

“I will send a check to St. Albans to-night, Miss Glynn.”

And she did. A check for two hundred dollars with a box of yellow roses — Sunrise roses they were called.

CHAPTER XIX

THERE are times in life, especially when one is young, that high peaks are the only landmarks in sight. Priscilla Glenn felt that henceforth her Road was to be a highway constructed in such a fashion that airy bridges would connect the lofty altitudes, and all below would exist merely as views.

Her first thought, on the day following her interview with Margaret Moffatt, was to get to John Boswell, and, as she laughingly put it, pay off her debts!

"Two hundred dollars and a full month's money from St. Albans! Gordon Moffatt certainly could not feel richer than she. And then the months ahead! Well — one could get dizzy on one's own heights. So Priscilla calmed herself by a day of strenuous shopping and looked forward to the evening with Boswell.

A dim drizzle set in late in the afternoon, and there was a chill in the air that penetrated sharply. The mist transformed everything, and, to tired, overexcited nerves, the real had a touch of the unreal. The park glistened: the tender new green on tree, bush, and grass looked as if it had just been polished, and the early flowers stood crisply on their young stalks.

At the point where once she had met poor Jerry-Jo McAlpin, Priscilla paused and was taken into control by memory and the long-ago Past. Quite unaccountably, she longed to have her mother, even her father, know of her wellbeing. Surely they would forgive everything if they knew just how things had turned out for her! She almost wished she had decided to go back to the In-Place before she started on her trip abroad. She could have made them understand about her and poor Jerry-Jo. Was old Jerry waiting and waiting? Something clutched Priscilla sharply. The loneliness and silence of the Place Beyond the Winds enfolded her like a compelling dream. How they could patiently wait, those home folks of hers! And how dear they suddenly became, now that she was going into the new life that promised her her Heart's Desire!

Then she decided: since she could not go to them she must write to Master Farwell, he had never answered her last letter, and beg him to tell them all about it. He would go, she felt sure, and, by some subtle magic, she seemed to see him passing along the red-rock road, his long-caped coat flapping in the soft wind, his hair blowing across his face, the dogs following sociably. He'd go first to old Jerry's, and then afterward, an hour, maybe, for it would

be hard for Jerry McAlpin — he would go to Lonely
Farm by way of the wood path that led by the
shrine in the open place — was the skull still there
with the long-dead grasses in its ears? It would be
night, perhaps, when the master reached the farm;
maybe the star would be shining over the hemlock ———

At this point Priscilla paused and caught her
breath sharply. She had come out of the park by
the gateway opposite Boswell's apartment, and just
ahead of her, across the street, was a thin, stooping
figure with caped coat flapping in the rising wind,
and hair blowing across a bent face.

"I — I am dreaming!" The words came brokenly. "I am bewitched!"

But with characteristic quickness of thought and
action she put her doubt to the test. Running across
the space between her and that slow-stepping figure
she panted huskily:

"Master Farwell! Master Farwell!"

He turned and fixed his deep, haunting eyes upon
her.

"It's Priscilla Glenn!" he whispered, as if to reas-
sure himself; "little Priscilla of the In-Place."

By some trick of over-stimulated imagination Priscilla tried to adjust the gentle, kindly man she
knew and loved to the strange creature into which
he had evolved since last she met him, but she could
not! To her he would always be the friend and

helper, the understanding guide of her stormy girl-hood. The rest was but shadows that came and went, cast by happenings with which she had nothing to do.

They were holding each other's hands under the window from which Boswell was, perhaps, at that very moment watching and waiting.

"Oh! my Master Farwell!" The tears rolled from the glad eyes. "I did not know how far and how sadly I had gone until this minute!"

"But you have not forgotten to be little Priscilla Glenn. My dear! my dear! how glad and thankful I am to see you. You have grown — yes; you have grown into the woman I knew you would. Your eyes are — faithful; your lips still smile. Oh! Priscilla, the world has not"—he paused and his old, quivering laugh rang out cautiously — "the world has not — doshed you!"

And then Priscilla caught him by the arm.

"You have not seen — him?" she looked upward.

"No. I was getting up my courage. The bird just freed from its cage — is timid."

"Come! A minute will not matter. I must know about my home people."

They walked on together. Then, because her heart was beating fast and the tears lying near, she drew close to her deepest interest by a circuitous way.

"Tell me of — of Mrs. McAdam and Jerry Mc-Alpin?"

"Mrs. McAdam is famous and rich. The White Fish Lodge has a waiting list every summer. The — the body of Sandy drifted into the Channel a month after you left. Bounder found it. You remember how he used to know the sound of Sandy's engine? The day the body was washed up he — seemed to know. One grave is filled, and Mary McAdam has put a monument between the two graves with the names of both boys. Jerry McAlpin has grown old and — and respectable. He has a fancy that Jerry-Jo will come back a fine gentleman. All these years he has been preparing for the prodigal. The young devil has never sent a line to his father. A bad lot was Jerry-Jo."

And then Priscilla told her story with many a catch in her voice.

"You see — he did it for me, Master Farwell. He was not all bad. Who is, I wonder? He lies in a quiet spot Mr. Boswell and I found far out in the country. There's a hemlock nearby and a glimpse of water. I — I think I will not let old Jerry know. While he waits, he is happy. While he is getting ready, life will mean something to him. And oh! Master Farwell, when — when Jerry-Jo went, he thought he was going through the Secret Portage to the Big Bay. I believe he will — welcome his father in the open some day. I will not send word back to the In-Place."

Farwell frowned.

"Boswell has touched you with his fanciful methods," he muttered; "is it — for the best?"

"I am sure it is. And — my — my people, Master Farwell, my mother?"

At this Farwell started and stepped back. The light from an electric lamp fell full on the girl's quivering, brilliant face. He had told Boswell of the mother's death.

"You — you did not know?" he asked. "She died ——"

"Died? Master Farwell, my mother dead!"

"You see — how it hurts when Boswell plays with you?"

A note of bitterness crept into the voice.

"When the day of reckoning comes — it hurts, it hurts like — hell!"

He had forgotten the girl, the white, frantic face.

"Tell me, tell me when she, my poor mother, died?"

The words brought him back sharply, and with wonderful tenderness he told her.

"Long Jean was with her. She would have her and no other, because she said Jean had helped you into the world and only she should help her out. It is a beautiful story they tell in Kenmore of your mother's passing. She thought she was going to you. She seemed quite happy once she found the way!

"'I have found her!' she cried just at the last, "'and she — understands!'"

"And I did, I did!" sobbed Priscilla.

A passerby noticed the sound and paused to look at the two sharply.

"Come, come," Farwell implored her; "we will arouse suspicion. Let us get back to — to Boswell. I haven't much time, you see. I have promised Pine to be back in ten days. Ten days!"

"You promised — Pine?"

"And you never knew?" Farwell gave an ugly laugh. "Well, I carried the ball and chain without a whimper, I can say that for myself. Pine is my ball and chain. Because he isn't all devil, because he knows I am not, he went off to play on Wyland Island. You know they kill the devil there the second week in June. Have you forgotten? Well, Pine has gone to take a stab at satan, and I'm free — for ten days. Free!"

"And then?"

"And then I'm going back voluntarily, and — assume the ball and chain!"

"Master Farwell!"

"Do not pity me! It doesn't matter now. I only wanted to — settle with Boswell. I've been in town — three days."

They were nearing the big apartment house; lights from the windows were showing cheerily through the misty fog. A chill fear shook Priscilla as she began to comprehend the meaning of Farwell's words. In her life Boswell, and this man beside her, stood for friendship in its truest, highest sense, and she felt that she must hold them together in spite of everything. She stood still and gripped Farwell's arm.

"You — you shall not go to him," she whispered, "until you tell me — how you are to pay him — for what he has done!"

Farwell's white, grim face confronted her.

"How does one pay another for lying to him, cheating him, and — and playing with him as though he were an idiot or a child?"

"Why did he do it, Master Farwell, why did he do it?"

"Because ——" But for very shame Farwell hesitated. "It makes no difference," he muttered. "I'm no fool and Boswell shall find it out."

"He has told me — the story." Priscilla still stayed the straining figure. "All his life he has given and given to you all that was in his power to give. He is the noblest man I ever knew, the gentlest and kindest, and I never knew a man could love another as he has loved you. What have you given to him — really? The smiles and jokes of the days long ago that were heavenly to him — what did they cost you? He gave, and gave his heart's best; he lied and cheated you, that you might have — some sort of peace in — in Kenmore. Oh! if you only knew how he has hated it all, how he has struggled to keep up the play even when he was so weary that the soul of him almost gave out! And now you come to — to pay him with hate and revenge when you have the only thing he wants in all the world at your command — to give him!"

The impassioned words fell into silence; the uplifted face with its shining eyes, mist-wet and indignant, aroused Farwell at last.

"And that is?" he asked.

"Yourself! your faith! See, that is his light. He is waiting — for me, because, since you sent me to him, he has been kind, heavenly kind to me, for your sake! Everything is, has always been, for your sake. Go to him, Master Farwell — go alone. I will come by and by; not now. Pay him for all he has done for you — all these lonely years!"

Farwell no longer struggled. He took Priscilla's hands in a long, close clasp.

"What a woman you have become, Priscilla Glenn! Thank you."

Without a word more they parted: Farwell to go to the reckoning; Priscilla to walk in the mist for a bit longer.

All that occurred in Boswell's library Priscilla was never to know.

There had been a moment of shock when Boswell, raising his eyes to greet Priscilla, saw Farwell Maxwell standing in the doorway.

"You have come!" Boswell gasped, with every sacred thing at stake.

"I — have come."

"For — what — Max?"

"To — to thank you, if I can. To — to tell you my story."

In the outer room Toky artistically held the dinner back. The honourable master and his strange but equally honourable friend must not be disturbed. Something was happening; but after a time Boswell laughed as Toky had never heard him laugh; so it was well, and the dinner could bide its time.

Then Priscilla came, wet and white-faced, but with the "shine-look" in her eyes that Toky, despite his prejudices and profession, had noted and respected.

"We will have the dinner now, Mees?" as if Toky ever considered her to that extent!

"I will — see Mr. Boswell."

"He has — honourable friend."

"My friend, Toky. The honourable friend is mine, also! And, oh! the flowers, Toky! There are no roses like the June roses. How wonderfully you have arranged them! A rose should never be crowded."

Toky grinned helplessly.

"Tree hours I take to make — look beautifully. One hour for each — rosy. That why it look beautifully."

"Yes, that is why it looks — beautifully. Three hours and — you, Toky!"

Boswell and Farwell were sitting in front of the grate, upon which the wood lay ready to light. Their faces were pale and haggard, but their eyes turned to Priscilla without shame or doubt.

"There is much — to talk about," said Boswell with his ready friendliness; "Max — your Farwell and mine — has told me ——"

"After dinner, dear friends. I am hungry, bitterly hungry and — cold!"

"Cold?"

"Yes; see, I am going to set the wood to burning. By the time we come back the room will be ready for us."

"To be sure!" Boswell sidled from his deep chair, the pinched look on his face relaxing.

"A fire, to be sure. Now, Max, no one but a woman would have thought of a fire in June."

"No one but Priscilla!" Farwell added.

They talked before the fire until late that evening. Priscilla's plans were discussed and considered. So full was she of excitement and joy that she did not notice the shock of surprise that Farwell showed when the names of Ledyard and Travers passed her lips. Seeing that she either did not connect the men with her past, or had reasons for not referring to it, Farwell held his peace. It was long afterward that he confided his knowledge to Boswell, and that wise friend bade him keep his secret.

"It's her life, and she's treading her Road," he said; "she has an odd fancy that her Heart's Desire lies just ahead. I cannot see that either you or I have the right to awaken her to realities while she lives so magically in her dreams."

After Priscilla's own plans were gone over and over again, Boswell said quietly:

"I'm going back to that blessed In-Place of yours, Butterfly. You remember how I told you, the first day I met you, that I could not understand any one choosing the dangerous Garden when he might have — the Place Beyond the Winds?"

Priscilla leaned forward, her breath coming sharply.

"You mean — you are going to — to live in Kenmore?"

"Yes! *Live!* That is a bright way of putting it. Live! live! The Beetle is — going to live!"

Priscilla looked about at the rich comfort of the room, thought of what it meant to the delicate cripple crouching toward the blaze, his deep eyes flame-touched and wonderful. Then she looked at Master Farwell, whose lips were trembling.

"He — he calls that — living!" he said slowly. "Tell him, Priscilla, of the bareness and hardness of the life. I have tried to, but he will not listen."

The tears, the ready, easy tears filled Priscilla's eyes, and her heart throbbed until it hurt.

"He will love the hemlocks and the deep red rocks," she said, as if speaking to herself; "he will love the Channel and the little islands, he will love the woods — and the wind does not blow hard there — he will be glad of that."

"But the ugly, wretched bareness of my hut, Priscilla! For heaven's sake, make him see that!"

"But the — fireplace, Master Farwell!"

"And — the friend beside it!" Boswell broke in; "and no more loneliness. A beetle that has crawled in the Garden so long will thank God for a real place — of its own. 'Tis but a change of scene for the Property Man."

"I love the Garden!" murmured Priscilla, sitting between the two men, her clasped hands outstretched toward the fire, which was smouldering ruddily.

"That is because you have wings, Butterfly," Boswell whispered.

"And no fetter on your soul," Farwell said so softly that only Boswell heard.

"I see," Priscilla childishly wandered on, "such a lovely trail leading, leading — where?"

"Where, indeed?" Boswell was watching her curiously.

"That is the beauty of it! I cannot see beyond the next step. All my life I have tried to keep my yearnings within bounds; now I — just follow. It's very, very wonderful. Some day I am going back to the In-Place. I shall find you both sitting by

Master Farwell's beautiful fire, I am sure. It will be the still morning time, I think, and you will be so glad to see me, and I shall tell you — all about it!"

"Heaven keep you!"

Boswell's voice was solemn and deep.

"Life will keep her safe," Farwell said with a laugh. "Life will take no liberties with her. She got her bearings, Jack, before the winds knocked her. Let us both walk home with her. What sort of a night is it?"

Priscilla went to the window.

"It's rather black," she returned; "as black as the big city ever is. The mist is clearing; it's a beautiful night."

CHAPTER XX

O F COURSE," Priscilla leaned back in her deep-cushioned chair and laughed from sheer delight, "I was a better girl in my former life than I ever had any idea of, or I wouldn't have been given this ——"

She and Margaret Moffatt were sitting on the piazza of a little Swiss inn. Below them lay a tiny lake as blue and as clear as a rare gem; round about them towered snowy peaks, protectingly. All that was past — was past! There did not seem to be any future; the present was sufficient.

"I think you must have been rather a good child, back there," Margaret Moffatt said, looking steadfastly at the girl near her; "and, anyway, you ought to have a rich reward for your hair if for no other reason."

"A recompense, you mean?"

"Heavens! no! I was thinking, as I often do when I see the lights in your hair, that for making people so cheerful and contented nothing is too good for you. I'm extremely fond of you, Priscilla Glynn! It's only when you put on your cap and apron manner that I recall — unpleasant things. Just tuck

them out of sight and let us forget everything but —
this! Isn't it divine?"

"It's — yes, it is divine, Miss Moffatt."

"Now then! Along with the cap and apron, please
pack away Miss Moffatt and Miss Glynn. Let us
be Priscilla and Margaret. This is a whim of mine,
but I have a fancy for knowing what kind of *girls* we
are. No one can tamper with us here. Dear old
Mousey never gets above a dead level, or below it.
Practically we are alone and detached. Let us
play — girls! Nice, chummy girls. Do you know,
I never had a friend in my life who wasn't labelled
and scheduled? I was sent to school where just such
and such girls were sent — girls proper for me to
know. Often they were not, but that was not considered so long as they wore their labels. It wasn't
deemed necessary for me, or my kind, to go to college: our lines of action were chosen for us. Certain
labelled men were presented; always labels, labels!
Even when I was running about with my label on
I used to have mad moments of longing to snatch
all the hideous things off — my own as well as
others — and find out the truth! And here we are,
you and I! I do not want to know anything about
you; I want to find out for myself, in my own way.
I want you to forget that I ever wore a tag. Did
you ever have a girl chum?"

"I think I know, now," Priscilla said quietly,
"why this particular little heaven was given to me.

I never, in all my life, had a girl friend. Think of that! I did not realize what I was missing until I — came into your life. Actually, I never had a girl or woman friend in the sense you mean. I was a lonely, weird little child; and then I — I came to the training school; and the girls there did not like me — I was still weird ——"

"Now, Priscilla, I do not want to know anything more about you! I intend to find you out for myself. Come, there's a boat down there, big enough for you and me. Do you row?"

"Yes, and paddle."

"You lived near the water! Ha! ha!"

"And you do — not row, Margaret?"

"No."

"Then you have never lived at all. You must learn to use oars and a paddle. It's when you have your own hand on the power that makes you go — that you live."

Margaret Moffatt turned and looked at Priscilla.

"You say, haphazard, the most Orphic things. There are times when I can imagine you before some shrine making an offering and chanting all sorts of uncanny rites. Of course it is when one has her hand on her own tiller, and is heading for what she wants, that she begins to — live. I declare, I haven't felt so young in — twenty years! I'm twenty-five, Priscilla. My father considers me on the danger-line. Poor daddy!"

"I'm ——"

"I do not want to know your age, Priscilla. Mythological characters are ageless."

Those were the days when Priscilla Glenn and Margaret Moffatt found their youth. Safeguarded by the faithful old housekeeper, who, happily, could understand and sympathize, they played the hours away like children.

"We'll travel by and by," promised Margaret. "It's rather selfish for me to hold you here when all the world would be fresh to you."

"I take root easily," Priscilla returned, "and I'm like a plant we have in my old home. My roots spread, and time is needed to strengthen them; suddenly I shoot up and — flower. The little Canadian blossom doesn't seem to justify the strong, spreading roots. I hope you will not find me disappointing, Margaret."

Margaret Moffatt smiled happily.

"Just to think," she said, "that my real self and your real self were waiting for us here behind the white hills! All along, through generations and generations, they have been acquainted and have loved and trusted each other, and then we, the unreal selves, came! Sometimes I wonder" — Margaret looked dreamy — "what they think of us, just between themselves? I am sure your true self must be prouder of you than mine can be of me, for, with everything at my command, what am I? While you — oh, Priscilla, how you have made everything tell!"

But Priscilla shook her head.

"Still," Margaret went on, "things were not at my command. They were all there, but pigeon-holed and controlled. Such and such things were for nice little girls like me! After a time I got to believe that, and it was only when, one day, I touched something not intended for me that my soul woke up. Priscilla, did you ever feel your soul?"

"Yes."

"Isn't it wonderful? It makes you see clearly your — your ——"

"Ideal?" suggested Priscilla.

"Yes; the thing you want to be; the thing that seems best to *you* without the interpretation of others. It stands unclouded and holy; and nothing else matters."

"And you never forget — never!"

"No. Your eyes may be blinded for a moment, but you do not forget — ever!"

They were out on the gemlike lake now, and Priscilla was sternly instructing Margaret how to handle an oar.

"It will never go the way you want it to," Margaret protested, making an ineffectual dab at the water.

"When it does you will know the bliss! Get a little below the surface, and have faith in yourself."

And that was the day that Priscilla caught a new light on Margaret's character. They landed at a tiny village across the lake and wandered about, Margaret talking easily to the people in their own tongue, Priscilla straining to follow by watching faces and gestures. While they stood so, discussing the price of some corals, a little child came close to them and slipped a deliciously dimpled, but very dirty little hand in Margaret's. At the touch the girl started, turned first crimson and then pale, and looked down. Suddenly her eyes deepened and glowed.

"The darling!" she whispered, and bent to catch what the child was saying. Presently she looked up, tears dimming her eyes, and said to Priscilla, "She says a new baby came to their house last night. She wanted to tell — me!"

"And ten already have been there," broke in a brown-faced native woman.

"But she is glad, and she wanted *me* to know! Come, my sweet, tell me more about the baby, and then we will go and see it."

They sat down under a clump of trees, and the dirty little maid nestled close to Margaret, while with uplifted head and unabashed confidence she told of the mystery.

Priscilla watched Margaret Moffatt's face. She was almost awed by the change that had come over it. The aloofness and pride which often marked it had disappeared as if by magic; the tenderness, passionate in its intentness, cast upon the little child, moved her to wonder and admiration. Later they went to the poor hovel and bent beside the humble bed on which the mother and child lay. Then it was that Priscilla played her part and made comfortable and grateful the overburdened creature, worn and weak from suffering.

" 'Twas the good God who sent you," murmured she.

" 'Twas your little maid," smiled Margaret, tucking a roll of bills under the hard, lumpy pillow. "Take time to love the babies — leave other things — but love them and enjoy them."

"Yes, my lady."

On the way back in the boat Margaret was very silent for a time as she watched Priscilla row; finally she said:

"Did it surprise you — my show of feeling for the — the child?"

"It was very beautiful. I did not know you cared so much for children, and this one was so — dirty."

"But so real! You see I have never had real children in my life. The kinds passed out to nice girls like me were sad travesties. Since I saw the darling of to-day I've been wondering — do not laugh, Priscilla — but I've been wondering what poor, cheated little morsel of humanity, in the unreal world, would find herself in that eleventh miracle of the wretched hovel? And what an art yours is, dear Priscilla! How you soothed away the suffering by your touch. I loved you better as I realized how that training of yours knows neither high nor low when it seeks to heal."

Priscilla thought of the operation on Margaret Moffatt's father, and her quick colour rose.

"And I loved you better when I saw how your humanity knows neither high nor low — just love!"

"Only toward little children. I cannot explain it, but when I touch the babies, their littleness and helplessness make me weak and trembling before — well, before the strength comes in a mighty wave. There is a physical sensation, a thrill, that comes with the first contact, and when they trust me, as that darling did this morning, I feel as if — God had singled me out! Only lately have I begun to understand what this means in me. It is one reason why I came away. I had to think it out. I suppose" — she paused and looked steadily at Priscilla — "I suppose the maternal has always been a master passion in me, and I've rebelled at being an only child; at having no children but the — specialized kind. I have been hungry for so many things I am realizing now."

"In my training I have seen — what you mean. All sorts drift in — to pay the price of love or the penalty of passion, as Doctor Ledyard used to express it; but" — and Priscilla's eyes grew darker

— "I used to find — a nurse gets so much closer, you know, than a doctor can — I found that sometimes it was the penalty of love and the price of passion. Those sad young creatures, with only blind instinct to uphold them, were so — divinely human, and paid so superbly. When it comes to the hour of a life for a life, one thing alone matters, I am afraid, and it is the thing *you* mean, Margaret."

"Yes. And what a horrible puzzle it all is. The thing I mean should be always there — always. The world's wrong when it is not."

Suddenly Priscilla, sending the light boat forward by the impulse of her last stroke, said, as if it were quite in line with all that had gone before:

"There's Doctor Travers on the wharf!"

He heard her, and called back:

"Quite unintentionally, I assure you. I was waiting for the boat to take me across. I've been wandering about, sleeping where I could. I simply find myself — here!"

At this both girls laughed merrily.

"This is the place of Found Personalities," Margaret Moffatt said, jumping lightly to the wharf. "Perhaps you'll come to the inn and have luncheon with us — that is, if you are sure Doctor Ledyard did not send you here to spy on me."

"I haven't seen him since I left America. My mother is with me; she's in a crack of the hills in

Italy. She wanted to be alone. Doctor Ledyard will join us later."

"Then come to the house. They serve meals on a dangerously poised balcony over the lake; we curb our appetites for fear our weight may be the one thing the structure cannot stand. Our old house-keeper waits upon us, but is in no wise responsible for the food which is often very bad and lacking in nourishment."

"You seem to thrive on it." Travers looked at the two before him. "I wonder just what it is this air and place have done to you?"

"Tell him, Priscilla."

"Oh, like you, Doctor Travers, we simply found ourselves — here! That's all."

Travers did not leave the inn that night, nor for many days thereafter.

"Doctor Ledyard will join my mother and me early in August," he explained; "until then I'm a floating proposition. I wish you'd let me stay on a while, Miss Moffatt, right here. I want to analyze the food, it puzzles me. Why just this kind of con-glomeration should achieve such results is interest-ing. I've gained five pounds in six days."

"And lost ten years," Margaret broke in. "I never thought of you as young, Doctor Travers; professional men never do seem youthful; but *here* you're rather a good sort."

And Travers remained, much to the delight of the

old housekeeper, who, with a nurse and a doctor in command, cast all responsibility aside.

"Young Miss looks well," she confided to the proprietor's wife, who, fortunately, could understand a word or so of English; "but folks is like weather: the fairer they seem, the nearer a storm. When a day or a person looks uncommonly fair — a weather breeder, says I, and generally, nine times out of ten, I'm right. My young lady is too changed to be comfortable. It's either a breaking up, or ——" But here a shout for "Mousey," silenced further prophecy.

The days ran along without cloud or shadow. Quite naturally, perhaps, Priscilla began to think that a drama of life was being enacted in the quiet, detached village. They three were always together, always enjoying the same things, but certainly no man, so she thought, could be with Margaret Moffatt long without falling at her feet. Gradually to Priscilla Glenn this girl stood for all that was fine and perfect. In her she saw all women as women should be. With the adoration she was so ready to give to that which appealed to her, Priscilla lavished the wealth of her affection upon Margaret Moffatt. Surely it was because of Margaret that Doctor Travers stayed on, and became the life of the party. To be sure he was tact itself in making Priscilla feel at ease; but that only confirmed her in her belief that he wanted to please Margaret to the uttermost. Often Priscilla recalled, with keener appreciation, John Boswell's description of Anton Farwell's conception of friendship. In like manner Margaret Moffatt claimed for her companion all that justly belonged to herself. Dispassionately, vicariously, Priscilla learned to know and admire the man who undoubtedly in time would win her one friend. It was all beautiful and natural, and in the lovely detachment it grew and grew. The long walks and drives, the rows upon the lake by sunlight and moonlight, all conspired to perfect the comradeship. They read together, sang together — very poorly to be sure — and once, just to vary the charm, they travelled to a nearby town and danced at a village fête. An odd thing happened there. Owing to high spirits and a sense of unconventionality, they entered into the sports with abandon. Travers even begged a reel with a pretty Swiss maiden, and led her proudly away, much to Margaret's and Priscilla's delight. Later, the men and women of the place came forward, and, entering a little ring formed by admiring friends, performed, separately, the native dances.

Travers watched Priscilla with a puzzled look in his eyes. She trembled with excitement; seemed hypnotized by the exhibition, much of which was delightfully graceful and picturesque. Then, suddenly, to the surprise of every one, she took advantage of a moment's pause and ran into the ring.

"Whatever possesses her?" whispered Margaret

to Travers; "she looks bewitched. See! she is — dancing!"

Travers watched the tall, slim figure in the thin white gown over which a light scarf, of transparent crimson, floated as the evening breeze and the girl's motions freed it. At first Priscilla took her steps falteringly, her head bent as if trying to recall the measure and rhythm; then with more confidence she swung into the lovely pose and action. With uplifted eyes and smiling lips, seeming to see something hidden from others, she bent and glided, curtesied and tripped, this way and that.

The lookers-on were wild with delight. The beauty of the thing itself, the willingness of the foreigners to join in the sport, aroused the temperamental enthusiasm, and the clapping and cheering filled the hall with noise. Suddenly the musicians dropped their instruments. They were but human, and, since they could not keep in time with this new and amazing dance, they drew near to admire.

"Play!" pleaded Priscilla, past heeding the sensation she was creating. "The best is yet to come!"

Carried out of himself, entering now wholly into the adventure, Travers caught up a violin near him and sent the bow over the strings with a master touch. He hardly knew what he played; he was himself, carried away on a wave of enchantment.

"Ah!"

The word escaped Priscilla like a cry of glad response.

"Now!"

They two, the musician and the dancer, seemed alone in the open space. The flashing eyes, the cheering voices, the clapping hands, even Margaret Moffatt, pale, puzzled, yet charmed, were obliterated. It was spring time in the Place Beyond the Winds, and the dance of adoration was in full swing, while the old tune, never out of time with the graceful, whirling form, played on and on. And then — the ring melted away, the lights grew dim, and Priscilla stood still.

"I'm — I'm tired," faltered she. A hand was laid upon her arm, some one guided her out of the heated, breathless room; they were alone, she and he, under wide-spreading trees, and a particularly lovely star was pulsing overhead.

"You are crying!" Travers's voice was low and tense. "Why?"

"It — it was the music! It was like something I had heard, and — and I was so tired. I was very foolish. Can you, can Margaret, forgive me?"

"Forgive you? Why, you were — I dare not tell you what you were! Here, sit down. Do not tremble so! Tell me, where did you learn to dance as you do?"

Priscilla had dropped upon the rough rustic seat; she did not seem to notice the hand that rested upon her clasped ones under the thin scarf. She no longer cried, but the tears shone on her long lashes.

"I — I never learned. It — it is I, myself. I thought I had grown into something else, but — I shall always be the same — when I let myself go."

"Let yourself go? Good heavens! Why not let yourself go — forever?" Travers's voice shook. "You have brought joy and youth to us all — to me, who never had youth. What — who are you?" he laughed boyishly. She sat rigidly erect and turned her sad eyes upon him.

"I'm Priscilla Glynn — a nurse! And you? Oh! you are Doctor Travers! Can you not see my beautiful, happy, happy life is ended — must end? Margaret, you, everything this joyous summer has made me — forget. Soon I am going back — where there is no dancing!"

"And — cease to be yourself?"

"Yes. But I shall always remember. Not many have had the wonderful glimpse I have had — not many."

"I — I will not let you go back! You belong in the light; in love and the giving of love. You have given me a glimpse of myself — as I should be. I have stayed in this magic place without a past and a future — for your sake! I see it now. I love —— "

"Oh! please, please stop. We are both mad, and when to-morrow comes and the day after, and the day after that, we will both be sorry, and, oh! I want all my life to — to — be glad because of this night."

"You shall — remember it — all your life as — your happiest night, if I can make it so!"

His face was bent close to hers. For the first time Travers was overpowered by the charm of woman, and all the pent passion and love of his life broke bonds like a wild, primeval thing that education and conventions had never touched.

"I — I want you! I want you without knowing any more than if you and I had been born anew in this wonderful life. Look at me! You believe I can offer you — the one perfect gift a man should offer a woman?"

She looked long and tenderly in his eyes. She was — going to leave him; she could afford the truth. She was brave now.

"Yes," she whispered.

"And I know you to be — what I want. Isn't that enough? Can we not trust each — for the rest?"

"Yes, if the white hills could shut us forever from the other things."

"Other things?"

"Yes, the things of to-morrow. Duty, the demands that lie — over the Alps."

"I — renounce them all!"

"But they will not renounce us!"

Travers felt her slipping from him. A man whose

youth has been denied, as his had, is a puppet in Fate's hands when youth makes its claims.

"I — mean to have you! Do you hear me? I mean to have you."

And just then Margaret Moffatt drew near. Calmly, smilingly, she came like one playing her part in a perfectly arranged drama.

"You are here? Ready for home? Wasn't it sublime and exactly as it should be? We are so nice and friendly with our real selves."

There was no surprise; no suggestion of disapproval. The world in which they were all playing could have only direct and simple processes. But, having lived in a past world where her perceptions had been made keen and vital, Margaret Moffatt understood what she saw. She had noticed every letting down and abandonment of Travers since he had joined them. She was too wise not to know the effect of such a woman as Priscilla upon such a man; such a denied and almost puritanical man as Travers. She knew his story from her father. An artistic triumph was hers that night. The splendid elements of primitive justice had been set in motion, and almost gleefully she wondered what they would do with Richard Travers and Priscilla Glynn.

For herself? Well, she had put herself to the test and had come out clear-visioned and glad to a point of dangerous excitement. Only two or three mighty things mattered, if one were to gain in the marvellous game. She meant to hold to them and let the rest go!

But Travers had not passed through Ledyard's school and come out untouched. After leaving Priscilla, silent and white, he had gone to his room and flung himself down upon a low couch by the window. Then his old self took him in hand while he stubbornly resisted every attack that reason, as trained by Ledyard, made upon him.

"Think of — your mother! What has she not done and suffered that you might stand before the world — a free man? And your profession; your future! They are all your mother holds to for her peace and joy. And I? Well, I do not claim anything for myself; but you know the game as well as I. If you toss to the winds all that has been gained for you, professionally and socially, you are done for! Your renunciation and restraint, what have they amounted to, unless you accept them as stepping-stones and go — on?"

And then Travers clenched his hands and had his say.

In that moment his own mother rose clear and radiant beside him and made her appeal. She pleaded for justice, but she showed mercy. He must not forget or forego anything that had been gained for him; but he was her child, the child of her love — unasking, unfettered love — and the passion that was throbbing in him was pure and instinctive; he must not deny it or the rest would be shucks! Non-essentials must not hamper him. Alone, unsought, a strange and compelling force had made him captive. All that others, and himself, had achieved for him must make holy this simple but all-powerful desire.

Then she faded, that poor, little, half-forgotten mother! But she left, like the fragrance of rare flowers that had been taken from the dim, moon-lighted room, a memory of happiness and sweetness and content.

CHAPTER XXI

B Y ALL the deductions of experience the three people in the little inn should have, in the light of the morning after, been reduced to common sense; but the day laughed common sense to scorn and fanned the fires of the previous evening to bright flame.

"I must write a letter," announced Margaret after breakfast, "a letter so momentous that it will take me — an hour and a half! But my plans and yours are all laid. Now, Priscilla, none of your cap and apron look. You'll do exactly what I tell you to do; and you, too, Doctor Travers."

"I haven't the slightest intention of disobeying. And as for my cap and apron, I've burned them!" Priscilla tossed her head.

Travers looked at her, and her loveliness seemed enhanced in her trim white linen gown with its broad collar of Irish lace. How magnificent her throat was! What a perfect woman she was! And *what* hair!

"There is a train that leaves here at nine-thirty, a mad little ramshackle train that goes to The Ghost and back in an hour and a half. We've all yearned to climb The Ghost, or as much of it as we dared. Now you two, with Mousey and a servant, are to go on the nine-thirty. I'll finish my destruction of the social system and catch the eleven o'clock train. We'll have picnic lunch. They say there's a dreadful cavern at the base of The Ghost that is corking for picnics, and then we'll explore until we have to return. Any objections?"

There were none.

"Very well! It's nine now! Priscilla, wear the roughest, heaviest things you've got. You always have your hours of remorse too late. The Ghost will chill your blood."

When the little party reached the small station at the mountain foot the servants started at once to the cavern to build a fire and prepare for the luncheon.

"Let us walk a bit up the trail," suggested Travers. "I always feel like the Englishman who said the views halfway up a mountain are more enjoyable than those on top. At least, you have life enough left to enjoy them. This particular trail is a mighty wicked one. There ought to be guides, for safety. I know the way perfectly; my mother and I once stayed here some years ago. She meant to come here this summer early, but has decided to wait until Doctor Ledyard joins us. I feel as if I were taking the cream off the thing. Will you trust me — Priscilla?"

There was challenge and command in the use of her name.

"Absolutely."

"Come, then! I want you to go first. The rise is easy for a half-mile or so. I can better watch out for you and catch you — if you make a misstep. The stones are loose and mischievous; the path is ridiculously near the edge of things. If one should — now do not get nervous, but if you should go over, just clutch the bushes, the sturdy little clumps, and nothing can really happen."

"I never get nervous in high places. Being used to dead levels, I have the courage of the ignorant. Doesn't the air make one ——"

"Heady?"

"Yes. I suppose that is it. Heady and — light-hearted."

Travers had his eyes fixed on the form ahead in its dark blue mountain skirt and corduroy waist.

"I wish you would take off your hat," he said.

Priscilla obeyed.

"Thank you! Will you let me — love you?"

He noticed a tremor run the length of her body.

"Is — that in my giving?" Priscilla meant to play just a little longer, only a little, and then she must make him see that because this sudden and great thing had come to them both, they must prove themselves worthy of it by unselfish recognition of deep truths.

"No. But I would like to have you say — yes!.
I meant all I said last evening; you said nothing. I
mean to have you, because I love you; because I
know you love me, and because nothing else matters.
It's only fair to warn you. You *do* love me?"

"Is it love — when everything else is swept aside?"

"Yes."

"All but the longing — for the best?"

"Yes. That is love."

"Then, I love you."

"On ahead there is a tiny bluff, do not speak again
until we reach it. A strange and wonderful thing
came to me there once — years ago. I want to
tell you about it, my beloved!"

Travers watched her as he spoke. Again that
tremor ran through Priscilla.

It was nearly noon when they stopped, at Travers's
word. They had come, silently, up the trail, only
their footsteps and their quicker breathing breaking the awesome stillness. Their separate thoughts
were bringing them dangerously nearer together,
trampling caution, warning, and purpose beneath
their young yearning for the vital meaning of life.
When they faced each other at last it was as if they
had indeed been transfigured.

"Mine!" whispered Travers, stretching out his
hands. "You are mine! Do not struggle."

Priscilla put her hands in his, but did not
speak.

"And now let us sit here. I want you to understand. You will try to understand?"

"Yes."

All her life Priscilla was to look back on that moment as the first perfect one of her life. She felt no shame in taking it. It belonged to her, and she meant to prove herself to him.

"I feel as if there were a new heaven and a new earth, Priscilla, and that you and I had just been created — the first man, the first woman. Dear heart, rest your head, so, against my knee." He was sitting above her. "Your hair holds all the glory of the sunlight, and how white and warm your throat is!" His fingers touched it reverently. "Let us cling to this one hour that has given us to each other. Are you happy?"

"It means — something more than that — this moment ——" Priscilla spoke as if held by a dream.

"You are — content?"

"Yes. That is it. I am — content. I shall never ask for anything more, anything better. I have everything — the world and — and God, has to give."

"My darling! Now let me tell you. Years ago I came here after a hard struggle for health. I had never had childhood or boyhood, in the real sense; but I was well at last! I saw that I was going to have a man's life, with all that that means, and for months the emotions and cravings, that generally go to the years of making a child and boy, had been crowding and pushing me to a sense of having been defrauded, and I meant to have my turn at last: my joy and pleasure. It seemed just and right to me that I should taste and revel in all that I had been deprived of. I had even been deprived of the longing, had not even had the glory of conquest. I had been such a meaningless creature, I thought I could afford even to be selfish. I shrank from being *different* — I had been forced to in the past — but I meant to make up for lost time and take my place among my fellows.

"One morning, just such a morning as this, I found myself alone — here! Then I had it out with myself. More distinctly than anything had ever come to me before I realized that life meant one thing, and one thing only: the biggest fight or the meanest defeat! I knew that every passion that burned and flayed me was a warhorse that, if controlled, would carry me safely through the battle; if succumbed to, would trample me under its relentless feet. This I knew with my brain, while tradition, inclination, and longing called me — fool! Well, I was given strength to follow my head; but every year has been a struggle. I found that to be different meant contempt often, misunderstanding always. Sometimes it has not seemed worth while; the victories were so lonely and useless; but I thanked

God last night, when I saw your face as you danced, that I could offer you a love that need not make the pitiful plea for mercy from your love. Through temptation and the long fight it has always seemed to me that no man should ask for pure love without the equivalent to offer in return.

"Can you understand when I say that this battle of mine has brought me closer to men and women, with no bitterness in my heart; has left me free, not to despise them, but to help them?"

"Yes, oh, yes; all my life I could understand those who — fight. I, too, have fought and fought."

Travers's hand was pressing upward the head against his knee so that he could look in the up-lifted eyes.

"My love! as free man and woman, let us give ourselves to each other!"

Then he bent and kissed the smiling mouth.

"Speak to me, my — wife."

"Yes! But let me think, dear heart. I must speak; the half has only been told." She moved a bit away from him. Travers let her go with no fear.

"Now, strange little thing, since you cannot speak in my arms, have your will!" he whispered.

"There is a to-morrow." The even voice had no strain of pain or sorrow in it. "And we must not forget that. We have played and played until we have made ourselves believe — such wonderful things; but to-morrow — we will wake up and be

what we have been made! I have heard, oh! so
many people, tell of your future, your honours. I
have seen Doctor Ledyard's eyes upon you; I know
you have a mother who adores you. I do not know
your world; I could not touch your place but to mar
it, and, because I love you so — oh! so absolutely,
and because I would want, and must have, glory in
my own love — we must stop playing! We have
not" — and now the eyes dimmed — "we have not
played for keeps!"

"You poor, little girl! How you use the old,
foolish arguments, thinking yourself — wise. Do you
imagine I could let you dim the sacred thing that
has come to us — by such idle prating? There are
only you and I and — the future. You darling child,
come here!"

In reaching toward her, Travers's foot pressed too
heavily against the stone upon which she sat; it
moved, slipped, and Priscilla escaped his clutch.
Not realizing her danger, she smiled up at him radiantly. She meant what she had said, but youth
could not relinquish its rights without a struggle, and
his eyes were so heavenly kind.

"My God! Clutch the bushes, Priscilla!"

"What — is the matter?" But with the question
came the knowledge. She was going down, down, and
every effort he made to save her sent her farther
along the awful slope! She held to a nearby bush
but uprooted it by the force with which she gripped

it. Faster, faster, with that terrified face above her!

"My precious one! Try again! Do not be afraid!"

"No."

And then they both heard the hoarse whistle of the little shuttle train nearing The Ghost, with Margaret Moffatt on board!

Travers realized the new danger. Very steep was the grade of the mountain, and it ended on — the tracks!

He shut his eyes; he could do no more. Every move he made imperilled the woman he would give his life to save. The only comfort he knew was that he, too, was losing, losing. They would be together at the last.

Priscilla understood also. She looked up and saw him close his eyes; then fear fled, as it does when the last hope takes it. It would soon be over for them, and — nothing in all the world could separate them. There was nothing but him and her! He had seen that; but now she saw it, too. Him and her! him and her!

"I — love you so!" she whispered. "I am not afraid. I'm sorry. I would have given myself to you! I would indeed!"

She wanted him to know. He opened his eyes and smiled a twisted, hideous smile.

"I — meant — to have you." The words came to her faintly. A nearer shriek of the whistle, and a deafening clang of the bell! Some one at the throttle of the engine had an inspiration and sent the crazy thing shooting ahead.

Then it was past, and upon the tracks over which the car had but just gone lay Priscilla Glenn quite unconscious!

Travers came to himself at once, and took her head on his knee where but a short time ago it had lain so happily.

"You, Priscilla!" It was Margaret Moffatt who spoke. The train had stopped; the few passengers had come back to see what had happened.

"Yes; my God! Yes! Miss Moffatt, will you see if she is dead? I dare not trust — myself."

It was late that night, in Priscilla's room at the inn, that she and Margaret had their talk.

Priscilla lay upon her bed weak and bruised, but otherwise safe. Margaret sat beside her, her hand in Priscilla's.

"Doctor Travers has pulled himself together at last," she said. "I never saw a strong man so shattered. And you, dear, you are sure you have told me the truth — you are not suffering?"

"No, only a little dazed. That's natural after looking death in the face for hours and hours while everything slipped away from you — things you had always thought meant something."

"Yes, poor girl!"

"And they — meant nothing. They never do."

"No. You found that at death's door; I found it at life's. I want to tell you something, dear, that will make you forget yourself — and think of me. You are sure you cannot sleep?"

"I do not want to sleep."

"Priscilla, I have given myself to love! You can understand. Travers has just told me — about him and you!"

A faint colour touched the face on the pillow.

"It was the telling that brought him around. He's superb, and you're a daffy little goose, Cilla. Imagine a man like Travers letting a girl like you slip through his fingers."

"He did!" weakly interrupted Priscilla.

"But he followed you right down, and into — hell!"

"Into life and joy, you mean, Margaret — life!"

"Well, at any rate, he was with you. It is magnificent to see a man, or a woman, big enough, brave enough, and sensible enough to sweep the senseless rubbish of life aside, and get each other! Oh! it's life as God meant it. Priscilla, the letter I wrote to-day was to — *my* man. He's as splendid as yours. I told you once how I — I loved children. I had taken that love for granted until something happened. A friend of mine married — one of the girls my people thought was the kind for me to know. She didn't understand life any more than I did; she just took one of the men who wore the same label she did. Her child came — a year after; a horrible little creature — diseased; dreadful — can you understand?"

"Yes" — Priscilla had turned toward the girl by her side — "yes, I know what you mean. I have been a nurse."

"That was the first time things we should have known — were known by my friend and me!" Margaret's voice was low and hard.

"She — she cursed him, her husband — and left him! It was terrible! I was frightened, more frightened than I had ever been. Everything seemed tottering around me. I thought — I must die; I dared trust nothing. Just then — some one told me — he loved me; and I — I had loved him. But I was more afraid of him than of any one in God's world. I thought I was going mad, and then — I went to Doctor Ledyard and told him all about it. I just threw my whole burden of doubt and ignorance upon him — he is such a *good* man! Sometimes I weep when I think of him. He was father, friend, and physician, all in one. He understood. He told me to go away; he got you for me. He told me to play like a little girl, with only the real and beautiful things of life; to forget the worries, and he would make sure!

"Priscilla, he has made sure! My love is safe. I can give myself to my love and let it have its way with me, and in the beautiful future, our future, his and mine, little children cannot — curse us by their suffering and deformity.

"This *must* be the heritage a woman should be able to give her children, or she has no right to her own love. God has been so good to me — he has not asked for sacrifice; but" — here she spoke fiercely — "I was ready to sacrifice my love — for I had seen my friend's baby!

"I had never known God before as I know him now. He came to me with love and faith and my glorious life. Before, my God was a prayer-book God; a dead thing that only rustled when we touched him; and now, oh! Cilla, he is alive and breathing in good men and women, in little children, in all the beautiful, real things. They did not bury my God, or yours, long ago; they only set him free for us to find and love and follow."

They clung to each other in a passion of reverence and happiness, and then kissed each other good night.

CHAPTER XXII

M Y GIRL," said Travers a week later, "how shall it be? May I tell every one how madly happy I am? May I take you to that little shrine a mile up the mountain yonder and make you — mine — and then show them all *why* I am so happy? Or —— "

"Yes. Or —— " Priscilla lay quite contentedly in his arms, her eyes on the shining outlines of The Ghost.

"And that means, my sweet?"

"That we should keep this blessed secret just a little longer — to ourselves. I feel as if I could not bear to have it explained, defended, or justified, and all that must follow, my very dear man, when the play is over and we return to — to school. I shall be glad and ready to do all this a little later on; proud to have you do it for me, and — we'll face the music. It is going to be music, dear, I am sure of that. But some very stern questions will be asked by that sweet mother of yours, and she shall have her answer. Then Doctor Ledyard, with all the prayer gone from his eyes, will call me up for judgment and demand to know what right a nurse, even a white nurse, had to lay hands upon a young physician who was on the road to glory! It will be hard to answer him; but never mind!"

"And then, dear lady of mystery, what then?"

"Why, then I'm going to beckon to you and we'll dance —— "

"Dance, my darling?"

"Yes, dance away and away to a holy place I know, and then I'm going to tell you the whole story of Priscilla —— "

But at that moment Margaret Moffatt came upon the scene. The miracle of love had transfigured the girl. She looked, as Travers had said to Priscilla, like the All Woman: large, fine, and noble, with unashamed surrender in her splendid eyes.

"And that is what she is!" Priscilla had replied, "the All Woman. I could die for her, live for her, do anything for her. For me, she is the first, the one woman, in all the world."

"Young devotee, could you, would you, give your — love up for her?" Travers had asked, and then Priscilla spoke words that Travers remembered long afterward.

"I could not give my love up for — that is — I, myself; just as the dance is — just as my soul is — but I could; yes, I know I could give up — my happiness for her, if by so doing I could spare her one shadow. Her glorious nature could reach where mine never could."

"Yours reaches to me, little girl."

"But hers — oh! my dear man, hers reaches to — the world. If you knew her as I know her!"

But Margaret was whimsical and witchy as she came upon the two in the small arbour by the lake.

"Folks," she said, "let us keep our nice little surprises to ourselves for a while, like miserly creatures. My dear old daddy-boy is fretting and fussing about me, 'dreading the issue,' as he told Doctor Ledyard, and behold — I'm going to do exactly what my daddykins desires! And you, Doctor Richard Travers, you are wanted by your lady mother. Here's a telegram. The girl in the office always tells what is in a telegram, to spare shock. And Cilla, my shining-headed chum, you and I are going to scamper about a bit before we go home. I'd be a miserable defaulter, indeed, if I did not give you your share of this experience. Oh! I know you've snatched bits that in no wise were included in the program, but we're all grafters. I want to play fair. Will you flit over the continent with me and Mousey, dear little — pal?"

And three days later they began their trip, while Travers returned to Helen. It was a charming trip the girls made, but their hearts were elsewhere.

In October they were in New York again, and the inevitable happened. Margaret was returned to her world, and, for the moment, was absorbed. Priscilla lost sight of her, though she heard constantly from her by telephone or delicately worded notes.

A sad occurrence kept Richard Travers abroad. Helen contracted fever and for weeks lay between life and death. Doctor Ledyard waited until the danger was past, and then left the two together in Paris, while Helen recovered, with Travers to watch and care for her.

The letters that came to Priscilla were all that kept her eyes shining and her heart singing.

"I shall go on as usual," she wrote to Richard. "When you come, then we'll make the wonderful announcement. I see now that we have no right to our secret alone; but with the ocean between us, it is best."

During those months Priscilla learned to know Helen Travers through Travers's letters. Woman-like, she read between the lines and caught a glimpse of Helen's nobility and simple sweetness. Her loved ones were so sacred to her that no personal demands could ever cause her to raise objections. Once she was sure that they she worshipped wanted anything for their true happiness, her energies were bent to that end.

"And she will love you, my girl; will learn to depend upon you as I do. As for Doctor Ledyard, when he is cornered, he is the best soul that ever drew breath, and mother can bully him into anything."

It was in February that Priscilla was called up by Doctor Hapgood, a man of high repute.

"Are you on duty?"

"No, sir."

"Any immediate engagement?"

"None until March."

"I would like to have you take a case of mine that requires tact as well as efficiency. Can you take it?"

"Yes, sir."

"Report then at 60 West Eighty-first Street this afternoon, at four."

Priscilla found herself promptly at four o'clock in the waiting-room of a palatial bachelor apartment, and there Doctor Hapgood joined her.

"Before we go upstairs," he said, drawing his chair close to Priscilla's and lowering his voice, "I wish to say to you what, doubtless, there is no real need of saying. I simply emphasize the necessity. The young man who requires your services is Clyde Huntter. This means nothing to you, but it does to many others. He is supposed to be in — Bermuda. You understand?"

"Yes, Doctor Hapgood."

"The case is a particularly tragic one, such an one as you may encounter later on in your career. It demands all your sympathy, encouragement, and patience. Mr. Huntter is as fine a man, as upright a one, as I know, his ideals and — and present life are above reproach. He is paying a bitter debt for youthful and ignorant folly. I believed this impossible, but so it is. I am thankful to say, however, that he has every reason to hope that the future, after this, is secure. I have chosen you to care for him, because I know your ability; have heard of your powers of reticence and cheerfulness. I depend upon you absolutely."

"Thank you, Doctor Hapgood."

Priscilla's face had gone deadly white, but never having heard Huntter's name before, she was impersonal in her feeling.

"I will do my best."

The days following were days of strain and torture to Priscilla. Her patient was a man who appealed to her strongly, pathetically. There were hours when his gloom and depression would almost drag her along to the depths into which he sank; then again he would beg her to pardon him for his brutal thoughtlessness.

"Sit there, Miss Glynn," he said one day. "The sunshine is rather niggardly, but when it rests on your hair — it lasts longer."

"Oh, my poor hair!"

"Poor? It looks like a gold mine." Then: "I wish you would read to me. No; nothing recent or superficial. Something from the old, cast-iron writers who knew how to use thumb screws and rack. There's something wholesome in them; something you buck up against. They make you writhe and groan, but they leave you with the thought that — you've lived through something."

Again, another day, after a bad night:

"I think you'd better go into the next room, Miss Glynn, and take a nap. I'd feel less brutally selfish if I could see your eyes calmer. Besides, being shut away here from all I'm dying to have makes an idiot of me. If you stay any longer, looking at me with those queer eyes of yours, I may break down and tell you all about it, just for the dangerous joy of easing my own soul by dumping a load on yours. Good God! Miss Glynn, such women as you should not be nurses; it isn't fair. I'd give — let me see — well, I'd give six months of my life — since Hapgood says I stand a fair chance for ninety years — to talk to you, man to woman, and get your point of view — about something. There are moments, after a bad night, when I think you women haven't had all they say you should have had. We men have been too blindly sure we could play your game as well as our own. Run now! If you stay another minute I'll regret it, and so will you."

"Shall I shake your pillow before I go, Mr. Hunter?"

"Yes. Thank you. You manage to shake more whim-whams out of the creases than you know."

He stayed her by a wistful, longing, and half-boyish smile.

"Say," he said, "you see you didn't run quick enough, and now I'm going to ask you something. You must have seen a good deal of women as well as men in your calling."

"Yes, I have."

"Seen them with their masks off?"

"Yes."

"What does love count for in the big hours of life? Does it stand everything, anything?"

Priscilla felt her throat contract. She longed to say something that would reach Huntter without arousing his suspicions.

"No; love — at least, woman's love, doesn't stand everything — always."

"What doesn't it stand? The essence, I mean."

"It doesn't stand unfair play! Women understand fair play and for it would die. They may not say much, but — they never forgive being — tricked."

"Oh! of course. How graphic you are, Miss Glynn. You sound as if we were discussing a game of — of tennis or bridge. Gentlemen do not trick ladies." He frowned a bit.

"Don't they, Mr. Huntter?"

"Certainly not! What I meant was this: You seem, for a trained woman, very human and — and — well, what shall I say? — observing and rather a — thoroughbred. If *you* loved, now, loved really, is there anything you would not forgive a man?

That is, if his love for you was the biggest thing in
his life?"

Priscilla stood quite still and looked at the pale,
handsome face on the pillow.

"My love — yes; my love could and would forgive anything, if it related only to — to — the man
I loved and — me!"

The frown deepened on Huntter's face; he turned
uneasily.

"After all," he muttered, "a man and woman see
things so differently. There is no use!"

"I wonder — if things would not seem plainer if
they saw them — together?"

But Priscilla saw she had gone too far. The whimsical mood in Huntter had passed. He was himself
again, and she was his nurse — his nurse who knew
too much! More fretfully than he had ever spoken
to her, he said:

"I wish to be alone, Miss Glynn."

Priscilla passed out, leaving the door between the
rooms ajar, and lay down upon the couch.

To Doctor Hapgood she was a machine merely;
an easy-running one, a dependable one, but none
the less a machine. To Huntter, shut away from
society, gregarious, friendly, and kindly, she had
meant much more. Her recent experience abroad,
with all the exquisite touches of human interest and
uplift, had left her peculiarly sensitive to her present
environment.

She liked the man in the room next her. There was much that was noble and fine about him, but he was a type that had never entered her life before, and often, by his kindliest word and gesture, drew her attention to a yawning space between them. She was at her ease, perfectly so, when near him, but she knew it was because of the distance that separated them. Still, she was confronted by a certain grim fact, and that ugly knowledge held him and her together. By some strange process of reason she wanted him to live up to the best in him. There were two markedly different sides of his nature; she trembled before one; before the other she gave homage as she did to Travers, to John Boswell, and Master Farwell.

The day before, Huntter had had a long talk with Doctor Hapgood while she was off duty. That conversation had doubtlessly caused the bad night; she wondered about it now. It had evidently upset Huntter a good deal.

Then Priscilla, losing consciousness gradually, thought of Travers, of Margaret Moffatt, who believed her to be out of the city. She smiled happily as she relived her blessed memories of good men and women. They justified and sanctified life, love, and happiness, and they made it possible for her, poor, struggling, little white nurse as she was, with all her professional knowledge, to trust and sympathize, and faithfully serve.

She must have slept deeply, for it took her a full moment to realize that some one in the next room was talking and — saying things!

"No, she's asleep, Huntter. She looks worn out. We must get a night nurse. Well, I have only this to say: God knows I pity you, but my duty compels me to say that — you should not marry! The chances are about even; but — you shouldn't take the risk."

A groan brought Priscilla to her feet, alert and quivering. Like a sudden and blinding shock she understood, what seemed to her, a whole life history. She stumbled to the door and faced Dr. Hapgood, hat in hand, keen-eyed, but detached.

"You slept — heavily?"

"Yes, Doctor Hapgood."

"I am going to send a night nurse to relieve you. When did you say your next engagement began?"

"March fifth."

"Well, you will need a week to recuperate. Make your plans accordingly. Do you understand?"

"Yes."

Did he suspect? Did he warn her? But his next words were kindness alone.

"There should have been two nurses all along. One forgets your youth in your efficiency. Good morning."

When Priscilla stood beside Huntter again his wan face, close-shut eyes, and grim mouth almost frightened her.

"I want to sleep," he said briefly. "Draw down the shades."

The night nurse became a staple joke between her and Huntter.

"Lord!" he exclaimed one day as Priscilla entered; "you're like the morning: clear, fresh, and hopeful. Do you know, that to escape the nightmare that haunts my chamber after you go, I have to play sleep even if I'm dying with thirst or blue devils? She's religious! Think of a nurse with religion that she feels compelled to share with a sick man! I'm going to get up to-day, Miss Glynn. I've bullied Hapgood into giving permission, and I've done him one better. I'm going to have a visitor! I'm back from Bermuda, you know. After you've fixed me up — isn't it a glorious day? — open the windows, and — I've ordered a lot of flowers. Put them in those brass bowls. My visitor is a lady. She likes yellow roses. By the way, Miss Glynn, Doctor Hapgood tells me that you've been in — Bermuda, too? Thorough old disciplinarian he! You must have been lonely. And you leave me next week? I want to thank you. I shall thank you ceremoniously every time you enter after this. You've been — a good nurse and a — good friend. I couldn't say more, now could I?"

"No, Mr. Huntter. And you've been — a very brave man! I know you will always be that, and make light of it. I rather like the half-joking way you do your kindest things. Here are the flowers! Oh, what beauties!"

Priscilla turned from helping Huntter and began arranging the glorious mass of roses in the brass bowls.

"What time is it, Miss Glynn?"

"Eleven o'clock."

"And my friend is due at eleven-thirty. She will be here on the minute. I feel like a boy, Miss Glynn. One gets the doldrums being alone and convalescing. How the grim devils catch and hold you while they try to distort life! I must have been a sad trial to you, but I'm myself again. Tell me, honest true, Miss Glynn, just how have I come out in your estimation? A man is no hero to his valet. What is he to his trained nurse?"

"You have been very patient and considerate." Priscilla's back was turned to Huntter; her face was quivering.

"Negative virtues! Had I been a brute you would have gone. I might have had the night nurse for twenty-four hours. I dared not run the risk of letting you go."

"I've come out pretty well in your estimation? That's a feather in my nice, white cap," she said.

"I wonder why I care what you think of me?"

"I do not know, Mr. Huntter, except that we all care for the good opinion of those who wish us well."

"You wish me well?"

"With all my heart."

"I'd like" — Huntter turned his face toward the window and the glorious winter day — "I'd like to be worthy of every well-wisher. I feel quite the good boy this morning. I've been — well, I've been rather up against it, I fear, and a trial to you, for all that you say to the contrary; but I am going to make amends to you — and the world! Now, when my friend comes, you won't mind if I ask you to leave us alone for a few moments? I can call you when I need you."

"Yes, Mr. Huntter."

"The lady is — you may have guessed — my fiancée. I have important things to say to her, and —— "

Priscilla's heart beat madly. She felt she was near a deeper tragedy than any that had ever entered her life. And just then, as the clock struck the half hour, came a tap on the door:

"Come!" cried Huntter, in a tone of joy; "Come!" And in burst Margaret Moffatt!

She did not notice the rigid figure by the bowl of flowers; her radiant face was fixed upon Huntter, and she ran toward him with outstretched arms.

"My beloved!" she whispered. "Oh! my dear, my dear! How ill you have been! They did not tell me. I shall never forgive them. When did you get back from Bermuda?"

Priscilla slipped from the room and closed the door

noiselessly behind her, but not before she had seen Margaret Moffatt sink into Huntter's arms; not before she heard the sigh of perfect content that escaped her.

Alone in the anteroom, the hideous truth flayed Priscilla into suffering and clear vision.

"What shall I do?" she moaned, clasping her hands and swaying back and forth. All the burden and responsibility of the world seemed cast upon her. Then reason asserted itself.

"He will tell her! He is telling her now! Killing her love — killing her! Oh, my God!"

Then she shrank from the thought that she would, in a few moments, have to face her friend! How could she, when she remembered that holy night of confession in the little Swiss village? Again she moaned, "Oh! my God!" But she was spared that scene. Moments, though they seemed ages, passed, and then Huntter called:

"Miss Glynn!"

She hardly recognized his voice. It was — triumphant, thrilling. It rang boldly, commandingly. When she entered, Huntter was alone. Gone was the guest; gone the mass of golden roses. Huntter turned a face glowing and confident to her.

"Just because you are you, Miss Glynn, and because I'm the happiest man in New York, I want you to congratulate me. That was Miss Moffatt. She and I are to marry — in the spring."

"Did you — mention my name to her?"

Priscilla's haggard face at last attracted the man.

"No. I was inhumanly selfish. You must forgive me. I meant to tell her of your faithful care; I meant to have you meet her. I forgot."

"Never mention — me to her! She is my — one friend in all the world; my one woman friend."

They faced each other blankly, fiercely. Then:

"Good Lord, Miss Glynn!" and Huntter — laughed!

CHAPTER XXIII

THE week of recuperation Doctor Hapgood recommended was one of prolonged torture to Priscilla Glenn. Thinking of it afterward, she realized that it was the Gethsemane of her life — the hour when, forsaken by all, she fought her bitter fight.

The drift of the ages confronted her. Her own insignificance, her humbleness, accentuated and betrayed her. Who would listen? How dared she speak! Who would heed her?

One, and one only. Margaret Moffatt!

From her Priscilla shrank and hid until she could gain courage to go and — by saving her, kill her! Yes, it meant that. The killing of the beautiful All Woman, as Travers had called her. After the telling there would be only the shadow of the splendid creature that God had meant to be so happy, if only the wrong of the world had not come between!

There were moments when, worn by struggle and wakeful nights, Priscilla felt incapable of sane thought.

Why should she interfere, she asked herself. Professional silence was her only course. And —

there was the chance — the chance! Against it stood, pleading, Margaret's radiant love and Huntter's strength and devotion.

Who could blame her if she — forgot? But oh! how they would curse her if she spoke! They might not believe; they might ruin her!

Then faith laid its commanding touch upon her spirit. It had been given her to know a woman who, for high principles and all the sacred future, was prepared to sacrifice her love if needs must be!

They two, Margaret of the high-soul, and she, Priscilla Glenn of the understanding devotion, seemed to stand apart and alone, each, in her way, called upon to testify and act.

"It must be done!" moaned Priscilla; "she must know and — decide! But how? how?"

John Boswell and Master Farwell were gone to the In-Place. The sanctuary overlooking the river was closed. There was no one, no place, to which Priscilla could go for comfort and advice, and her secret and her duty left her no peace or rest.

She had taken a tiny suite in a family hotel. The rooms had the comfort needed for her physical wants, but she tossed on the bed nights and slept brokenly. She ate poorly and grew very thin, very pale. She walked, days, until her body cried out for mercy. She cancelled her engagement, for she was unfitted for service, and intuitively she knew that, for her, a great change was near.

When she was weak from weariness and lonely to the verge of exhaustion, she thought of Kenmore — not Travers — with positive yearning. The woman of her, madly defending, or about to defend, woman, excluded even her own love and her own man. It was sex against sex; the world's injustice against all that woman held sacred! If Margaret were to be sacrificed, so was she, for she blindly felt that Travers would not uphold her! How could he when tradition held him captive? How could he when his oath bound him like a slave? Doctor Hapgood had done his part, had spoken his word — to man! But that was not enough. Man had flaunted it, was willing to take — the chance without giving the woman intelligent choice. Oh! it was cruel, it was unjust, and it must be defied. She and Margaret must stand side by side, or life never again would taste sweet and pure!

Priscilla had not heard from Travers in ten days, and this added to her sense of desolation. Then, one evening, coming in from a long tramp in the park, snow covered and bedraggled, she faced him in her own little parlour!

"My blessed child!" cried he, rushing toward her. "What have you been doing to yourself?"

She was in his arms; his hands were taking off her snow-wet coat and hat. He was whispering to her his love and gladness while he placed her in a chair and lighted the tiny gas log in the grate.

"It's a wicked shame!" he said laughingly; "but it will have to do. Now then, confess!"

"Oh! I have longed so for you! I have been — mad!"

Priscilla tried to smile, but collapsed miserably.

"I don't believe you have eaten a morsel since —— " Travers glared at her ferociously.

"Since I — I was in Switzerland." The sob aroused Travers to the girl's condition.

"You poor little tyke!" he said. "Now lean back and do as you're told. I'm going to ring for food. Just plain, homely food. I'm as hungry as a bear myself. I came to you from the vessel. I sent mother home in a cab. I had to see you. We'll eat — play; and then, my precious one, we'll talk business."

"How I have wanted you! needed you!" Again the pitiful wail.

"Now behave, child! When the waiter comes we must be as staid as Darby and Joan. You poor little girl! Heavens! how big your eyes are, and how frightened! Come in! Yes. This is the order; serve it here."

The waiter took the order wrapped in a good-sized bill, and departed on willing feet.

"Your hair is about all that's familiar; longing for me couldn't take the shine from that!" Travers kissed it.

"I see my next case," he laughed. "To get you

in shape will be quite an achievement. We both need — play. We thrive on that."

"Yes, my dear, my dear; but I have forgotten how!"

"Nonsense! Here's the food. Put the table near the grate" — this to the man — "things smoking hot; that's good. The wine, please. Thanks! Miss Glynn, to your health!"

How Travers managed it no one could tell, but his own unfettered joy drove doubt and care from the little room. Priscilla, warmed and comforted, laughed and responded, and the meal was a merry one. But it was over at last, and the grim spectre stalked once more. Travers noticed the haunted look in the eyes following his every movement, and took warning. Something was seriously wrong, that was evident; but he had boundless faith in his love and power to drive the cloud away. After the room was cleared of dishes and the grateful waiter, Travers attacked the shadow at once.

He drew a stool to Priscilla's chair and flung his long body beside her.

"Now," he said, with wonderful tenderness, "let me begin my life work at once, my darling. You are troubled; I am here to bear it all — for you!"

"Oh! Will you bear — half, dear heart?"

"Yes, and that is better. We need not waste words, my tired little girl. Out with the worst and then — you and I are going to — my mother!"

"Your — mother?"

"My mother! God bless her! You know she came near slipping away. She will need and love you more than ever."

"Oh! how good it sounds! Mother! Oh, my love, my love! I've had so little and I've wanted so much! Your mother!"

"She'll be yours, too, Priscilla. But hurry, child! Just the bare structure; my love will fill in the rest."

"Do not look up at me, dear man! So, let me rest my face on your head. Can you hear me — if I whisper?"

"Yes."

"It's about Margaret — Margaret Moffatt."

"The All Woman, the happiest creature, next to what you're going to be, in all God's world?"

"No!"

"No? Priscilla, what do you mean?"

"Do not move. Please do not look up. She is — engaged to — to Clyde Huntter!"

"Well?"

"I did not know; she never mentioned his name. While we played, names did not matter — his, mine, no one's." An hysterical gasp caused Travers to start.

"No, please keep your face turned. I must tell you in my way. I have just taken care of — Mr. Huntter. He is not — fit to marry any woman — he cannot marry — Margaret! Doctor Hapgood told him, but — he — means to marry! She came to see him; she did not see me; she does not know; but she *must* know!" fiercely; "she must know! That is the one thing above all else that would matter to her; she told me so! She does not live for the — the now; she was made for — for bigger things!"

"My God!" Travers was on his feet, and he dragged Priscilla with him. He held her close by her wrists and searched her white, agonized face. Truth and stern purpose were blazoned on it. She had never looked so beautiful, so noble, or so — menacing.

"You heard Doctor Hapgood say that?"

"I did."

"In your presence?"

"No." Then she described the little scene graphically.

"But Ledyard —— " Then he paused. Ledyard's confidence must be sacred to him.

"And Huntter — Huntter knows that you know; does he know that you are Margaret's friend?"

"Yes."

"And — he trusts you?"

"He thinks I do not count, but I do — with Margaret."

"Priscilla, this is no work for you, poor child!"

"It is — hers — and mine, and God's!" determinedly.

"Darling, you are overwrought. You must trust me. You know what I think of such things; you can safely leave this to me. Ledyard is Huntter's physician. Why he called Hapgood in, I do not know. I will go to Ledyard. Can you not see — that they would not believe — you?"

"Margaret will!"

"But her father! You do not understand, my precious. You dear, little, unworldly soul! Margaret Moffatt's marriage means a ninth wonder. Any meddling with that would have to be sifted to the dregs. And when they reached you, my own girl, they would grind you to atoms!"

"Not — Margaret!"

Priscilla drew herself away from the straining hands. She was quite calm now and terribly earnest.

"When all's told, it is Margaret and I — and God!"

"No. There are others, and other things. All the world's forces are against you."

"No, they are not! They are turning with me. I feel them; I feel them. I am not afraid." Then she took command, while Travers stood amazed. She put her hands on his shoulders and held him so before the bar of her crude, woman-judgment.

"Answer me, my beloved! You believe — what I have told you?"

"I do."

"You know Doctor Hapgood will do no more?"

"He — cannot."

"If you go to Doctor Ledyard — and he knows and believes — what will he do?"

"He has been Huntter's physician for years. If he has been mistaken, he will go to Huntter."

"Go to — Huntter! And what then? Suppose Mr. Huntter — still takes the chance?"

"Ledyard will — he will forbid it!"

"And what good will that do?" A pitiful bitterness crept into Priscilla's voice; her lips quivered.

"It is all Huntter! Huntter! All men! men! and there stands my dear — alone! No one goes to her to let — *her* choose; no one but me! Don't you see what I mean? Oh! my love, my love! My good, good man, can you leave her there in ignorance, all of you? Through the ages she has not had her say — about the chance, and that is why —— "

Priscilla paused, choked by rising passion.

"Little girl, listen! What do you mean?" Travers was genuinely alarmed and anxious.

"I mean" — the white, set face looked like an avenger's, not a passionately loving woman's — "I mean — that because women have never had an opportunity to know and to choose, you and I, and all people like us, stand helpless with our own great heaven-sent love at peril!"

"At peril! Oh, my dear girl!"

"Yes, at peril. We do not know what to do, where to turn. You see the great injustice clearly

as I do; but you — all men have tried to right it by
themselves, in their way, while all women, through
all the ages, have stood aside and tried to think
they were doing God's will when they accepted —
your best; your *half* best! Now, oh! now something
— I think it is God calling loud to them — is waking
them up. They know — you cannot do this thing
alone; it is their duty, too — they must help you,
for, oh!" — Priscilla leaned toward him with tear-
blinded eyes and pleading hands — "For the sake of
the — the little children of the world. Oh! men
are fathers, good fathers, but they have forgotten
the part mothers must take! We women cannot
leave it all to you. It is wicked, wicked for women
to try! There is something mightier than our love
— we are learning that!"

Travers took her in his arms. She was weeping
miserably. His heart yearned over her, for he
feared she was feeling, as women sometimes did, the
awful weight of injustice men had unconsciously,
often in deepest love, laid upon them.

"Priscilla, you trust me; trust my love?"

"Yes."

"You believe me when I say that I see this — as
you do — but that we only differ as to methods?"

"I — I hope I see that and believe it."

"Then" — and here Travers did his poor, blind
part to lay another straw upon the drift of burden —
"leave this — to me. I know better than you do

the end of any such mad course as you, in your
affection and sense of wrong, might take. Little
girl, let me try to show you. Suppose you went to
Margaret Moffatt. You know her proud, sensitive
nature; her loyalty and absolute frankness. After
the shock and torture she would go to her father
with the truth — for she would believe you — and
announce her unwillingness — I am sure, even
though her heart broke, she would do this — to marry
Huntter. Then the matter would lie among men;
men with the traditional viewpoint; men with much,
much at stake. If Huntter has, as you say, taken
the chance, in his love for Margaret — and he does
love her, poor devil! — he will defend himself and
his position."

"How?" Priscilla was regaining her calm; she
raised her head and faced Travers from the circle
of his arms.

"He will — send Moffatt to — to — Hapgood."

"And he — what will he do?"

"What does the priest do when the secrets of the
confessional are attacked?"

"Yes, yes — but then?"

"Then — oh! my precious girl! Can you not
see? You will come into focus. You, my love, my
wife, but, nevertheless, a woman! a trained nurse!
Hapgood would flay you alive, not because he has
anything against you, but professional honour and
discipline would be at stake. Between such a man

as Hapgood and — Priscilla Glynn — oh! can you not see my dear, dear girl?"

"Yes, I begin to see. And — I see I dare not trust even you!" The hard note in Priscilla's voice hurt Travers cruelly. "And — you, you and Doctor Ledyard — how would you stand?" she asked faintly.

Travers held her at arm's length, and his face turned ashen gray.

"Besides being men, we, too, are physicians!" he said. "Brutal as this sounds, it is truth!"

The light burned dangerously in Priscilla's eyes.

"When you are physicians — you are *not* men!" she panted, and suddenly, by a sharp stab of memory, Ledyard's words, back in the boyhood days at Kenmore, stung Travers. They were like an echo in his brain.

"You — you of all women, cannot say that and mean it, my darling!" he cried, and tried to draw her to him. She resisted.

"Our love, the one sacred thing of our very own," he pleaded, "is in peril." He saw it now. "Can you not see? Even if it is woman against woman, what right have you, Priscilla, to cloud and hurt our love?"

"It is not — woman against woman — any more." The words came sweetly, almost joyously; something like renunciation tinged them. "It is woman *for* woman until men will take us by the hands, trustingly, faithfully, and work with us for what belongs equally to us both!"

The radiance of the uplifted eyes frightened Travers. So might she look, he thought, had she passed through death and come out victorious.

"Now, just for a time," the tense, thrilling voice went on, "she and I — women — must stand alone, and do our best as we see it. It is no good leaving it to — to any man. I see that! And our love, yours and mine! Oh! dear man of my heart, that can never die or be hurt. It is yours, mine! God gave it. God will not take it away. God will not take Margaret's either. She will understand, and, even alone, far, far from *her* love, she will be true, as I will be. That is what it means to us!" Then she paused and smiled at Travers as across a widening chasm.

"I — am going now!"

"Going? My beloved — going — where?"

"To Margaret."

"You — dare not! You shall not! You are — mad!"

"No. I am — going, because, as things are, I cannot — trust you, even you! That is our penalty for the world's wrong. Long, long ago some one — oh! it was back in the days when I did not know what life meant — some one told me — never to let any one kill my ideal! No one ever has! It goes on before, leading and beckoning. I must follow. I do not know where he is, he who told me, but I know, as sure as I know that I shall always love you, that he is following *his* ideal, and living true and sure. Good night."

Unable to think or act, Travers saw Priscilla take up her still damp coat and hat. Like a man in a nightmare he saw her turn a deadly white face upon him, and then the door closed and he was alone in her little room!

He looked about, dazed and emotionless. He felt *her* in every touch of the lonely place; her books, her little pictures, herself! Some women are like that: they leave themselves in the presence of them they love — forever!

"Kill her ideal!" The words rang in the empty corners of his heart and mind. "Somewhere he is following his ideal, and living true and sure!"

Unconsciously, as men do in an hour of stress, Travers turned to action. Presently he found himself setting the tiny room in order as one does after a dear one has departed, or a spirit taken its flight. And while he moved about his reason was slowly readjusting itself, and he felt poignantly his impotency, his inability to use even his love for dominance. Being a just and honest man, he could not deny what Priscilla had said; truth rang in every sentence, chimed in with the minor notes of his life. No thought of following or staying her entered his mind; she had set about her business, woman's business, and, to the man's excited fancy, he seemed to see her pressing forward to the doing of that to which her soul called her. Then it was her beautiful shining hair he remembered, and his passion cried out for its own.

"This comes," he fiercely cried, setting his teeth hard, "of our leaving them behind — our women! Through the ages their place has been beside us as we fought every foe of the race. We set them aside in our folly, and now" — he bowed his head upon his folded arms — "and now they are waking up and demanding only what is theirs!"

A specimen of the new man was Travers, but inheritance, and Ledyard's teaching, had left their seal upon him. Bowed in Priscilla's little room he tried to see his way, but for a time he reasoned with Ledyard's words ringing in his ears. Had he not gone over this with his friend and partner many a time?

"Yes, I know the cursed evil, know its power and danger! Yes, it threatens — the race, but it has its roots in the ages; it must be tackled cautiously. If we take the stand you suggest" — for Travers had put forth his violent, new opposition — "what will happen? The quacks and money-making sharks will get the upper hand. Do you think men would come to us if exposure faced them? It's the devil, my boy; but of the two evils this, God knows, is the least. We must do what we can; work for a scientific and moral redemption, but never play the game like fools." — "But the women," Travers had put in feverishly, "the women!" — "Spare me, boy! The women have clutched the heart of me — always. The women and the — the babies. I've used them to flay many men into remorse and better living. I am thinking of them, as God hears me, when I take the course I do!"

And so Travers suffered and groaned in the small, deserted room.

Above and beyond Ledyard's reasoning stood two desolate figures. They seemed to represent all women: his Priscilla and Margaret Moffatt! One, the crude child of nature with her gleam undimmed, leading her forth unhampered, though love and suffering blocked her way; the other, the daughter of ages of refinement and culture, who had heard the call of the future in her big woman-heart and could leave all else for the sake of the crown she might never wear, but which, with God's help, she would never defile.

On, on, they two went before Travers's aching eyes. The way before them was shining, or was it the light of Priscilla's hair? They were leaving him, all men, in the dark! It was to seek the light, or —— And then Travers got up and left the room with bowed head, like one turning his back upon the dead.

He went to Ledyard at once, and found that cheerful gentleman awaiting him.

"At last!" he cried. "Helen telephoned at seven. She thought you were on your way here. Did you get lost?"

"Yes."

"What's the matter, Dick? You look as if you had seen a ghost."

"I have. An army of them."

"Are you — ill?"

"No."

"Sit down, boy. Here, take a swallow of wine. You're used up. Now then!"

"Doctor Ledyard, you were wrong — about Huntter! You remember what you told me, before Margaret Moffatt announced her engagement?"

"Yes." Ledyard poured himself a glass of wine and walked to his chair across the room.

"You were wrong; he is not what you think."

"What do you mean? I haven't seen Huntter for — for a year or more. I took care, sacred care, though, to — to trace him from the time he first came to me, more than ten years ago. No straighter, more honourable man breathes than he. He was one of the victims of ignorance and crooked reasoning, but, thank God! he was spared the worst."

"He was — not."

"Dick, in God's name, what do you mean?"

"Hapgood was called in. Huntter has not been in Bermuda; he has been right here in New York, under Hapgood's care."

"And Hapgood — told you?"

A purplish flush dyed Ledyard's face.

"No."

"Who, then? No sidetracking, Dick. Who?"

"The — the nurse."

"She-devil! Fell in love with her patient? I've struck that kind —— "

"Stop!"

Both men were on their feet and glaring at each other.

"You are speaking of my future — wife!"

Ledyard loosened his collar and — laughed!

"You're mad!" he said faintly, "or a damned fool!"

"I'm neither. I am engaged to marry Priscilla Glynn; have been since the summer. I meant to tell you and mother to-night. I went to her from the vessel. Priscilla Glynn took care of Huntter without knowing of his connection in the Moffatt affair. Above all else in the world" — Travers's voice shook — "she adores Margaret Moffatt, knows her intimately, and wishes, blindly, to serve her as she understands her. There are such women, you know, and they are becoming more numerous. She has gone to — tell Margaret Moffatt."

"Gone?" Ledyard reeled back a step. "And you permitted that?"

"I had no choice. You do not know — my — my — well, Miss Glynn."

"Not know her? The young fiend! Not know her? I remember her well. I might have known that no good could come from her. But — we can crush her, the young idiot! I do not envy you your fiancée, Dick."

The telephone rang sharply and Ledyard took up the receiver with trembling hand.

"It's your mother," he said; "you had better speak for yourself."

"So you are there, Dick?"

"Yes, mother."

"There was a message just now. Such a peculiar one. I thought you had better have it at once. It was only this: 'She knows' and a 'good-bye.'"

"Thanks, mother. I understand."

Ledyard watched the unflinching face and noted the even voice. He was so near he had caught Helen's words.

"And that is all, mother?"

"All, dear."

"I'll be home soon. Good night."

Then he looked up at Ledyard, and the older man's face softened.

"You'll find this sort of thing is a devil of a jigsaw. It cuts in all directions," he said, laying his hand on Travers's shoulder.

"Yes, doesn't it? But, Doctor Ledyard, I want to tell you something. She's right — that girl of mine, and Margaret Moffatt, too — and you know it as well as I do! If I can, I'm going to have my love and my woman; but even if I go empty hearted to my grave I shall know — they are right! Besides being women, and our loves, they are human beings, and they are beginning to find it out. The way may lead through hell, but it ends in —— "

"What?" Ledyard breathed; his eyes fixed on the stern young face.

"In understanding.   It leads to the responsibility all women must take.   Good night, old friend."

CHAPTER XXIV

PRISCILLA had gone straight from Margaret Moffatt's to her own little apartment. She had no sense of suffering; no sensation at all. She must pack and get away! And like a dead thing she set to work, although it was midnight and she had been so weary before; and then she smiled quiveringly:

"Before!"

She stood and stretched out her arms to the empty space where Travers had been.

"Oh! my dear, dear man!" she moaned. "My beloved!"

She had set the spark to the powder; by to-morrow the devastation would be complete. That, she knew full well. And he — the man she loved above all else in life — in order to escape must seek safety with those others! All those others — men! men! men! Only she and Margaret, suffering and alone, would stand in the ruins. But from those ruins! Her eyes shone as with a vision of what must be.

"I wish I could tell you — all about it!" the weak, human need called to the absent love. The whispered words brought comfort; even his memory was a stronghold. It always would be, even when she was far away in her In-Place, never to see him again.

How thankful she was that he did not know, really. He could not follow; she would not be able to hurt him — after to-morrow. Her changed name had saved her!

"Priscilla Glynn," she faltered, "hide her, hide her forever, hide poor Priscilla Glenn."

Then her thoughts flew back to the recent past. She had found Margaret alone in her own library.

"Now how did you know I wanted you more than any one else in the world?" Margaret had said. "When did you get back? You baddest of the bad! Why did you hide from me? Where were you?"

"In — Bermuda." How ghastly it sounded, but it caught Margaret's quick thought.

"Sit down, you little ghost of bygone days of bliss. You'll have to play again. Work is killing you. In Bermuda? What doing?"

"Wearing — my cap and apron, dear, dear —— "

"Your cap and apron? I thought you burned them! I shall tell Travers, you deceitful, money-getting little fraud! Well, who has taken it out of you so? You are as white as ivory. Do you know the Traverses came in on the *St. Cloud* to-day?"

"Yes. Doctor Travers came to see me."

"Ha! ha! He doesn't seem to have cheered you much. I wager he's told you what he thinks of you, tossing to the winds all the beautiful health and spirits of the summer! When are you to be married? I must tell him to bully you as — as my dear love is bullying me! Has Doctor Ledyard growled at you? I can twist him easily! He is a darling, and just wears that face and voice for fun in order to scare little redheaded nurses. Cilla, dear heart, I'm going to be married in June! Dear, old-fashioned June, with roses and good luck and — oh! the heaven seems opening and the glory is pouring down! There, girlie! cuddle here! I'm going to tell you everything; even to the mentioning of names! I've always hated to label my joy before. But, first, take some chocolate; it's hot and piping. Now! Whom did you nurse in Bermuda? I'm going to tell him, or her, what I think of him!"

"I — nursed — Mr. Clyde Huntter. We were in New York all the time. That is why — I had to keep — still —— "

"Mr. Clyde Huntter?" Margaret set the cup she held, down sharply. The quick brain was alert and in action.

"Mr. Clyde Huntter?" And then Margaret Moffatt came close to Priscilla, and looked down deep into the unfaltering eyes raised to hers.

"Mr. Clyde Huntter — is the man I am to marry!" she said in a voice from which the girlish banter had gone forever. It was the voice of a woman in arms to defend all she worshipped.

"Yes, I know. I was in his room the day you called. I thought I should die. I hoped he would tell you. I was ready to stand beside you; but he did not tell!"

"Tell — what? As God hears you, Priscilla, as you love me, and — and as I trust you, tell me what?"

And then Priscilla had told her. At first Margaret stood, taking the deadly blow like a Spartan woman, her grave eyes fixed upon Priscilla. Slowly the cruel truth, and all it implied, found its way through the armour of her nobility and faith. She began to droop; then, like one whose strength has departed, she dropped beside Priscilla's chair and clung to her. It had not taken long to tell, but it had lain low every beautiful thing but — courage!

"Back there," Margaret had said at last, "back there where we played, I told you I was ready for sacrifice. I thought my God was not going to exact that, but since he has, I am ready. Priscilla, I still have God! I wonder" — and, oh! how the weak, pain-filled voice had wrung Priscilla's heart — "I wonder if you can understand when I tell you that I love my love better now — than ever? Shall always love him, my poor boy! Can you not see that he did not mean — to be evil? It was the curse handed down to him, and when he found out — his love, our love, had taken possession of him, and he could not let me — go! I feel as if — as if I were his mother! He cannot have the thing he would die for, but I shall love him to the end of life. I shall try to make it up to him — in some way; help him to be willing and brave, to do the right; teach him that my way is the only — honourable way. I am sure both he and I will be — glad not — not to let others, oh! such sad, little others, pay the debt for us. Our day is — is short at best, but the — the eternity! And you, dear, faithful Cilla! You, with your blessed love, how will it be when I have done what I must do? I must go to — to father and tell the truth, and then ———"

"I know," Priscilla had said. "Doctor Travers told me what would follow. I shall not be here for him to suffer for; I am going ———"

"Where, my precious friend?"

"To — the Place Beyond the Winds! You do not understand. You cannot; no one can follow me; but I cannot bear the hurting blasts any more. I want the In-Place."

Then it was over, and now she was back in her lonely rooms. She packed her few, dear possessions, and toward morning lay down upon her bed. At daylight she departed, after settling her affairs with the night clerk and leaving no directions that any one could follow.

"It is business," she had cautioned, and the sleepy fellow nodded his head.

The rest did not matter. She would travel to the

port from which the boats sailed to Kenmore. Any boat would do; any time. Some morning, perhaps, at four o'clock, if the passage had not been too rough, she would find herself on the shabby little wharf with the pink morning light about her, and the red-rock road stretching on before.

Then Priscilla, like a miser, gripped her purse. Never before had money held any power over her, but the hundreds she had saved were precious to her now. Her father's doors were still, undoubtedly, closed to her. She could not be a burden to the two men living in Master Farwell's small home. There was, to be sure, Mary McAdam! By and by, perhaps, when the hurt was less and she could trust herself more, she would go to the White Fish Lodge and beg for employment; but until then ——

The morning Priscilla departed, Ledyard, unequal to any further strain, was called upon to bear several. By his plate, at the breakfast table, lay a scrawled envelope that he recognized at once as a report from Tough Pine.

"What's up now?" muttered he. "This thing isn't due for — three weeks yet."

Then he read, laboriously, the crooked lines:

I give up job. Dirty work. Money — bad money. I take no more — or I be damned! He better man — than you was; you bad and evil, for fun — he grow big and white. No work for bad man — friend now to good mens.

PINE.

"The devil!" muttered Ledyard; but oddly enough the letter raised, rather than lowered, his mental temperature. Those ill-looking epistles of Pine's had nauseated him lately. He had begun to experience the sensation of over-indulgence. Some one had told him, a time back, of Boswell's leaving the city, and he had been glad of the suspicion that arose in him when he heard it.

Later in the day the forces Priscilla had set in motion touched and drew him into the maelstrom.

"Ledyard" — this over the telephone — "my daughter has just informed me that she is about to break her engagement. May I see you at — three?"

"Yes. Here, or at your office?"

"I will come to you."

They had it out, man to man, and with all the time-honoured and hoary arguments.

"My girl's a fool!" Moffatt panted, red-faced and eloquent. "Not to mention what this really means to all of us, there is the girl's own happiness at stake. What are we to tell the world? You cannot go about and — explain! Good Lord! Ledyard, Hunter stands so high in public esteem that to start such a story as this about him would be to ruin my own reputation."

"No. The thing's got to die," Ledyard mused. "Die at its birth."

"Die in my girl's heart! Good God! Ledyard, you ought to see her after the one night! It wrings my heart. It isn't as if the slander had killed her love for him. It hasn't; it has strengthened it. 'I must bear this for him and for me,' she said, looking at me with her mother's eyes. She never looked like her mother before. It's broken me up. What's the world coming to, when women get the bit in their teeth?"

"There are times when all women look alike," Ledyard spoke half to himself; "I've noticed that." The rest of Moffatt's sentence he ignored.

"Why, in the name of all that is good," Moffatt blazed away, "did you send that redheaded girl into our lives? I might have known from the hour she set her will against mine that she was no good omen. Things I haven't crushed, Ledyard, have always ended by giving me a blow, sooner or later. Think of her coming into my home last night and daring ——" The words ended in a gulp. "Let me send Margaret to you," pleaded the father at his wits' end. "Huntter is away. Will not be back until to-morrow. Perhaps you can move her. You brought her into the world; you ought to try and keep her here."

At four Margaret entered Ledyard's office. She was very white, very self-possessed, but gently smiling.

"Dear old friend," she said, drawing near him and taking the rôle of comforter at once. "Do not think I blame you. I know you did your best with your blessed, nigh-to glasses on, but we younger folks have long vision, you know. Do you remember how you once told me to swallow your pills without biting them? I obeyed you for a long, long time; but I've bitten this one! It's bitter, but it is for the best. The medicine is in the pills; we might as well know."

"See here, Margaret, I'm not going to use your father's weapons. I only ask you — to wait! Do not break your engagement; let me see Huntter. Do not speak to him of this. I can explain, and —" he paused — "if the worse comes to the worst, the wedding can be postponed; then things can happen gradually."

"No," Margaret shook her head. "This is his affair and mine, and our love lies between us. I want — oh! I want to make him feel as I do, if I can; but above all else he must know that whatever I do is done in love. You see, I cannot hate him now; by and by it would be different if we were not just to each other."

"My poor girl! Do you women think you are going to be happier, the world better, because of — things like this? Men have thought it out!"

"Alone, yes. And women have let you bear the burden — alone. Happiness is — not all. And who can tell what the world will be when we all do the work God sent us to do? I know this: we cannot push our responsibilities off on any one else without stumbling across them sooner or later, for the

overburdened ones cannot carry too much, or forever!"

Ledyard expected Travers for dinner, but, as the
time drew near, he felt that his young partner would
not come. At six a note was handed to him:

KINDEST OF FRIENDS:
To-morrow, or soon, I will come to you; not to-night.
I have to be alone. I am all in confusion. I can see only
step by step, and must follow as I may. Two or three
things stand out clear. We haven't, we men, played the
game fair, though God knows we meant to. They —
she and such women as my girl — are right! Blindly,
fumblingly right. They are seeking to square themselves,
and we have no business to curse them for their efforts.

Lastly, I love Priscilla Glynn, and mean to have her,
even at the expense of my profession! You have set my
feet on a broad path and promised an honourable position.
I have always felt that to try and follow in your steps was
the noblest ambition I had. I know now that I could
not accomplish this. You have truth and conviction to
guide and uphold you. I have doubt. I must work
among my fellows with no hint of distrust as to my own
position. Forgive me! Go, if you will, to my mother —
to Helen. She will need you — after she knows. You
will, perhaps, understand when I tell you that, for a time
at least, I must be by myself, and I am going to the little
town where my own mother and I, long ago, lived our
strange life together. She seems to be there, waiting for me.

Ledyard ate no dinner that night; he seemed
broken and ill; he pushed dish after dish aside, and
finally left the table and the house.

Everything had failed him. All his life's work and hopes rustled past him like dead things as he walked the empty streets.

"Truth and conviction," he muttered. "Who has them? The young ass! What is truth? How can one be convinced? It's all bluff and a doing of one's best!"

And then he reached Helen Travers's house and found her waiting for him.

"I have a — a note from Dick," she said. Ledyard saw that she had been crying.

"Poor boy! He has gone to — his mother; his real mother. We" — she caught her breath — "we have, somehow, failed him. He is in trouble."

"I wonder — why?" Ledyard murmured. Never had his voice held that tone before. It startled even the sad woman.

"We have tried to do right — have loved him so," she faltered.

"Perhaps we have been too sure of ourselves, our traditions. Each generation has its own ideals. We're only stepping-stones, but we like to believe we're the — end-all!"

"That may be."

Then they sat with bowed heads in silence, until Ledyard spoke again.

"I'm going to retire, Helen. Without him, work would be — impossible. His empty place would be a silent condemnation, a constant reminder, of — mistakes."

"If he leaves me, I shall close this house. I could not live — without him here. I never envied his mother before. I have pitied, condoned her, but to-night I envy her from my soul!"

"Helen" — and here Ledyard got up and walked the length of the room restlessly; he was about to put his last hope to the test — "Helen, this world is — too new for us; for you and me. We belong back where the light is not so strong and things go slower! We get — blinded and breathless and confused. I have nothing left, nor have you. Will you come with me to that crack in the Alps, as Dick used to call it, and let me — love you?"

"Oh! John Ledyard! What a man you are!"

"Exactly! *What* a man I am! A poor, rough fool, always loving what was best; never daring to risk anything for it. I'm tired to death —— "

She was beside him, kneeling, with her snow-touched head upon his knee.

"So am I. Tired, tired! I could not do without you. I have leaned on you far too long; we all have. Now, dear, lean on me for the rest of the way."

He bent his grizzled head upon hers and his eyes had the look of prayer that Priscilla once discovered.

"Dick — has not told me his real trouble," Helen faintly said. "I know it is somehow connected with a — nurse."

"The redheaded one," Ledyard put in; "a regular

little marplot!" Then he gave that gruff laugh of
his that Helen knew to be a signal of surrender.

"It's odd," he went on, "how one can admire and
respect when often he disapproves. I disapprove of
this — redheaded girl, but, if it will comfort you any,
my child, I will tell you this: Dick's future, in her
hands, would be founded on — on everlasting rock!"

"Perhaps — she won't have him!"

"Helen" — and Ledyard caught her to him —
"you never would have said that if you had been
Dick's mother!"

"Perhaps — not!"

"No. You and I have only played second fiddles,
first and last; but second fiddles come in handy!"

The room grew dim and shadowy, and the two
in the western window clung together.

"Have you heard — John, that Margaret Moffatt
has broken her engagement to Clyde Huntter?"

"Yes. Where did you hear it?"

"She came — to see me; wanted to know how I
was. She was very beautiful and dear. She talked
a good deal about that — that —— "

"Redheaded nurse?" asked Ledyard.

"Yes. I couldn't quite see any connecting link
then, but you know Dick did go to that Swiss village
last summer. I fear the party wasn't properly chap-
eroned, for 'twas there he met — the nurse!"

"It — was!" grunted Ledyard.

"There is something sadly wrong with this broken

engagement of Margaret's, but I imagine no one will ever know. Girls are so — so different from what they used to be."

"Yes," but a tone of doubt was in Ledyard's voice. Presently he said: "Since Dick has left, or may leave, the profession, I suppose he'll take to writing. He's always told me that when he could afford to, he'd like to cut the traces and wollop the race with his pen. Many doctors would like to do that. A gag and a chain and ball are not what they're cracked up to be. The pen is mightier than the pill, sometimes, but it often eliminates the butter from the bread."

Helen caught at the only part of this speech that she understood.

"There's the little income I'm living on," she said; "it's Dick's father's. I wish — you'd let me give it to him — now. I am old-fashioned enough to want to live on my husband's money."

"Exactly!" Ledyard drew her closer; "quite the proper feeling. It can be easily arranged."

And while they sat in the gathering gloom, Travers was wending his way up a village street, and wondering that he found things so little changed.

While his heart grew heavier, his steps hastened, and he felt like a small boy again — a boy afraid of the dark, afraid of the mystery of night — alone! The boy of the past had always known a heavy heart, too, and that added reality to the touch.

There stood the old cottage with a sign "To Let" swinging from the porch. Had no one lived there since they, he and the pretty creature he called mother, had gone away?

There had been workmen in the house, evidently. They had carelessly left the outer door open and a box of tools in the living-room. Travers went in and sat down upon the chest, closed his eyes, and gave himself up to his sad mood. Clearly he seemed to hear the low, sweet voice:

"Little son, is that you?" Yes, it was surely he! "Come home to — to mother? Tired, dear?" Indeed he was tired — tired to the verge of exhaustion. "Suppose — suppose we have a story? Come, little son! It shall be a story of a fine, golden-haired princess who loves and loves, but — is very, very wise. And you are to be the prince who is wise, too. If you are not both very wise there will be trouble; and of course princesses and princes do not have trouble." The old, foolish memory ran on with its deeper truth breaking in upon the heart and soul of the man in the haunted room.

Then Travers spoke aloud:

"Mother, I will make no mistake if I can help it, and as God hears me, I will not cheat love. As far as lies in me, I will play fair for her sake — and yours!"

When he uncovered his eyes he almost expected to see a creaky little rocker and a sleepy boy resting on the breast of a woman so beautiful that it was no wonder many had loved her.

"Poor, little, long-ago mother!"

Then he thought of Helen and her strong purpose in life, her devotion and sacrifice.

"I must go to her!" he cried resolutely. "I owe her — much, much!"

CHAPTER XXV

THE pines and the hemlocks stood out sharply against a pink, throbbing sky in which the stars still shone faintly but brilliantly. It was five o'clock of a dim morning, and no one was astir in the In-Place as the little steamer indolently turned from the Big Bay into the Channel and headed for the wharf.

Not a breath of air seemed stirring, and the stillness was unbroken except by the panting of the engines.

Priscilla Glenn stood near the gangway of the boat. Now that she had left all her beautiful love and life, she was eager to hide, like a hurt and bruised thing, in the old, familiar home. Leaning her poor, tired head against the post near her, she thought of the desolate wreck behind, and the tears came to the deep, true eyes.

"I could have done — nothing else!" she murmured, as if to comfort the sad thing she was. "It had to be! Margaret knew that; she understood. By now she is as bereft as I; poor, dear love! Oh! it seems, just sometimes it seems, like an army of men on one side and all of us women on the other.

369

Between us lies the great battlefield, and they, the men, are trying to fight alone — fight our battle as well as theirs. And — they cannot! they cannot!''

Just then the boat touched the wharf, and a sleepy man, a stranger to Priscilla, materialized and looked at her queerly.

"For the Lodge?" he grunted.

"Yes — I suppose so. Yes, the Lodge."

"Up yonder." Then he turned to the freight. Once she was on the Green, Priscilla paused and looked about.

"For which?" Then she smiled a ghost of her bright, sunny smile.

"My father's doors are shut to me," she sighed; "I cannot go to the Lodge, yet! I must go — to —— " Something touched her hand, and she looked down. It was Farwell's dog, the old one, the one who used to play with Priscilla when she was a little girl.

"You dear!" she cried, dropping beside him; "You've come to show me the way. Beg, Tony, beg like a good fellow. I have a bit of cake for you!"

Clumsily, heavily, the old collie tried to respond, but of late he had been excused from acting; and he was old, old.

"Then take it, Tony, take it without pay. That comes of being a doggie. You ought to be grateful that you are a dog, and — need not pay!"

It was clear to her now that Farwell's home must

be her first shelter, and taking up her suit-case she passed over the Green and took the path leading to the master's house.

Some one had been before her. Some one who had swept the hearth, lighted a fire, and set the breakfast table. Pine had taken Toky's place and was vying with that deposed oriental in whole-souled service.

Priscilla pushed the ever-unlatched door open and went inside. The bare living-room had been transformed. John Boswell had transferred the comfort, without the needless luxury, from the town home to the In-Place — books, pictures, rugs, the winged chair and an equally easy one across the hearth. And, yes, there was her own small rocker close by, as if, in their detachment, they still remembered her and missed her and were — ready for her coming! Priscilla noiselessly took off her wraps and sat down, glad to rest again in the welcoming chair.

She swayed back and forth, her closely folded arms across her fast-beating heart. She kept her face turned toward the door through which she knew the men would enter. She struggled for control, for a manner which would disarm their shock at seeing her; but never in her life had she felt more defeated, more helplessly at bay.

The early morning light, streaming through the broad eastern window, struck full across her where she sat in the low rocker; and so Boswell and Farwell came upon her. They stopped short on the threshold and each, in his way, sought to account for the apparition. The brave smile upon Priscilla's face broke and fled miserably.

"I — I've been doshed!" she cried in a last effort at bravado, and then, covering her face with her hands, she wept hysterically, repeating again and again, "I've come home, come home — to — no home!"

They were beside her at once. Boswell's hand rested on the bowed head; Farwell's on the back of her chair.

"Dear, bright Butterfly!" whispered Boswell comfortingly; "it has come to grief in the Garden."

"Oh! I wanted to learn, and oh! Master Farwell, I said I was willing to suffer, and I have, I have!"

Then she looked up and her unflinching courage returned.

"I was tired!" she moaned; "tired and hungry."

"After breakfast you will explain — only as much as you choose, child." This from Farwell. "Make the toast for us, Priscilla. I remember how you used to brown it without blackening it. Boswell always gets dreaming on the second side of the slice."

After the strange meal Priscilla told very little, but both men read volumes in her pale, thin face and understanding eyes.

"Damn them!" thought Farwell; "they have taken it out of her. I knew they would; but they have not conquered her!"

Boswell thoughtfully considered her when her eyes were turned from him.

"She learned," he thought; "suffered and learned; but when she gets her breath she will go back. The In-Place cannot hold her."

Then they told her of the Kenmore folk.

"Your father has had a stroke, Priscilla," Farwell said in reply to her question; "it has made him blind. Long Jean cares for him. He will have no other near him."

"And — he never wants me?" Priscilla whispered.

"No; but he needs you!" Boswell muttered. "You must let your velvety wings brush his dark life; the touch will comfort him."

"And old Jerry?"

Farwell leaned forward to poke the fire.

"Old Jerry," said he, "has gone mildly — mad. All day he sits dressed in his best, ready to start for Jerry-Jo's. He fancies that scapegoat of his has a mansion and fortune, and is expecting his arrival. He amuses himself by packing and unpacking a mangy old carpet-bag. Mary McAdam looks after him and the village youngsters play with him. It's rather a happy ending, after all."

Many a time after that Priscilla packed and unpacked the old carpet-bag, while Jerry rambled on of his great and splendid lad to the "Miss from the States."

"It's weak I am to-day, ma'am," he would say,

"but to-morrow, to-morrow! 'Tis the Secret Portage I'll make for; the Fox is a bit too tricky for my boat — a fine boat, ma'am. I'm thinking the Big Bay may be a trifle rough, but the boat's a staunch one. Jerry-Jo's expecting me; but he'll understand."

"I am sure he will be glad to see you, sir." Priscilla learned to play the sad game. The children taught her and loved her, and all the quiet village kept her secret. Mary McAdam claimed her, but Priscilla clung to the two men who meant the only comfort she could know. They never questioned her; never intruded upon her sad, and often pitiful, reserve; but they yearned over her and cheered her as best they could.

Priscilla's visits to her father's house were often dramatic. At first the sound of her voice disturbed and excited the blind man pathetically.

"Eh? eh?" he stormed, holding to Long Jean's hand; "who comes in my door?"

"Oh! a lass — from the States," Jean replied with a reassuring pat on the bony shoulder.

"From the States?" suspiciously.

"Aye. She's taken training in one of them big hospitables, and is a friend to the crooked gentleman who bides with Master Farwell. The lass comes to give me lessons in my trade." Jean had a touch of humour.

"I'll have no fandangoing with me!" asserted Glenn, settling back in his chair. "Old ways are good enough for me, Jean, and remember that, if you value your place. I want no woman about me who has notions different from what God Almighty meant her to have. Larning is woman's curse. Give 'em larning, I've always held, and you've headed 'em for perdition."

But Priscilla won him gradually, after he had become accustomed to her disturbing voice. He would not have her touch him physically. She seemed to rouse in him a strange unrest when she came near him, but eventually he accepted her as a diversion and utilized her for his own hidden need.

One day, with a hint of spring in the air, he reached out a lean hand toward the window near which Jean had placed him, and said:

"Woman, are you here?"

"Jean's gone — erranding." The old mother-word attracted Glenn's attention.

"Eh?" he questioned.

"To the village. I'm waiting until she comes back. Can I do anything for you, sir?"

"No. Is — is it a sunny day?"

"Glorious. The ice is melting now — in the shady places."

"I thought I felt the warmth. 'Tis cold and drear sitting forever in darkness."

"I am sure it must be — terrible."

But Glenn resented pity.

"God's will is never terrible!" he flung back. Then:

"Are you one — who got larning?"

"I — learned to read, sir."

"And much — good it's done you — the larning! I warrant ye'd be better off without it. Women are. Good women are content with God's way. My wife was. Always willing, was she, to follow. God was enough for her — God and me!"

"I wonder!"

"Eh? What was that?"

"Nothing, sir. May I read to you?"

"Is the Book there?"

"Right here on the stand. What shall I read?"

"There's one verse as haunts me at times; find it in Acts — the seventeenth, I think — and along about the twenty-third verse. I used to conjure what it might mean more than was good for me. It haunts me now, though I ain't doubting but what the meaning will come to me, some day. Them as sits in darkness often gets spiritual leadings."

And Priscilla read:

"'For as I passed by, and beheld your devotions, I found an altar with this inscription, To the Unknown God. Whom, therefore, ye ignorantly worship, him I declare unto you?'"

A silence fell between the old, blind father and the stranger-girl looking yearningly into his face.

"I've conned it this way and that," Glenn said, with his oratorical manner claiming him. "It might be that some worship an Unknown God and the true God might pass by and set things straight. There be altars and altars, and sometimes even my God seems ——"

"An Unknown God?" Priscilla asked tenderly. "That must be such a lonely feeling."

"No!" almost shrieked Nathaniel, as if the suggestion insulted him; "no! The true God declared himself to me long since. But what do you make of it, young Miss?"

Priscilla turned her eyes to the open, free outer world, where the sunshine was and the stirring of spring.

"Sometimes," she whispered, "I love to think of God coming down from all the shrines and altars of the world, and walking with his children — in the Garden! They need him so. I do not like altars or shrines; the Garden is the holiest place for God to be!"

"Thou blasphemer!" Glenn struggled to an upright position and his sightless eyes were fixed upon his child. "Wouldst thou desecrate the holy of holies, the altars of the living God?"

"If he is a living God he will not stay upon an altar; he will come and walk with his children!"

The tone of the absorbed voice reached where heretofore it had never touched.

"I'll have none of thee!" commanded Nathaniel, his face dangerously purple. "Your words are of the — the devil! Leave me! leave me!" And for the second time Priscilla was ordered from her father's house.

It did not matter. It was all so useless, and the future was so blank. Still, to go back to Master Farwell's just then was impossible, and Priscilla turned toward the wood road leading to the Far Hill Place. She had no plan, no purpose. She was drifting, drifting, and could not see her way. The bright sun touched her comfortingly. In the shadow it was chilly; but the red rock was warm and luring. And so she came to the open space and the almost forgotten shrine where once she had raised her Strange God.

She sat down upon a fallen tree and looked over the little, many-islanded bay to the Secret Portage. Through that she seemed to pass yearningly, and her eyes grew large and strained. Then she stretched out her arms, her young, empty arms.

"My Garden!" she called; "my Garden, my dear, dear love and Margaret's God! Margaret's and mine!"

And so she sat for a while longer. Then, because the chill air crept closer and closer, she arose and faced the old, bleached skull. The winters had killed the sheltering vines that once hid it from all eyes but hers. It stood bare and hideous, as if demanding that she again worship it. A frenzy overpowered Priscilla. That whitened, dead thing brought back memories that hurt and stung by their very sweetness. She rushed to the spot and seized the forked stick upon which the skull rested.

"This for all — Unknown Gods!" she cried in breathless passion, and dashed the skull to the ground. "And this! and this!" She trampled it. "They shall not keep you upon shrines! They shall not keep you hidden from all in the Garden!" With that she took a handful of the shattered god and flung it far and wide, with her blazing eyes fixed on the Secret Portage.

Standing so, she looked like a priestess of old defying all falseness and traditional wrong.

Among the trees Richard Travers gazed upon the scene with a kind of horror gripping him.

He was not a superstitious man, but he was a worn and weary one, and he had come to the Far Hill Place, two days before, because, after much searching, he had failed to find Priscilla Glynn, and his love was hurt and desperate. He had wanted to hide and suffer where no eyes could penetrate. But he had discovered that for a man to return to his boyhood was but to undergo the torture of those who are haunted by lost spirits. It had been damnable — that dreary, dismantled house back on the hill! The nights had maddened him and left him unable to cope intelligently with the days. Nothing comforting had been there. The pale boy he once had been taunted him with memories of lowered ideals, unfilled promise and purpose. He had travelled a long distance from the Far Hill Place, and he was going back to fight it out — somehow, somewhere. He would stop at Master Farwell's and then take the night steamer for the old battle-ground. And just at that moment, in the open space, he saw the strange sight that stopped his breath and heart for an instant.

Of course his wornout senses were being tricked. He had known of such cases, and was now thoroughly alarmed. Like a man in delirium, he walked into the open and confronted the fascinated gaze of the girl for whom he had been searching for weeks.

"How came — you here?" he asked in a voice from which normal emotions were eliminated.

"And — you?" she echoed.

They came a step nearer, their hands outstretched in a poor, blind groping for solution and reality.

"Why — I am — I meant to tell you — some day. I am Priscilla Glenn — not Glynn — Priscilla Glenn of — Lonely Farm."

"My God!" Travers came a step nearer, his face set and grim. "Of course! I see it now — the dance! Don't you remember? The dance at the Swiss village?"

"And the — the tune that made me cry. Who — are —— How did *you* know that tune? How did you know — the In-Place?"

Their hands touched and clung now, desperately. Together they must find their way out.

"I am — I was — the boy of the Far Hill Place. I played for you — once — to dance — right here!"

Something seemed snapping in Priscilla's brain.

"Yes," she whispered, breathing hard and quick. "I remember now: you taught me music, and—and you taught me — love, but you told me not to let them kill my ideal; and, oh! I haven't! I haven't!"

She shut her eyes and reeled forward. She did not faint, but for a moment her senses refused to accept impressions.

Travers knelt and caught her to him as she fell. Her dear head was upon his knee once more, and he pressed his lips to the wonderful hair from which the little hat had fallen. Then her eyes opened, but her lips trembled.

"You — came all the way from the Place Beyond the Winds, little girl, to show me my ideal again; to strike your blow — for women." Travers was whispering.

"Your ideal? But no, dear love. Your ideal is back there — in the Garden."

"And yours? I — I do not understand, Priscilla. I am still dazed. What Garden?"

"The big world, my dear man; your world."

"My blessed child! Do not look like that. Do you think I'm going back without you? I've been looking for — Priscilla Glynn — fool that I was! And you were — great heavens! You were the little nurse in St. Albans!"

"Yes — and you and I — stood by Jerry-Jo Mc-Alpin's bed — you and I! That was his secret."

"Priscilla, what do you mean?"

Then she told him, clinging to him, fearing that he might fall from her hold as she had once fallen from his, on the mountain across the sea.

"And you danced before my eyes as only one woman on earth can dance — and I did not know! Tricked by a name and — and the change in me! You were always the same — the flame-spirit that I first saw — here!"

"And you played—that tune, and you were divinely good; and I — I did not know."

"But we drifted straight to each other, my girl!"

"Only — to part."

"To part? Never! It's past the Dreamer's Rock for us, my sweet, and out to the open sea. We'll slip our moorings to-night, and send word after! I must have you, and at once. I know what it means to see you escaping my hold. Flame-spirits are elusive."

"And — and Margaret?"

"She — needs you. A fortnight ago I saw her, and this is what she said, smiling her old, brave smile: 'I think I could bear it better if her dear, shining head was in sight. Greater love hath no woman! Find her and bring her back!' That's your place, my sweet. Out there where the fight is on. Such as you can show us — that 'tis no fight between men and women, but one against ignorance and tradition. You'll trust yourself to me, dear girl?"

"I did — long ago!"

"To think" — Travers was gaining control of himself; the shock, the readjustment, had been so sudden that sensation returned slowly — "to think, dear blunderer, of your coming among us all, striking your blow, and then rushing to your In-Place! But love is mightier than thou; mightier than all else!"

"Not mightier than honour — such honour as Margaret knows!" Then fiercely: "What right have I to my — joy, when she —— "

"She told me that only by your happiness being consummated could she hope for peace."

Travers's voice was low and reverent.

"What — a girl she is!" Priscilla faltered.

"The All Woman."

"Yes, the All Woman."

The sun began to drop behind the tall hemlocks. Priscilla shivered in the arms that held her.

"Little girl, I wish I could wrap you in the old red cape you wore once, before the shrine."

"It is gone now, like the shrine. Oh! my love, my love, to think of the Garden makes me live again." The fancy caught Travers's imagination.

"The Garden!"

'Twas a day for dreamy wandering, now that they had come to a cleared space from which they could see light.

"The Garden, with its flowers and weeds."

"And its men and women!" added Priscilla, her eyes full of gladness. "Oh! long ago, I told Master Farwell that I felt Kenmore was only my stopping-place; I feel it now so surely."

"Yes, my sweet, but you and I will return here to polish our ideals and catch our breaths."

"In the Place Beyond the Winds, dear man?"

"Exactly! Those old Indians had a genius for names."

"And in the Garden — what are we to do?" Priscilla asked, her eyes growing more practical. "They will have none of — Priscilla Glynn, you know. And you, dear heart, what will they do to you, now that you have defied their code?"

"Priscilla Glynn has done her best and is — gone! There will be a Priscilla Travers with many a stern duty before her."

"Yes, but you?"

"I shall try to keep your golden head in sight, little girl! For the rest — I have a small income — my father's. I must tell you about him and my mother, some day; and I shall write — write; and men and women may read what they might not be willing to listen to."

"I see! And oh! how rich and bright the way on ahead looks! Just when I thought the clouds were crushing me, they opened and I saw —— "

"What, Priscilla?"

"You!"

"And now," Travers got upon his feet and drew her up; "do you know what is going to happen?"

"Can anything more happen to-day?"

"We are going to Master Farwell's, you and I. We are going to take him with us to the little chapel down the Channel; there we'll leave Priscilla Glenn, and, in her place, bring Priscilla Travers forth."

The colour rose to the thin, radiant face.

"And may we take John Boswell, too?"

"Boswell? Is he here?"

"Yes, with my Master Farwell."

Travers rapidly put loose ends of the past together, then exclaimed:

"God bless him; God bless Master Farwell!"

"I only know" — Priscilla's eyes were dim — "I only know — they are good men — both!"

"Yes, both! And to-night," Travers came back to the present, "I will take my wife away with me on the steamer."

"A poor, vagabond wife. Nothing but a heart full of love — as baggage."

"The Garden is a rich place, my love."

"And one can get so much for so little there." Priscilla meant to hold to her dear old joke.

"And so little — for so much!"

"That's not the language of the Garden, good man!"

It was so easy to play, now that Travers was leading the way from the wrecked shrine.

"You are right, my girl!" Then Travers stopped and faced her, his eyes glowing with love and courage. "And to-morrow — is not yet touched!" he said.

THE END

AMELIA E. BARR'S STORIES
DELIGHTFUL TALES OF OLD NEW YORK

THE BOW OF ORANGE RIBBON. With Frontispiece.

This exquisite little romance opens in New York City in "the tender grace" of a May day long past, when the old Dutch families clustered around Bowling Green. It is the beginning of the romance of Katherine, a young Dutch girl who has sent, as a love token, to a young English officer, the bow of orange ribbon which she has worn for years as a sacred emblem on the day of St. Nicholas. After the bow of ribbon Katherine's heart soon flies. Unlike her sister, whose heart has found a safe resting place among her own people, Katherine's heart must rove from home—must know to the utmost all that life holds of both joy and sorrow. And so she goes beyond the seas, leaving her parents as desolate as were Isaac and Rebecca of old.

THE MAID OF MAIDEN LANE; A Love Story. With Illustrations by S. M. Arthur.

A sequel to "The Bow of Orange Ribbon." The time is the gracious days of Seventeen-hundred and ninety-one, when "The Marseillaise" was sung with the American national airs, and the spirit affected commerce, politics and conversation. In the midst of this period the romance of "The Sweetest Maid in Maiden Lane" unfolds. Its chief charm lies in its historic and local color.

SHEILA VEDDER. Frontispiece in colors by Harrison Fisher.

A love story set in the Shetland Islands.
Among the simple, homely folk who dwelt there Jan Vedder was raised; and to this island came lovely Sheila Jarrow. Jan knew, when first he beheld her, that she was the one woman in all the world for him, and to the winning of her love he set himself. The long days of summer by the sea, the nights under the marvelously soft radiance of Shetland moonlight passed in love-making, while with wonderment the man and woman, alien in traditions, adjusted themselves to each other. And the day came when Jan and Sheila wed, and then a sweeter love story is told.

TRINITY BELLS. With eight Illustrations by C. M. Relyea.

The story centers around the life of little Katryntje Van Clyffe, who, on her return home from a fashionable boarding school, faces poverty and heartache. Stout of heart, she does not permit herself to become discouraged even at the news of the loss of her father and his ship "The Golden Victory." The story of Katryntje's life was interwoven with the music of the Trinity Bells which eventually heralded her wedding day.

GROSSET & DUNLAP, 526 WEST 26th ST., NEW YORK

CHARMING BOOKS FOR GIRLS

WHEN PATTY WENT TO COLLEGE, By Jean Webster.
Illustrated by C. D. Williams.

One of the best stories of life in a girl's college that has ever been written. It is bright, whimsical and entertaining, lifelike, laughable and thoroughly human.

JUST PATTY, By Jean Webster.
Illustrated by C. M. Relyea.

Patty is full of the joy of living, fun-loving, given to ingenious mischief for its own sake, with a disregard for pretty convention which is an unfailing source of joy to her fellows.

THE POOR LITTLE RICH GIRL, By Eleanor Gates.
With four full page illustrations.

This story relates the experience of one of those unfortunate children whose early days are passed in the companionship of a governess, seldom seeing either parent, and famishing for natural love and tenderness. A charming play as dramatized by the author.

REBECCA OF SUNNYBROOK FARM,   By Kate Douglas Wiggin.

One of the most beautiful studies of childhood—Rebecca's artistic, unusual and quaintly charming qualities stand out midst a circle of austere New Englanders. The stage version is making a phenominal dramatic record.

NEW CHRONICLES OF REBECCA, By Kate Douglas Wiggin.
Illustrated by F. C. Yohn.

Additional episodes in the girlhood of this delightful heroine that carry Rebecca through various stages to her eighteenth birthday.

REBECCA MARY, By Annie Hamilton Donnell.
Illustrated by Elizabeth Shippen Green.

This author possesses the rare gift of portraying all the grotesque little joys and sorrows and scruples of this very small girl with a pathos that is peculiarly genuine and appealing.

EMMY LOU: Her Book and Heart, By George Madden Martin.
Illustrated by Charles Louis Hinton.

Emmy Lou is irresistibly lovable, because she is so absolutely real. She is just a bewitchingly innocent, hugable little maid. The book is wonderfully human.

THE NOVELS OF
STEWART EDWARD WHITE

THE RULES OF THE GAME. Illustrated by Lajaren A. Hiller

The romance of the son of "The Riverman." The young college hero goes into the lumber camp, is antagonized by "graft" and comes into the romance of his life.

ARIZONA NIGHTS. Illus. and cover inlay by N. C. Wyeth.

A series of spirited tales emphasizing some phases of the life of the ranch, plains and desert. A masterpiece.

THE BLAZED TRAIL. With illustrations by Thomas Fogarty.

A wholesome story with gleams of humor, telling of a young man who blazed his way to fortune through the heart of the Michigan pines.

THE CLAIM JUMPERS. A Romance.

The tenderfoot manager of a mine in a lonesome gulch of the Black Hills has a hard time of it, but "wins out" in more ways than one.

CONJUROR'S HOUSE. Illustrated Theatrical Edition.

Dramatized under the title of "The Call of the North."

"Conjuror's House is a Hudson Bay trading post where the head factor is the absolute lord. A young fellow risked his life and won a bride on this forbidden land.

THE MAGIC FOREST. A Modern Fairy Tale. Illustrated.

The sympathetic way in which the children of the wild and their life is treated could only belong to one who is in love with the forest and open air. Based on fact.

THE RIVERMAN. Illus. by N. C. Wyeth and C. Underwood.

The story of a man's fight against a river and of a struggle between honesty and grit on the one side, and dishonesty and shrewdness on the other.

THE SILENT PLACES. Illustrations by Philip R. Goodwin.

The wonders of the northern forests, the heights of feminine devotion, and masculine power, the intelligence of the Caucasian and the instinct of the Indian, are all finely drawn in this story.

THE WESTERNERS.

A story of the Black Hills that is justly placed among the best American novels. It portrays the life of the new West as no other book has done in recent years.

THE MYSTERY. In collaboration with Samuel Hopkins Adams

With illustrations by Will Crawford.

The disappearance of three successive crews from the stout ship "Laughing Lass" in mid-Pacific, is a mystery weird and inscrutable. In the solution, there is a story of the most exciting voyage that man ever undertook.

GROSSET & DUNLAP, 526 WEST 26th ST., NEW YORK